5th International Workshop on Health Text Mining and Information Analysis

(Louhi 2014)

Held at the 14th Conference of the European Chapter of the Association for Computational Linguistics

Gothenburg, Sweden
27 April 2014

ISBN: 978-1-63266-406-8

Printed from e-media with permission by:

Curran Associates, Inc.
57 Morehouse Lane
Red Hook, NY 12571

Some format issues inherent in the e-media version may also appear in this print version.

Printed by Curran Associates, Inc. (2014)

For permission requests, please contact the Association for Computational Linguistics at the address below.

Association for Computational Linguistics
209 N. Eighth Street
Stroudsburg, Pennsylvania 18360

Phone: 1-570-476-8006
Fax: 1-570-476-0860

acl@aclweb.org

Additional copies of this publication are available from:

Curran Associates, Inc.
57 Morehouse Lane
Red Hook, NY 12571 USA
Phone: 845-758-0400
Fax: 845-758-2634
Email: curran@proceedings.com
Web: www.proceedings.com

Introduction

Welcome to Louhi 2014: The Fifth International Workshop on Health Text Mining and Information Analysis, in Gothenburg, Sweden. The Louhi workshop series is an international, scientific, forum for researchers and practitioners in the multidisciplinary area of health text mining and information analysis. This research area has progressed and grown since the First Louhi workshop in Turku, 2008, addressing challenging research issues in the health and biomedical domain, leading to more openly available annotated corpora, tools, terminologies, etc. Moreover, work on other languages than the previously dominating English is both increasing and maturing.

The importance of accurate and specific information extraction and classification from diverse health and biomedical documents such as Electronic Health Records (EHRs), scientific literature and online health forums is evident for several differing purposes, e.g. detecting drugs and medications, adverse events, building timelines, understanding information needs. Ontologies and terminologies for such tasks are also crucial. The papers presented in this workshop all address these issues from different perspectives, and on different languages such as Basque, Spanish, French, Danish, Swedish, German and English. The Fifth Louhi workshop will provide a platform for important and useful discussions in this vivid research area, and hopefully lead to many more fruitful endeavours.

We received in total 21 submissions from 11 countries and three continents, and after a rigorous double-blind peer-review process we could accept 17 of these submissions (nine long papers and eight short papers) to be published in the 2014 Louhi proceedings. The acceptance rate for long papers was 60%, while the overall acceptance rate for the workshop was 81%.

A short description of each paper follows in order of appearance.

Long papers:

Medical queries in a Swedish health portal are studied from the perspective of supporting information needs by using semantic- and graph-based methods (*Moradi et al.*).

Collier et al. experiment with five strategies for mitigating the impact of near domain transference for biomedical named entity recognition. Distributional dissimilarities of domains need to be adequately compensated during learning, or else lower performance and higher annotation costs are expected.

Zhao and Tou Ng also address domain adaptation, but in the area of coreference resolution, using active learning methods and target domain instance weighting.

Discourse parsing is addressed in the paper by *Stepanov and Riccardi*, where cross-domain evaluation of a discourse relation parser trained on one domain generalises well across domains with feature-level domain adaptation.

Perez-de-Viñaspre and Oronoz present initial work on semi-automatically translating SNOMED CT into Basque, using the English version of SNOMED CT as source and then adapting the terms to Basque utilizing various rules.

A method for building FrameNet-like corpora using ontologies is described in the paper by *Tan*. The system includes algorithms for selecting and describing appropriate concepts to be translated into semantic frames.

Quan and Ren describe work on gene-disease association extraction by combining information filtering, grammar parsing and network analysis. With breast cancer as testing disease, they achieve 83.9% accuracy for the testing genes and diseases and 74.2% accuracy for the testing genes.

Segura-Bedmar et al. describe work on detecting drugs and adverse events from Spanish health social media posts. A gold standard is created for evaluation, and a multilingual text analysis engine, Textalytics, was applied for automatic detection, achieving 80%/56% precision, and 87%/85% recall for drugs/adverse events.

The paper by *Moen et al.* presents several methods for information retrieval, focusing on care episode retrieval based on textual similarity using distributional semantics and ICD-10 codes of diagnoses, to retrieve the most similar care episodes among the records.

Short papers:

Engel Thomas et al. present work on text mining of Danish health records, with a focus on handling spelling and ending variations, gaps and shuffling of terms, as well as negation identification and scope. Spelling variation was found to be the most important functionality.

A new annotated corpus for identifying phenotype information for congestive heart failure is presented by *Alnazzawi et al.* This corpus is unique in that it integrates information both from electronic health records and literature articles.

Medication extraction, as defined in the 2009 i2b2 challenge, is addressed by using agile text mining methods in the paper by *Shivade et al.* They report results of 92% precision and 71.5% recall.

Roller and Stevenson describe work using the Unified Medical Language System (UMLS) for distantly supervised relation extraction.

Casillas et al. describe work on extracting cause-effect relations between drugs and diseases, applied on Spanish health records.

Semantic relations are integrated in a vector space model to tackle the problem of context-unawareness and applied on an electronic health record corpus (*Périnet and Hamon*).

Kreuzthaler and Schulz present work on disambiguating period characters in German clinical discharge summaries. An accuracy of 93% is reported for abbreviation detection and sentence delimitation.

The Heideltime system is used for identifying time expressions in English and French in the paper by *Hamon and Grabar*. Results of 0.94 (French) and 0.85 (English) F-measure are reported on their adapted version of the system.

Dear reader, most welcome to study these proceedings, which we hope will raise interest, open new perspectives and generate new exciting research questions in health text mining and information analysis.

Stockholm and San Diego, March 2014

Sumithra Velupillai, Martin Duneld, Maria Kvist and Hercules Dalianis

Chair:

Sumithra Velupillai, DSV/Stockholm University

Program Chairs:

Hercules Dalianis, DSV/Stockholm University
Maria Kvist, DSV/Stockholm University
Martin Duneld, DSV/Stockholm University

Local Organizing Committee:

Maria Skeppstedt, DSV/Stockholm University
Aron Henriksson, DSV/Stockholm University

Publication Chair:

Martin Duneld, DSV/Stockholm University

Program Committee:

Anette Hulth, Swedish Institute for Infectious Disease Control, Karolinska Institutet, Sweden
Antti Airola, University of Turku, Finland
Beáta Megyesi, Uppsala University, Sweden
David Martinez, NICTA, Australia
Dimitris Kokkinakis, University of Gothenburg, Sweden
Filip Ginter, University of Turku, Finland
Gintaré Grigonyté, Stockholm University, Sweden
Hanna Suominen, NICTA, Australia
Henning Müller University of Applied Sciences Western Switzerland, Switzerland
Jon D. Patrick, Health Language Laboratories, Australia
Jong C. Park, KAIST Computer Science, Korea
Jussi Karlgren, KTH, Royal Institute of Technology, Sweden
Mats Wirén, Stockholm University, Stockholm
Özlem Uzuner, MIT, U.S.
Pierre Zweigenbaum, LIMSI, France
Richárd Farkas, Institute of Informatics, Hungary
Sabine Bergler, Concordia University, Canada
Sampo Pyysalo, University of Tokyo, Japan
Sanna Salanterä, University of Turku, Finland
Sophia Ananiadou, University of Manchester, U.K.
Stefan Schulz, Graz General Hospital and University Clinics, Austria
Tapio Salakoski, University of Turku, Finland
Thomas Brox Røst, Norwegian University of Science and Technology, Norway

Invited Speaker:

Sophia Ananiadou, University of Manchester, U.K.

Table of Contents

Keynote: Supporting evidence-based medicine using text mining
Sophia Ananiadou 1

A Graph-Based Analysis of Medical Queries of a Swedish Health Care Portal
Farnaz Moradi, Ann-Marie Eklund, Dimitrios Kokkinakis, Tomas Olovsson and Philippas Tsigas 2

The impact of near domain transfer on biomedical named entity recognition
Nigel Collier, Mai-vu Tran and Ferdinand Paster 11

Domain Adaptation with Active Learning for Coreference Resolution
Shanheng Zhao and Hwee Tou Ng 21

Towards Cross-Domain PDTB-Style Discourse Parsing
Evgeny Stepanov and Giuseppe Riccardi 30

Translating SNOMED CT Terminology into a Minor Language
Olatz Perez-de-Viñaspre and Maite Oronoz 38

A System for Building FrameNet-like Corpus for the Biomedical Domain
He Tan 46

Gene–disease association extraction by text mining and network analysis
Changqin Quan and Fuji Ren 54

Negation scope and spelling variation for text-mining of Danish electronic patient records
Cecilia Engel Thomas, Peter Bjødstrup Jensen, Thomas Werge and Søren Brunak 64

Building a semantically annotated corpus for congestive heart and renal failure from clinical records and the literature
Noha Alnazzawi, Paul Thompson and Sophia Ananiadou 69

Precise Medication Extraction using Agile Text Mining
Chaitanya Shivade, James Cormack and David Milward 75

Applying UMLS for Distantly Supervised Relation Detection
Roland Roller and Mark Stevenson 80

Adverse Drug Event prediction combining shallow analysis and machine learning
Sara Santiso, Arantza Casillas, Alicia Perez, Maite Oronoz and Koldo Gojenola 85

Reducing VSM data sparseness by generalizing contexts: application to health text mining
Amandine Périnet and Thierry Hamon 90

Disambiguation of Period Characters in Clinical Narratives
Markus Kreuzthaler and Stefan Schulz 96

Tuning HeidelTime for identifying time expressions in clinical texts in English and French
Thierry Hamon and Natalia Grabar 101

Detecting drugs and adverse events from Spanish social media streams
Isabel Segura-Bedmar, Ricardo Revert and Paloma Martínez 106

Care Episode Retrieval
Hans Moen, Erwin Marsi, Filip Ginter, Laura-Maria Murtola, Tapio Salakoski and Sanna Salanterä
116

Workshop Program

Sunday 27 April 2014

08:45	Opening Remarks by Sumithra Velupillai, Department of Computer and Systems Sciences (DSV), Stockholm University
	Keynote Talk
09:00	*Keynote: Supporting evidence-based medicine using text mining* Sophia Ananiadou
	Session I
10:05	*A Graph-Based Analysis of Medical Queries of a Swedish Health Care Portal* Farnaz Moradi, Ann-Marie Eklund, Dimitrios Kokkinakis, Tomas Olovsson and Philippas Tsigas
10:30	Coffee
	Session II
11:00	*The impact of near domain transfer on biomedical named entity recognition* Nigel Collier, Mai-vu Tran and Ferdinand Paster
11:25	*Domain Adaptation with Active Learning for Coreference Resolution* Shanheng Zhao and Hwee Tou Ng
11:55	*Towards Cross-Domain PDTB-Style Discourse Parsing* Evgeny Stepanov and Giuseppe Riccardi
12:20	Lunch Break

Sunday 27 April 2014 (continued)

Session III

13:45 *Translating SNOMED CT Terminology into a Minor Language*
Olatz Perez-de-Viñaspre and Maite Oronoz

14:10 *A System for Building FrameNet-like Corpus for the Biomedical Domain*
He Tan

14:35 *Gene–disease association extraction by text mining and network analysis*
Changqin Quan and Fuji Ren

Poster Session (with coffee 15:30-16:00)

Negation scope and spelling variation for text-mining of Danish electronic patient records
Cecilia Engel Thomas, Peter Bjødstrup Jensen, Thomas Werge and Søren Brunak

Building a semantically annotated corpus for congestive heart and renal failure from clinical records and the literature
Noha Alnazzawi, Paul Thompson and Sophia Ananiadou

Precise Medication Extraction using Agile Text Mining
Chaitanya Shivade, James Cormack and David Milward

Applying UMLS for Distantly Supervised Relation Detection
Roland Roller and Mark Stevenson

Adverse Drug Event prediction combining shallow analysis and machine learning
Sara Santiso, Arantza Casillas, Alicia Perez, Maite Oronoz and Koldo Gojenola

Reducing VSM data sparseness by generalizing contexts: application to health text mining
Amandine Périnet and Thierry Hamon

Disambiguation of Period Characters in Clinical Narratives
Markus Kreuzthaler and Stefan Schulz

Tuning HeidelTime for identifying time expressions in clinical texts in English and French
Thierry Hamon and Natalia Grabar

Sunday 27 April 2014 (continued)

Session IV

16:00 *Detecting drugs and adverse events from Spanish social media streams*
Isabel Segura-Bedmar, Ricardo Revert and Paloma Martínez

16:25 *Care Episode Retrieval*
Hans Moen, Erwin Marsi, Filip Ginter, Laura-Maria Murtola, Tapio Salakoski and Sanna Salanterä

16:50 Closing Remarks by Sumithra Velupillai, Department of Computer and Systems Sciences (DSV), Stockholm University

Keynote: Supporting evidence-based medicine using text mining

Sophia Ananiadou
School of Computer Science, University of Manchester, UK
sophia.ananiadou@manchester.ac.uk

Evidence-based medicine uses systematic reviews to identify relevant studies to answer specific research questions. An underlying principle of the approach is the importance of specifying a priori the research question to drive the review process. Such reviews have a central role in health technology assessments, development of clinical guidelines and public health guidance, and evidence-informed policy and practice. However, public health questions are complex and often need to be described using abstract, fuzzy terminology. Understanding the scope of evidence often emerges during a review and cannot be defined a priori. Can text mining support a dynamic and multidimensional definition of relevance using interactive, exploratory searching under uncertainty? Can text mining help reviewers to explore evidence of interconnections between different factors, diseases and human behaviour?

A Graph-Based Analysis of Medical Queries of a Swedish Health Care Portal

Farnaz Moradi[1], **Ann-Marie Eklund**[2], **Dimitrios Kokkinakis**[2], **Tomas Olovsson**[1], **Philippas Tsigas**[1]
[1]Computer Science and Engineering, Chalmers University of Technology, Sweden
[2]Språkbanken, Department of Swedish Language, University of Gothenburg, Sweden
{moradi,tomasol,tsigas}@chalmers.se[1]
{ann-marie.eklund,dimitrios.kokkinakis}@gu.se[2]

Abstract

Today web portals play an increasingly important role in health care allowing information seekers to learn about diseases and treatments, and to administrate their care. Therefore, it is important that the portals are able to support this process as well as possible. In this paper, we study the search logs of a public Swedish health portal to address the questions if health information seeking differs from other types of Internet search and if there is a potential for utilizing network analysis methods in combination with semantic annotation to gain insights into search behaviors. Using a semantic-based method and a graph-based analysis of word co-occurrences in queries, we show there is an overlap among the results indicating a potential role of these types of methods to gain insights and facilitate improved information search. In addition we show that samples, windows of a month, of search logs may be sufficient to obtain similar results as using larger windows. We also show that medical queries share the same structural properties found for other types of information searches, thereby indicating an ability to re-use existing analysis methods for this type of search data.

1 Introduction

Query logs which are obtained from search engines contain a wealth of information about the language used in the logs and the behavior of users. Searching for health and medical related information is quite common, and therefore analysis of query logs of medical websites can give us insight into the language being used and the information needs of the users in the medical domain.

In this study, we analyze 36 months of query logs from a Swedish health care portal, which provides health, disease, and medical information. On one hand, we perform a semantic enhancement on the queries to allow analysis of the language and the vocabulary which has been used in the queries. On the other hand, we perform a graph-based analysis of the queries, where a word co-occurrence graph is generated from the queries. In a word co-occurrence graph each node corresponds to a word and an edge exists between two words if they have co-occurred in the same query.

Our study reveals that a word co-occurrence graph generated from medical query logs has the same structural and temporal properties, i.e., small world properties and power law degree distribution, which has been observed for other types of networks generated from query logs and different types of real-world networks such as word association graphs. Therefore, the existing algorithms and data mining techniques can be applied directly for analysis of word co-occurrence graphs obtained from health search.

One of the widely studied structural properties of real-world networks is the communities in these networks. In this study, we apply a state-of-the-art local community detection algorithm on the word co-occurrence graph. A community detection algorithm can uncover a *graph community* which is a group of words that have co-occurred mostly with each other but not with the rest of the words in the network. The community detection algorithm used in this study is based on random walks on the graph and can find overlapping communities.

The communities of words, identified from the graph, are then compared with the communities of words obtained from a semantic analysis of the queries. In semantic enhancement, if a word or term in a query exists in medical oriented semantic resources, it is assigned a label. The words and terms which have co-occurred with these labels are used to create a *semantic community*. We have compared the obtained semantic communities with the graph communities using a well-known similarity measure and observed that the communities identified from these two different approaches overlap. Moreover, we observed that the graph communities can cover the vast majority of the words in the queries while the semantic communities do not cover many words. Therefore, the graph-based analysis can be used to improve and complement the semantic analysis.

Furthermore, we study the effect of the time window lengths for analysis of log queries. Our goal is to investigate whether short snapshots of log queries also can be useful for this type of analysis, and how the increase in the size of the log files over time can affect the results.

The reminder of this paper is organized as follows. In Section 2 we review the related work. Section 3 presents the Swedish log corpus used for this study. Section 4 describes the semantic enhancement on the query logs. In Section 5 we describe the graph analysis methods. Section 6 summarizes our experimental results. Finally, Section 7 concludes our work.

2 Related Work

In this paper, we study the co-occurrence of words in medical queries and perform both a semantic and graph analysis to identify and compare the communities of related words. In this section, we briefly present a number of related works which deal with analysis of query logs.

Query logs have been previously studied for identifying clusters of similar queries. In (Wen et al., 2001) a method was described for clustering similar queries using different notions of query distance, such as string matching of keywords. In (Baeza-Yates et al., 2004) clicked Web page information (terms in URLs) was used in order to create term-weight vector models for queries, and cosine similarity was used to calculate the similarity of two queries based on their vector representations.

Several previous works have also dealt with graph analysis of query logs. In (Baeza-Yates, 2007) several graph-based relations were described among queries based on different sources of information, such as words in the text of the query, clicked URL terms, clicks and session information. In (Herdagdelen et al., 2009) vector space models were compared, by embedding them in graphs, and graph random walk models in order to determine similarity between concepts, and showed that some random walk models can achieve results as good as or even better than the vector models. In (Gaillard and Gaume, 2011), it was shown that drawing clusters of synonyms in which pairs of nodes have a strong confluence is a strong indication of aiding two synonymy graphs accommodate each others' conflicting edges. Their work was a step for defining a similarity measure between graphs that is not based on edge-to-edge disagreement but rather on structural agreement.

3 Material - a Swedish Log Corpus

The Stockholm Health Care Guide, `http://www.vardguiden.se/`, is the official health information web site of the County of Stockholm, sponsored by the Stockholm County Council and used mostly by people living in the Stockholm area and provides information on diseases, health and health care. In January 2013 the Stockholm County Council reported that vardguiden.se had two million visitors per month. As of November 2013, vardguiden.se and another similar portal, 1177.se (which was a common web site for Swedish regions and counties, and the official national telephone number for health information and advice), are merged into one called 1177 Vårdguiden, sharing the same interface and search engine. The corpus data used in this study consists of the search queries for the period October 2010 to the end of September 2013. The data is provided by vardguiden.se, through an agreement with the company Euroling AB which provides indexing and searching functionality to vardguiden.se. We obtained 67 million queries in total, where 27 million are unique before any kind of normalization, and 2.2 million after case folding. Figure1 shows an example of a query log.

Information acquisition from query logs can be useful for several purposes and potential types of users, such as terminologists, infodemiologists, epidemiologists, medical data and web analysts, specialists in NLP technologies such as information retrieval and text mining, as well as, public officials in health and safety organizations. Analysis of web query logs can provide useful information regarding when and how users seek information for topics covered by the site (Bar-Ilan et

```
Q 929C0C14C209C3399CAE7AEC6DB92251 1377986505 symptom brist folsyra hidden:meta:region:00 = 13 1 -N - sv =
Q 2E6CD9E0071057E4BEDC0E52B0B0BDAC 1377986578 folsyra hidden:meta:region:00 = 36 1 -N - sv =
Q 527049C35E3810C45B22461C4CCB2C23 1377986649 kroppens anatomi hidden:meta:region:01 = 25 1 -N - sv =
Q F86B6B133154FD247C1525BAF169B387 1377986685 stroke hidden:meta:region:00 = 320 1 -N - sv =
Q 17CCB738766C545BFE3899C71A22DE3B 1377986807 diabetes typ 2 vad beror på hidden:meta:region:12 = 61 1 -N - sv =
```

Figure 1: Example queries. A query consist of (Q)uery, session ID, time stamp, search query, metadata, number of links returned, the batch ID of the visited link, (N)o spelling suggestions, Swedish search.

al., 2009). Such information can be used both for a general understanding of public health awareness and the information seeking patterns of users, and for optimizing search indexing, query completion and presentation of results for improved public health information. For an overview of some common applications and methods for log analysis see (Oliner et al., 2011).

Deeper mining into queries can reveal more important information about search engine users and their language use and also new information from the search requests; cf. (Medelyan, 2004). The basis for Search Analytics is made of different kinds of logs of search terms and presented and chosen results by web site users (Mat-Hassan and Levene, 2005). At a syntactic level queries may contain e.g., synonyms and hyponyms, and to be able to study patterns of search behavior at a more abstract level, we map the syntactic terms to semantic concepts. To our knowledge this is the first of its kind resource for Swedish and as such it can be used as a test bed for experimental work in understanding the breadth and depth of usage patterns, the properties of the resource and the challenges involved in working with such type of data. The only study we are aware of using Swedish log data, in the context of health-related information, is described by (Hulth et al., 2009). In their study, three million search logs from vardguiden.se (June 05 to June 07) were used for the purpose of influenza surveillance in Sweden, and seven symptoms, roughly corresponding to cough, sore throat, shortness of breath, coryza (head cold), fever, headache, myalgia (muscle pain) were studied.

4 Semantic Enhancement

Description of various corpus analytics that enables us to gain insights into the language used in the logs; e.g., terminology and general vocabulary provide, to a certain degree, an indication of the search strategies applied by the users of the web site service from where the logs are obtained. Findings can serve as background work that, e.g., can be incorporated in search engines or other web-based applications to personalize search results, provide specific site recommendations and suggest more precise search terms, e.g., by the automatic identification of laymen/novices or domain experts. The logs have been automatically annotated with two medically-oriented semantic resources (Kokkinakis, 2011) and a named entity recognizer (Kokkinakis, 2004). The semantic resources are the Systematized Nomenclature of Medicine - Clinical Terms (SNOMED CT) and the National Repository for Medicinal Products (NPL, `http://www.lakemedelsverket.se/`)[1]. We perceive all these resources as highly complementary for our task since the Swedish SNOMED CT does not contain drug names and of course none of the two contain information about named entities.

4.1 SNOMED CT and NPL

SNOMED CT provides a common language that enables consistency in capturing, storing, retrieving, sharing and aggregating health data across specialties and sites of care. SNOMED CT provides codes and concept definitions for most clinical areas. SNOMED CT concepts are organized into 18 top-level hierarchies, such as Body Structure and Clinical Finding, each subdivided into several sub-hierarchies and contains around 280,000 terms. More detailed information about SNOMED CT can be found at the International Health Terminology Standards Development Organisation's web site, IHTSDO, at: `http://www.ihtsdo.org/snomed-ct/`.

The NPL is the official Swedish product registry for drugs and contains 11,250 entries. Every product in the registry contains metadata about

[1]Named entities have not been used for this study. However, we intend to use them in future studies. Nevertheless, the named entity annotation includes the ontological categories location, organization, person, time, and measure entities. Such entities can capture a wide range of entities searched by in such logs such as addresses to health care centers and various health care organizations.

its substance(s), names, dosages, producers and classifications, like prescription and Anatomical Therapeutic Chemical codes (ATC). For instance, for the question "missbruk st göranssjukhus" ("abuse st göran hospital") from the query "Q \t C7ED234574EE24 \t 1326104437 \t missbruk st göranssjukhus meta:category:PageType;Article \t = \t 0 \t ..." (here "\t" signals a tab separation), we add three new tab-delimited columns (named entity label, SNOMED-CT, NPL or N/A if no match can be made) to each query. In this case, the three added columns for this particular query will get the labels "FUNCT-ENT", "finding–32709003–missbruk" and "N/A" (no annotation), where the first stands for a FUNCTional-ENTity, the second for a finding category with concept-id "32709003" and "missbruk" as the recommended term.

4.2 Semantic Communities

We use the semantic labels obtained from the semantic enhancement to group words into communities. Communities can be used for getting insight into the language and the related words being used for medical search. The words which are matched with the same semantic label are clearly relevant to each other as they belong to the same semantic hierarchy. For each semantic label, we create a set of all the words in the queries which received this label. In other words, the words in queries that co-occurred with the same label are assumed to belong to the same community.

We have generated such communities only from SNOMED CT and NPL labels and refer to them as *semantic communities* in the rest of the paper. As an example, the community {borrelia, serologiska, blodprover, test, serologisk, testning} was obtained from the queries which received the label "qualifier value–27377004–serologisk".

5 Graph Analysis

Query log data can be modeled using different types of graphs (Baeza-Yates, 2007). In this study, we have generated a word co-occurrence graph, in which each node corresponds to a word and two nodes are connected with an edge if they have appeared in the same query. The generated graph is undirected and unweighted and has no multiedges. To generate the graph we have used the words as they appeared in the logs, i.e., we did not replace words with their synonyms, correct misspellings, or translate non-Swedish words to Swedish. For example, "eye", "öga", "ögat", "ögon", and "ögonen" appear as five different nodes in the graph but mean the same thing.

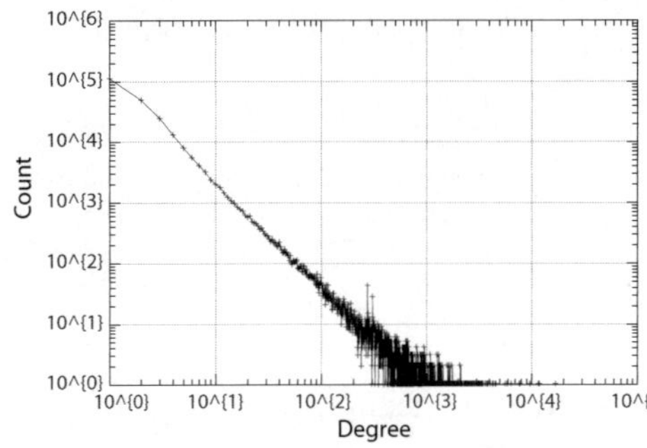

Figure 2: The degree distribution of the co-occurrence graph.

The graph $G(V, E)$ generated from the queries which contained two or more words has $|V| =$ 265,785 nodes and $|E| =$ 1,555,149 edges. The words in one-word queries which did not co-occur with any other words could not be considered for the graph analysis. The generated graph consists of 6,688 connected components. A connected component is a group of nodes where a path exists between any pair of them. The largest connected component of the graph, also known as giant connected component (GCC), contains around 95% of the nodes in the graph.

It was shown in (Ferrer i Cancho and Solé, 2001), that a graph generated from the co-occurrence of words in sentences in human languages, exhibit two structural properties that other types of complex networks have, i.e, the graph is a *small world* network and it has a *power-law degree distribution* (Barabási and Albert, 1999). Later studies on different types of word graphs have also been shown to follow the above properties. In this paper, we also show that a word co-occurrence graph generated from medical queries exhibits the same structural properties.

In small world networks, there is a short path connecting any pair of nodes in the GCC of the network. This property can be examined by calculating the *effective diameter* of the network (Leskovec et al., 2007). Small word networks also are highly clustered and therefore have a high *clustering coefficient* value. The effective diameter of our co-occurrence graph is 4.88, and it has an average clustering coefficient of 0.34. These values confirm that our word co-occurrence graph is a small world network.

Table 1: Structural properties of the word co-occurrence graph over time.

Time window	$\lvert V \rvert$	$\lvert E \rvert$	$\lvert V_{GCC} \rvert$	clustering coeff.	effective diameter
1 month	16,045	52,403	14,877	0.29	5.47
3 months	30,681	168,045	29,220	0.30	5.42
6 months	48,229	298,331	46,435	0.31	5.38
12 months	69,380	414,643	67,245	0.32	4.97
36 months	265,785	1,555,149	251,597	0.34	4.88

The degree distribution of the co-occurrence graph is shown in Figure 2. It can be seen that the degree distribution follows a power law distribution. This observation is similar to the observations presented by (Baeza-Yates and Tiberi, 2007) that almost all the measures of a graph generated from query log files follow power laws. Therefore, the user behavior in medical search does not seem different from general search behavior. In addition to networks of word relations, power law degree distributions have also been observed in social, information, and interaction networks where there are many nodes with low degrees and a few nodes with very high degrees (Clauset et al., 2009). The word with the highest degree in our graph is "barn" (child/children) which has 17,086 edges. Some other high-degree nodes are "sjukdom" (disease), "behandling" (treatment), "ont" (pain), "gravid" (pregnant), and "feber" (fever).

We have also looked into how the structural properties of the word co-occurrence graph change over time as the graph increases in size with an increasing number of queries. Table 1 summarizes the results. It can be seen that similar to many other networks, the diameter of the graph shrinks when more nodes become connected and its average clustering coefficient does not change much as the graph becomes larger.

Overall, the structural properties of the word co-occurrence graph are similar to many other real-world networks. Although it was shown in (Yang et al., 2011) that the queries and information needs of medical practitioners in accessing electronic health records are different from users of general search engines, our analysis reveals that there are similarities between information seeking of general users on health data and on general data. Therefore, the algorithms introduced for analysis of such networks can be directly deployed for analysis of word co-occurrence graphs.

5.1 Graph Community Detection

One of the widely studied structural properties of real-world networks is their community structure. A community, also known as a cluster, is defined as a group of nodes in a graph which have dense connections to each other, but have few connections to the rest of the nodes in the network. There have been numerous studies on the community structure of social and information networks and a variety of algorithms have been proposed for identifying the communities in these networks. A thorough overview of different types of community detection algorithms can be found in (Fortunato, 2010; Xie et al., 2013).

Community detection algorithms can be divided into global and local algorithms. The global algorithms require a global knowledge of the entire structure of the network to be able to find its communities. Therefore, these types of algorithms do not scale well for log analysis since query logs are usually very large and are continuously growing. The local algorithms, on the other hand, only require a partial knowledge of the network and therefore can identify network communities in parallel. However, the identified communities might not cover all the nodes in a network.

Moreover, community detection algorithms can be divided into overlapping and non-overlapping algorithms. Traditional partitioning and clustering algorithms typically divide the nodes in a network into disjoint communities. But in many real networks, a node can actually belong to more than one community. For example, in a social network, a user can belong to a community of family members, a community of friends, and a community of colleagues. In a co-occurrence graph, a symptom can co-occur with different types of diseases. Therefore, a community detection algorithm which can identify overlapping communities is more suitable for analysis of the graphs generated from search queries.

For the analysis of log queries, we have used a local overlapping community detection algorithm. This algorithm is a random walk-based algorithm which uses an approximation of a personalized PageRank (Andersen and Lang, 2006; Andersen et al., 2006) and is shown to perform well in detecting real communities in social and interaction networks (Yang and Leskovec, 2012). The algorithm starts from a seed node and expands the seed into a community until a scoring function is optimized. One of the widely used functions for community detection is *conductance*. The conductance of a community C in a graph $G(V, E)$ is defined as $\phi(C) = \frac{\overline{m}(C)}{\min(vol(C), vol(V \setminus C))}$, where $\overline{m}(C)$ is the number of inter-cluster edges and $vol(C) = \sum_{v \in C} deg(v)$ is the volume of a community and corresponds to the sum of the degree of all the nodes in the community. The lower the conductance of a community, the better quality the community has. The complexity of this algorithm is independent of the size of the network and only depends on the size of the target communities.

6 Experimental Results

In this section we present our experimental results and discuss the possible applications for graph-based analysis of medical data.

6.1 Semantic and Graph Analysis

From the semantic enhancement, we have generated 16,427 unique semantic communities which cover less than 11% of the nodes in the network. This means that, the majority of the queries in the network did not contain words that match the medical concepts provided by of SNOMED CT and NPL. This observation suggests that a semantic enhancement of queries on its own is not adequate for understanding the relations between all the words used in medical search.

For the graph analysis, we have used the local overlapping community detection algorithm of (Yang and Leskovec, 2012) to identify the communities from the co-occurrence graph generated from the complete query logs. The algorithm identified 107,765 unique communities in the GCC of the graph with average conductance 0.74. This shows that the communities are not well separated from each other and that there are many edges between distinct communities. Moreover, the identified communities cover 93% of the nodes in the network which means that the graph analysis is more suitable for the study of the relations between the words than the semantic analysis.

The semantic communities and the graph communities are both dependent on the co-occurrence of words in queries, but identify communities differently. The semantic method places the nodes which belong to the same semantic hierarchy together with the words that co-occurred with them in the same community. However, the graph-based method places the words based on the structure of the generated network in the communities.

We have compared and calculated the similarity between the graph communities and the semantic communities using the *jaccard index* which is defined as $JI(C, S) = \frac{|C \cap S|}{|C \cup S|}$. The jaccard index shows the normalized size of the overlap between a graph community C and a semantic community S. Similarity functions, including Jaccard, have been used before for measuring the distance of two different queries. In this study we use similarity to assess the similarity of communities of words obtained from the two distinct methods.

We have compared each semantic community with all the graph communities and show the similarity distribution in Figure 3. It can be seen that the majority of the communities partially overlap. As an example, from the word "tandsjukdom" (dental disease) as the seed, we identified the graph community {tandsjukdom, licken, munhåleproblem, rubev, emalj, tändernaamelin, hypopla, permanentatänder, lixhen, hypoplazy, hipoplasy, hypoplazi, bortnött, hipoplazy}. From the semantic enhancement, "tandsjukdom" and "tandsjukdomar" both have received semantic label "disorder–234947003–tandsjukdom". From the queries which received this label we have generated the semantic community {tandsjukdom, emalj, olika, vanligaste, tandsjukdomar, licken, plack, ovanliga}. The similarity of these communities is low, i.e., 0.16, however, they both contain the words which are clearly relevant to teeth and dental diseases.

As another example, "osteoklast" and "osteoklaster" both receive the semantic label "cell–27770000–osteoklast". From the graph analysis, we have found {osteoklaster, osteoblster, osteocyter, osteoblaster} as a community with "osteoklaster" as the seed. We have also obtained the semantic community {osteoblaster, osteoklast, osteoporos, osteocyter, benskörhet, osteoklaster, osteoblster}. In this example, the graph community is a subset of the semantic community, and their similarity is 0.57. The above examples suggest that a graph-based analysis of medical queries can be used to complement the semantic analysis.

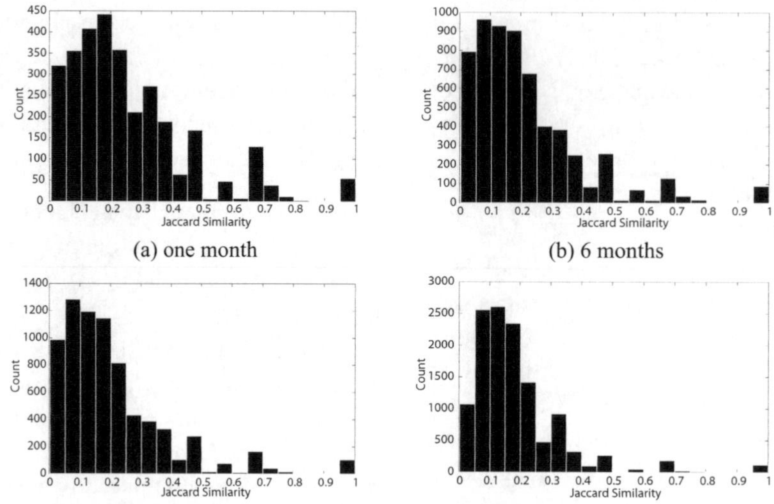

(a) one month (b) 6 months (c) 12 months (d) 36 months

Figure 3: The distributions of jaccard similarity of semantic-based and graph-based communities.

6.2 Frequent Co-Occurrence Analysis

In the query logs, we observed that there are many misspellings, meaningless words, etc. In order to clear the dataset, it is common in different studies of log files, to filter out queries which appeared less frequently. By removing such queries, we can dramatically reduce the number of such words.

In this study, we have generated another graph from the words which co-occurred frequently in different queries. We have only considered words that co-occurred five times or more, and the graph contains 32,449 nodes and 217,320 edges, with average clustering coefficient of 0.29 and effective diameter of 5.66.

In the GCC of this graph we found 22,890 graph communities with average conductance of 0.65 and coverage of 95%. Moreover, we have also used the words which co-occurred at least five times to generate the semantic communities. The similarity of these communities with graph communities using jaccard similarity was 0.16 in average which is slightly lower than when no filtering was used. Overall, our observations suggest that filtering can be used to reduce the noise in the datasets and allow us to perform a faster analysis on a smaller graph.

6.3 Time Window Analysis

Another property which we have empirically studied in this paper is the effect of time window length during which the queries are analyzed. We have observed that, in average, more than 31% of the nodes and 12% of the edges have reappeared in each month compared to their previous month. This suggests that the search content changes over time perhaps depending on the changes in the monthly or seasonal information requirements of the users. It also means that over time the size of the word co-occurrence graph increases (see Table 1), and since in each month new co-occurrences shape, the graph becomes more and more connected. Therefore, when the time window is long, the analysis requires more time and the identified communities do not have good conductance. When the time window is short, the small size of the graph speeds up the analysis but might affect the analysis result. In this section we investigate the effect of time window length on our analysis.

We started by setting the time window length to one month. From the queries which were observed during each month, we generated a co-occurrence graph and identified the graph communities and the semantic communities. As presented in Section 5, the structural properties of a graph generated from one month are quite similar to that of the complete graph. We have also observed that the average conductance of the communities identified by the community detection algorithm is around 0.5 which is lower than when the complete graph was used. This means that the communities in the graphs generated from one month of queries have better quality since they have fewer connections to the rest of the graph.

We observed that the similarities between graph communities and semantic communities are higher when a one-month window is used (in average 0.26). By increasing the length of the time window from one to three, six, twelve, and thirty-six months, we observed a reduction in the similarities (in average 0.23, 0.22, 0.21, and 0.19, respectively). The similarity distributions are shown in Figure 3. It seems that with more queries over time, more words get connected and it becomes more difficult to identify good communities. Therefore, using short time windows can improve the quality of the analysis. Moreover, analysis of different time windows can also shed light on how the word relations and user requirements are affected by the months or seasons of the year.

6.4 Discussion

Our empirical analysis of a large-scale query log of medical related search presented in this paper can be used to improve our knowledge of the terminology and general vocabulary, as well as the search strategies of the users. In addition to providing a background for language analysis, a potential application for community detection could be to provide better spelling suggestions to users. We have observed that there are communities with very low conductance which contain a number of words which seem to correspond to guessing attempts to find a correct spelling, e.g., {shoulder, froozen, frosen, cholder, sholder, fingers, frozen, scholder, shulder, schoulder, shoulders}. The low conductance of the community means that the community is very isolated and has very few edges outside it and therefore it can easily be cut from the graph. Therefore, the community detection can be used for identifying such cases.

Another potential application of our graph analysis method is to provide recommendations and suggest more precise search terms based on the words that appear in the same community as the keywords entered by the users. For example, since the communities can overlap, each word can belong to more than one graph community or semantic community. We observed that in average, in the complete graph (generated from 36 months of logs), each word belongs to 3.8 unique graph communities and 3.6 semantic communities. It means that a word which can be related to multiple groups of words or have different meanings, can belong to several communities. This knowledge can potentially be used to provide suggestions to the users and help them to select the intended meaning and therefore reducing the ambiguity in the searched queries.

Overall, in this paper, we have presented a promising approach for analysis of medical queries using co-occurrence graphs. As a future work, the following improvements could be of interest for complementing our empirical study:

- Representing different variations of the words with only a single node in the graph, e.g., "öga" for "ögat", and "ögon".
- Filtering out the non-medical related words such as person and location entities from the queries based on the semantic enhancement with name entities from NER. Overall, more than 136,000 queries contained a person name entity, and around 127,000 contained a place entity.
- Filtering out high frequency words/terms which do not have medical significance, e.g., "olika" (different).

7 Conclusions

Our analysis of a large-scale medical query log corpus is the first step towards understanding the language and the word relations in health/medical related queries. We have performed a semantic enhancement of queries based on medically related semantic resources to find the communities of words which have co-occurred with a semantic label. We have also performed a graph-based analysis of the word co-occurrences and have shown that since a word co-occurrence graph has similar structural properties to many types of real-world networks, existing algorithms for network analysis can be deployed for our study. We then have used a random walk-based community detection algorithm in order to identify communities of words in our graph. Our empirical results show that the communities identified from the semantic analysis and the graph analysis overlap, however the graph-based analysis can identify many more communities and achieves much higher coverage of the words in the queries. Therefore, the graph-based analysis can be used in order to improve and complement the semantic analysis. Our experiments also show that short time window lengths for analysis of query logs, such as a month, would suffice for graph-based analysis of medical queries.

8 Acknowledgments

We are thankful to Adam Blomberg, CTO, Euroling AB for providing the log data. We are also thankful for the support by the Centre for Language Technology (`http://clt.gu.se`).

References

Reid Andersen and Kevin Lang. 2006. Communities from seed sets. In *Proceedings of the 15th international conference on World Wide Web - WWW '06*, page 223. ACM Press.

Reid Andersen, Fan Chung, and Kevin Lang. 2006. Local Graph Partitioning using PageRank Vectors. In *2006 47th Annual IEEE Symposium on Foundations of Computer Science (FOCS'06)*, pages 475–486. IEEE.

Ricardo Baeza-Yates and Alessandro Tiberi. 2007. Extracting semantic relations from query logs. *Proceedings of the 13th ACM SIGKDD international conference on Knowledge discovery and data mining - KDD '07*, page 76.

Ricardo Baeza-Yates, Carlos Hurtado, and Marcelo Mendoza. 2004. Query Clustering for Boosting Web Page Ranking. In *Advances in Web Intelligence*, volume 3034, pages 164–175. Springer.

Ricardo Baeza-Yates. 2007. Graphs from Search Engine Queries. In *Theory and Practice of Computer Science*, volume 4362, pages 1–8. Springer.

Judit Bar-Ilan, Zheng Zhu, and Mark Levene. 2009. Topic-specific analysis of search queries. In *Proceedings of the 2009 workshop on Web Search Click Data - WSCD '09*, pages 35–42. ACM Press.

A.L. Barabási and R. Albert. 1999. Emergence of Scaling in Random Networks. *Science*, 286(5439):509.

Aaron Clauset, Cosma Rohilla Shalizi, and M. E. J. Newman. 2009. Power-Law Distributions in Empirical Data. *SIAM Review*, 51(4):661–703, November.

R Ferrer i Cancho and R V Solé. 2001. The small world of human language. *Proceedings. Biological sciences / The Royal Society*, 268(1482):2261–5, November.

Santo Fortunato. 2010. Community detection in graphs. *Physics Reports*, 486(3-5):75–174, February.

Benoît Gaillard and Bruno Gaume. 2011. Invariants and Variability of Synonymy Networks : Self Mediated Agreement by Confluence. In *Proceedings of the TextGraphs-6 Workshop (Graph-based Algorithms for Natural Language Processing)*, pages 15–23.

Amaç Herdagdelen, Katrin Erk, and Marco Baroni. 2009. Measuring semantic relatedness with vector space models and random walks. In *In Proceedings of the TextGraphs-4 (Graph-based Methods for Natural Language Processing)*, pages 50–53.

Anette Hulth, Gustaf Rydevik, and Annika Linde. 2009. Web queries as a source for syndromic surveillance. *PloS one*, 4(2):e4378, January.

Dimitrios Kokkinakis. 2004. Reducing the Effect of Name Explosion. In *In Proceedings of the LREC Workshop: Beyond Named Entity Recognition, Semantic Labelling for NLP tasks. Fourth Language Resources and Evaluation Conference (LREC)*, pages 1–6.

Dimitrios Kokkinakis. 2011. What is the Coverage of SNOMED CTon Scientific Medical Corpora? *MIE: XXIII International Conference of the European Federation for Medical Informatics. Studies in Health Technology and Informatics*, 169:814 – 818.

Jure Leskovec, Jon Kleinberg, and Christos Faloutsos. 2007. Graph Evolution: Densification and Shrinking Diameters. *ACM Transactions on Knowledge Discovery from Data*, 1(1):2–es, March.

Mazlita Mat-Hassan and Mark Levene. 2005. Associating search and navigation behavior through log analysis. *Journal of the American Society for Information Science and Technology*, 56(9):913–934, July.

Olena Medelyan. 2004. Why Not Use Query Logs As Corpora? In *Proceedings of the Ninth ESSLLI Student Session*, pages 1–10.

Adam Oliner, U C Berkeley, and Archana Ganapathi. 2011. Advances and Challenges in Log Analysis Logs contain a wealth of information for help in managing systems . *Queue - Log Analysis*, pages 1–11.

Ji-rong Wen, Jian-yun Nie, and Hong-Jiang Zhang. 2001. Clustering user queries of a search engine. In *Proceedings of the tenth international conference on World Wide Web - WWW '01*, pages 162–168. ACM Press.

Jierui Xie, S Kelley, and BK Szymanski. 2013. Overlapping community detection in networks: the state of the art and comparative study. *ACM Computing Surveys*, 45(4).

Jaewon Yang and Jure Leskovec. 2012. Defining and evaluating network communities based on ground-truth. In *Proceedings of the IEEE International Conference on Data Mining (ICDM)*, pages 1–8.

Lei Yang, Qiaozhu Mei, Kai Zheng, and David a Hanauer. 2011. Query log analysis of an electronic health record search engine. *AMIA ... Annual Symposium proceedings / AMIA Symposium. AMIA Symposium*, 2011:915–24, January.

The impact of near domain transfer on biomedical named entity recognition

Nigel Collier*
European Bioinformatics Institute
Hinxton, Cambridge, UK, and
National Institute of Informatics, Tokyo, Japan

Ferdinand Paster
University of Applied Sciences
Upper Austria
Hagenberg Campus, Austria

Mai-vu Tran
University of Engineering and Technology - VNU
Hanoi, Vietnam

Abstract

Current research in fully supervised biomedical named entity recognition (bioNER) is often conducted in a setting of low sample sizes. Whilst experimental results show strong performance in-domain it has been recognised that quality suffers when models are applied to heterogeneous text collections. However the causal factors have until now been uncertain. In this paper we describe a controlled experiment into near domain bias for two Medline corpora on hereditary diseases. Five strategies are employed for mitigating the impact of near domain transference including simple transference, pooling, stacking, class re-labeling and feature augmentation. We measure their effect on f-score performance against an in domain baseline. Stacking and feature augmentation mitigate f-score loss but do not necessarily result in superior performance except for selected classes. Simple pooling of data across domains failed to exploit size effects for most classes. We conclude that we can expect lower performance and higher annotation costs if we do not adequately compensate for the distributional dissimilarities of domains during learning.

1 Introduction

Model and feature selection are important experimental tasks in supervised machine learning for suggesting approaches that will generalise well on real world data. Research in biomedical named entity recognition (bioNER) often displays two features: (1) small samples of labeled data, and (2) an implicit assumption that the future data will be drawn from a similar distribution to the labeled data and hence that minimising expected prediction error on held out data will minimise actual future loss. Since expert labeling is time consuming and expensive, labeled data sets tend to be relatively small, e.g. (Kim et al., 2003; Tanabe et al., 2005; Pyysalo et al., 2007), in the region of a few hundred or thousand Medline abstracts. Despite the danger of intrinsic idiosyncracies such corpora are often used to demonstrate putative prediction error across the heterogeneous collection of 22 million Medline abstracts. Once this assumption is made explicit it is of interest to both researchers and users that the implications and limitations of such experimental settings are explored.

Cross domain studies have indicated an advantage for mechanisms that compensate for domain bias. For fully supervised learning, which is the scenario we explore here, recent methods include: feature augmentation (Daumé III, 2007; Arnold et al., 2008; McClosky et al., 2010), instance weighting (Jiang and Zhai, 2007; Foster et al., 2010), schema harmonisation (Wang et al., 2010) and semi-supervised/lightly supervised approaches (Sagae and Tsujii, 2007; Liu et al., 2011; Pan et al., 2013). More generally there is a wide body of work in transfer learning (also known as *domain adaptation*) that tries to handle discrepancies between training and testing distributions (Pan and Yang, 2010).

As an illustration of near domain bias consider the list of high frequency named entities in Table 1 drawn from two sub-domains in the research literature of hereditary diseases. A domain expert in hereditary diseases would have no difficulty in dividing them into two non-overlapping sets corresponding to the two near domains with one term t_5 *patients* shared by both: $\{t_1,t_6,t_8,t_9\}$ and $\{t_2,t_3,t_4,t_7,t_{10}\}$.

Previous studies have shown what happens when you radically change the domain and/or the

*collier@ebi.ac.uk

t_1	rheumatoid arthritis	t_6	human leukocyte antigen
t_2	lupus erythematosus	t_7	coronary heart disease
t_3	leopard syndrome	t_8	type 1 diabetes
t_4	Omapatrilat	t_9	T1D
t_5	patients	t_{10}	hypertension

Table 1: High frequency entities in the hereditory disease literature for auto-immune and cardio-vascular diseases.

annotation schema, e.g. from newswire to Medline or Web pages. But what happens when the annotation schema, the annotator and the primary domain stay the same? Although the notion of *domain* is difficult to formalise in the context of research literature, this study explores the condition where the variable factor is a shift to a *near domain* of literature as defined by biocurators and illustrated in the previous example. Our contribution to biomedical named entity recognition (bioNER) is in five areas:

1. We compare four data combination strategies for mitigating the impact of near domain transference and measure their effect on f-score performance against an in domain baseline.

2. We provide additional evidence for the effectiveness of (Daumé III, 2007)'s *frustratingly simple* strategy which provides both general and domain-specific features; in effect a joint learning model.

3. Expectedly, but not trivially, we show that a general loss of f-score occurs on bioNER when transfering to near domains. This loss is not uniform across all classes. We provide class-by-class drill down analysis to the underlying causal factors which make some entities more robust to near domain transference in biomedicine than others.

4. Our results challenge the notion that pooling small corpora, even when guideline differences are reconciled, leads to improved f-score performance (Wang et al., 2010; Wagholikar et al., 2013).

5. In addition to the usual biomedical entity types we introduce the class of phenotypes which are valued as indicators of genetic malfunction and characteristic of diseases. The phenotype class incorporates a complex dependency between classes, notably anatomical entities and genes.

This paper is organised as follows: Section 2 describes related work in cross domain transfer for biomedical NER, Section 3 discusses our approach including the two data sets used in our experiments, CRF model, feature choices and evaluation framework. In Section 4 we outline our experimental design. Finally in Section 5 we compare the performance of six data selection strategies that try to maximise f-score performance on domain entity classes in the target corpus.

2 Related work

It is surprising that there exists, to the best of our knowledge, no controlled study that has shed light on the issue of near domain transfer for bioNER in a straightforward manner. The closest approach to our investigation in the biomedical domain is (Wang et al., 2009). Wang et al. explore potential sources of incompatibility across major bioNER corpora with different annotation schema (GENIA - 2000 Medline abstracts, GENETAG - approximately 20,000 Medline sentences and AIMed - 225 Medline abstracts). They focus exclusively on protein name recognition and observe a drop in performance of 12% f-score when combining data from different corpora. Various reasons are put forwards such as differences in entity boundary conventions, the scope of the entity class definitions, distributional properties of the entity classes and the degree of overlap between corpora.

A follow up study by the authors (Wang et al., 2010) looked at increasing compatibility between the GENIA and GENETAG corpora by reorganising the annotation schema to unify protein, DNA and RNA NER under a new label GGP (Gene and Gene Product). However the best performance from the coarse grained annotations still do not improve on the intra-corpus data.

In earlier work, (Tsai et al., 2006) looked at schema differences between the JNLPBA corpus of 2000 Medline abstracts (Kim et al., 2004) and the BioCreative corpus of 15,000 Medline sentences (Yeh et al., 2005) and tried to harmonise matching criteria. They demonstrated that relaxing the boundary matching criteria was helpful in maximising the cross-domain performance.

In the clinical domain (Wagholikar et al., 2013), explore the effect of harmonising annotation guidelines on the 2010 i2b2 challenge with Mayo Clinic Rochester (MCR) electronic patient records. They concluded that the effectiveness of pooling - i.e. merging of corpora by ensuring a common format and harmonised semantics - is dependent on several factors including compatibility between the annotation schema and differences in size. Again they noticed that simple pooling resulted in a loss of f-score, 12% for MCR and 4% for i2b2. They concluded that the asymmetry was likely due to size effects of the corpora, i.e. MCR being smaller suffered a greater loss due to the classifier being biased towards i2b2.

Due to the formulation of these studies and their limited scope it has previously been difficult to understand the precise causual factors affecting performance. Our study sheds light on the expected level of loss under different combination strategies and more importantly highlights the non-uniform nature of that loss.

3 Approach

We assume two small labeled data sets $D^S = d^s_1..d^s_n$ and $D^T = d^t_1..d^t_m$. $d^s_i = \langle x_i \subset X, y_i \subset Y \rangle$ is drawn from an unknown distribution P^s and represents the source document examples. Similarly,$d^t_i = \langle x_i \subset X, y_i \subset Y \rangle$ is also drawn from an unknown distribution P^t and represents the target document examples. We assume that D^S has N examples and D^T has M examples where $N \approx M$. x_i represents a covariate or feature vector and y_i is a target or label that can take multiple discrete values. We have a learning algorithm that learns a function $h : X \rightarrow Y$ with minimal loss on the portion of D^T used for testing. Any combination of D^S and D^T which are not used in testing can be used to learn h. Our task is to explore various strategies for data selection and re-factoring labels/features in order to maximise held out performance.

3.1 Data

In this paper we aim to empirically test domain transferrence for bioNER under the condition that the test and training data are relatively small and drawn from near domains, i.e. from studies on different types of heritable diseases. To do this we selected Medline abstracts from PubMed that were cited by biocuration experts in the canonical database on heritable diseases, the Online Mendelian Inheritance of Man (OMIM) (Hamosh et al., 2005). We selected *auto-immune diseases* and *cardio-vascular diseases* for our two corpora which we denote as C1 and C2 respectively. By comparing performance of a single model, a single annotator and a single annotation scheme with a range of sampling techniques we hope to quantify the effects of domain transferrence in isolation.

The target classes for the entities are as follows:

ANA Anatomical structures in the body. e.g. *liver, heart.*

CHE A chemical or drug. e.g. *pristane, histamine, S-nitrosoglutathione.*

DIS Diseases. e.g. *end stage renal disease, mitral valve prolapse.*

GGP Genes and gene products. e.g. *KLKB1 gene, highly penetrant recessive major gene.*

PHE Phenotype entities describing observable and measurable characteristic of an organism. e.g. *cardiovascular abnormalities, abundant ragged-red fibers, elevated IgE levels.*

ORG A living organism. e.g.*first-degree relatives, mice.*

The two corpora were annotated by a single experienced annotator who had participated in the GENIA entity and event corpus annotation. We developed detailed guidelines for single span none-nested entities before conducting a training and feedback session. Feedback was conducted over two weeks by email and direct meetings with the annotator and then annotation took approximately two months. The characteristics of the two corpora are shown in Table 2. Because annotation was carried out by only one person we do not provide inter-annotator scores.

Importantly, we note four points at this stage: (1) We incorporate a new named entity type, phenotype, which is aligned with investigations into heritable diseases. Semantically it is interesting because phenotypes annotated in the auto-immune literature pertain more often to sub-cellular processes and those in the cardiovascular domain pertain more often to cells, tissues and organs; (2) It can be seen that two NE classes fall well below 500 instances - what we might arbitarily consider the necessary level of support for high levels of performance. These are ANA and CHE;

	C1	C2	a	b
Abstracts	110	80	-	-
Tokens	27,421	26,578	-	-
Av. length	32.57	29.93	-	-
ANA	194 (138)	195 (133)	0.33	0.26
CHE	44 (33)	147 (75)	0.08	0.07
DIS	892 (282)	955 (442)	0.39	0.27
GGP	1663 (928)	754 (511)	0.41	0.45
ORG	799 (429)	770 (323)	0.56	0.67
PHE	507 (423)	1430 (1113)	0.52	0.33

Table 2: Characteristics of the C1 auto-immune and C2 cardiovascular corpora: number of abstracts, number of tokens, average sentence length, frequency of each entity type. Figures in parentheses represent counts after removing duplication. a: probability that a word in an entity class X in C1 is also a word in entity class X in C2. b: probability that a word in an entity class X in C2 is also a word in entity class X in C1

(3) We calculated from Table 2 the average number of mentions for each entity form by class and noted that this is relatively stable across corpora, except for DIS which has less variation in C2 than C1 and CHE which has more variation in C2 than C1. When combining evidence from both corpora the approximate order of type/token ratio are $PHE < ANA < CHE, GGP < ORG < DIS$ indicating that on average PHE entities have the greatest variation. Average entity lengths in tokens (not shown) indicate that PHE are significantly longer than other entity mentions; and (4) We calculated the probability that a word token in an entity class from one corpus would appear in an instance of the same entity class in the other corpus, reported as columns a and b. Although the probability of an exact match in instances between entities in the two corpora is generally quite low (below 20% - data not shown) there appears to be significant vocabulary overlap in most classes except for chemicals.

3.2 Conditional Random Fields

As in (Finkel and Manning, 2009) we apply our approach to a linear chain conditional random field (CRF) model (Lafferty et al., 2001; McCallum and Wei, 2003; Settles, 2004; Doan et al., 2012) using the Mallet toolkit[1] with default parameters. CRFs have been shown consistently to be among the highest performing bioNER learners. The data selection strategies employed here though are neutral and could have been applied to any other fully supervised learner model.

3.3 Features

We made use of a wide range of features, both conventional features such as word or part of speech, as well as gazetteers derived from external classification schemes that have been hand crafted by experts. These are shown in Table 3. Previous studies such as (Ratinov and Roth, 2009) have noted that domain gazetteer features play a critical role in aiding classification. In order to show realistic model behaviour consistent with state-of-the-art techniques we have included gazetteers derived from: the Human Phenotype Ontology (HPO: 15,800 terms), the Mammalian Phenotype Ontology (MP: 23,700 terms), the Phenotypic Attribute and Trait Ontology (PATO: 2,200 synonyms), the Brenda Tissue Ontology (BTO: 9,600 synonyms), the Foundation Model of Anatomy (FMA: 120,000 terms), National Library of Medicine gene list (NLM: 9 million terms), UMLS disease terms (UMLS: 275,000 terms), Jochem chemical terms (JOCHEM: 320,000 terms).

The feature set is quite large and therefore there is a danger that the learner will be hindered. For feature selection, we conducted baseline test runs under the same experimental conditions as those reported here using a grid search on features F1 to F11 and found that f-score performance was uniformly lower when removing any feature (data not shown but available as supplementary material from the first author).

In order to characterise the contribution each feature is making in label prediction we wanted to provide a measure of similarity between the feature and the class label probability distributions. Here we use the Gain Ratio (GR) to estimate intra-corpus class prediction performance by each feature. GR was used as a splitting function in C4.5

[1] http://mallet.cs.umass.edu/

(Quinlan, 1993) and is defined as

$$GR(C, F) = IG(C, F)/H(F) \quad (1)$$

where C represents a class label and F represents a feature type. IG is information gain and defined as,

$$IG(C, F) = H(C) - H(C|X) \quad (2)$$

H is entropy and defined for feature types as,

$$H(F) = -\sum_{i=1}^{n} p(f_i) log_2(p(f_i)) \quad (3)$$

for n feature types $f_i \in F$. Further information can be found in (Quinlan, 1993). GR is used in C4.5 in preference to IG because of its ability to normalise for the biases in IG. Generally this results in GR having greater predictive accuracy than IR since it takes into account the number of feature values. Note that GR is undefined when the denominator is zero.

Several points emerge from looking at GR and IG values in Table 3:

- C1 (auto-immune) and C2 (cardio-vascular) have about the same information gain contribution from most features but C1 seems to benefit more from GENIA named entity tagging, Human Phenotype Ontology (HPO), Foundation Model of Anatomy (FMA) and Gene Ontology (GO) terms whereas C2 benefits more from the UMLS diseases and ChEBI terms.

- GO, containing terms about genetic processes, has a higher GR in C1 than C2. This supports what we already expected - that auto-immune diseases contain a higher proportion of information about genetic process phenotypes than cardiovascular.

- The GENIA POS tags seem to provide a slightly higher GR in C2 than in C1.

- Despite its large size, UMLS has a smaller GR on both corpora compared to some other resources like HPO or GO or MA. This is despite its high IG value.

3.4 Evaluation

Traditional re-sampling using *k-fold cross validation* (k-CV) divides the n labelled documents into k disjoint subsets of approximately equal size designated as D_i for $i = 1, .., k$. The NER learner is trained successively on $k - 1$ folds from D and tested on a held out fold over k iterations. In order to preserve independence between contexts in training and held out data we assume here that the unit of division is the document, i.e. a single Medline abstract. Estimated prediction error is calculated based on the learner's labels on the k held out folds. Whilst k-CV is known to be nearly unbiased it is a highly variable estimator. Several studies have looked at k-CV for small sample sets. For example, (Braga-Neto and Dougherty, 2004) found on classifier experiments for small microarray samples ($20 <= n <= 120$) that whilst k-CV showed low bias they suffered from excessive variance compared to bootstrap or resubstitution estimators.

One cause of variance has been identified as within-block and between-block training errors arising from the disproportionate effects of a single abstract appearing in the training set of many folds. In order to reduce this effect Monte Carlo cross validation was used (also called *CV with repetition*). 100 iterations were used to randomly reorder the documents in the corpora before 10-fold CV sampling was run (*cv10r100*). Sampling of documents is done without replacement so that the independence between training and testing sets are maintained. Stratification was not applied. Micro averaged f-scores for labeling accuracy were calculated based on the 1000 test folds for each model. Evaluation was done in both directions (training and testing) for each corpus C1 and C2 to show any asymmetrical effects. To minimse the time taken for each experiment a cluster computer was used with 48 nodes.

The matching criteria we employ is the exact match - i.e. the span of the system labeling and the held out data labels should be exactly the same. Although this is not a necessary criteria for some applications such as database curation we used it here as it is widely applied in shared evaluations and shows the clearest effects of modeling choice.

We evaluate using the named entity precision, recall and F-score calculated using the CoNLL 2003 Perl script. This was calculated as,

$$f - score = \frac{(2 \times precision \times recall)}{(precision + recall)} \quad (4)$$

where,

	Feature	$IG(C1, F_i)$	$GR(C1, F_i)$	$IG(C2, F_i)$	$GR(C2, F_i)$
F_1	Word	1.17	0.13	1.20	0.13
F_2	Lemma	1.15	0.13	1.18	0.13
F_3	POS tag	0.36	0.09	1.18	0.13
F_4	Chunk tag	0.22	0.12	0.26	0.10
F_5	GENIA NE^a	0.20	0.35	0.14	0.27
F_6	Orthography	0.15	0.08	0.16	0.08
F_7	Domain prefix	0.11	0.11	0.11	0.10
F_8	Domain suffix	0.08	0.11	0.08	0.11
F_9	Word length	0.13	0.05	0.16	0.06
F_{10}	Parenthesis	0.04	0.20	0.04	0.23
F_{11}	Abbreviation	0.08	0.22	0.06	0.24
F_{12}	HPO^b	0.07	0.41	0.09	0.33
F_{13}	MP^c	0.03	0.33	0.06	0.33
F_{14}	PATO^d	0.01	0.03	0.02	0.04
F_{15}	BTO^e	0.03	0.32	0.03	0.29
F_{16}	FMA^f	0.05	0.28	0.05	0.23
F_{17}	MA^g	0.02	0.31	0.02	0.29
F_{18}	PRO^h	0.02	0.12	0.03	0.15
F_{19}	ChEBI^i	0.01	0.15	0.03	0.20
F_{20}	JOCHEM^j	0.01	0.15	0.01	0.14
F_{21}	NCBI^k	0.01	0.14	0.01	0.14
F_{22}	UMLS^l disease	0.01	0.14	0.03	0.24
F_{23}	NCBI gene	0.02	0.18	0.02	0.19
F_{24}	GO^m	0.13	0.38	0.05	0.28
F_{25}	UMLS^n	0.48	0.12	0.52	0.11
F_{26}	45CLUSTERS^o	0.50	0.10	0.47	0.10

Table 3: Features used in the experiments. ^{a}The GENIA named entity tagger (Kim et al., 2003), ^{b}(Robinson et al., 2008), ^{c}(Smith et al., 2004), ^{d}(Gkoutos et al., 2005), ^{e}(Gremse et al., 2011), ^{f}(Rosse and Mejino, 2003), ^{g}(Hayamizu et al., 2005), ^{h}(Natale et al., 2011) , ^{i}(Degtyarenko et al., 2008), ^{j}(Hettne et al., 2009),^{k}(Federhen, 2012),^{l}(Lindberg et al., 1993),^{m}(Gene Ontology Consortium, 2000),^{n}133 categories from the UMLS,^{o}45 cluster classes derived by Richard Socher and Christoph Manning PubMed available at http://nlp.stanford.edu/software/bionlp2011-distsim-clusters-v1.tar.gz

$$precision = TP/(TP + FP) \quad (5)$$

and,

$$recall = TP/(TP + FN) \quad (6)$$

A true positive (TP) is a gold standard NE tagged by the system as an NE. A true negative (TN) is a gold standard none-NE tagged by the system as a none-NE. A false positive (FP) is a gold standard none-NE tagged by the system as an NE. Evaluation is based on correctly marked whole entities rather than tokens.

4 Experimental design

In this section we present the experimental conditions we used, starting with a description of the models which we designate M1 to M6 and describe below. All methods made use of 100 iterations of Monte Carlo 10-fold cross validation.

M1: IN DOMAIN We trained and tested on only the data for the source domain. This methods forms our baseline and represents the standard experimental setting.

M2: OUT DOMAIN We trained on the source domain and tested on the target domain. This method shows expected loss on near domain transferrence and represents the standard operational setting for users.

M3: MIX-IN We trained on 100% of the source domain and unified this with 90% of the folded in target domain data, leaving 10% for testing. This method reflects the pooling technique typically employed in corpus construction for bioNER.

M4: STACK We trained a CRF model on 100% of the source domain and stacked it with another CRF trained on 90% of the folded in target domain data. Stacking employs a meta-classifier and is a popular method for constructing high performance ensembles of classifiers (Ekbal and Saha, 2013). In this case we collected the output labels from the source domain-trained CRF on target sentences and added them as features for the target domain trained CRF.

M5: BINARY CLASS We re-labeled the complex class PHE as PHE-C1 in C1 and PHE-C2 in C2 and repeated M3. Afterwards we recombined PHE-C1 and PHE-C2 into PHE.

M6: FRUSTRATINGLY SIMPLE We followed the feature augmentation approach of (Daumé III, 2007). This method effectively provides a joint learning model on C1 and C2 by splitting each feature into three parts: one for sharing cross domain values and one for each domain specific value. We evaluated using the same regime as M3.

5 Experimental results and discussion

In Table 4 we show f-score performance from near biomedical domains with our six strategies. This section now tries to draw together an interpretation for the performance trends that we see and to drill down to some of the causal factors.

Held out tests performed in-domain (M1) on both corpora C1 and C2 indicate a relatively high level of performance, conservatively in line with state-of-the-art estimates. The broad trend in performance is for entity classes with more instances to out perform others with lower numbers. The class which most obviously breaks this trend is the complex entity type of PHE. To understand this consider that PHE is defined as an observable property on an organism and as such tends to be formed from a quality such as *malformed* that describes a structural entity such as *valve*. To see closer what is happening we looked at the confusion matrices for M1 on both corpora. For both C1 and C2 we observed that a substantial proportion of words inside PHE sequences were confused with GGP, DIS or ANA entities. Similarly a high proportion of words inside ANA sequences were confused with PHE entities. This indicates that dependencies within complex biomedical entities like PHE might better be modeled explicitly using tree-structures in a manner similar to events rather than using n-gram relations.

In the M2 out of domain experiments we see a generally severe loss of f-score performance across most classes. Training on C2 and testing on C1 results in a 19.1% loss (F1 69.9 to 50.8) and training on C1 and testing on C2 results in a 11.9% loss overall (F1 58.5 to 46.6). The results agree with Wang et al.'s experience on heterogeneous Medline corpora and extend the upper limit on all-class loss due to domain transferrence to 19%. The only NE class where we see a symmetric benefit from pooling entities in M3 is for ORG (F1 68.4 to 72.2, F1 73.2 to 77.4). Intriguingly the data from Tables 2 and 4 hint at a correlation between the success of M3 pooling for ORG and broad cross-domain compatibility on the vocabulary (over 50% of ORG vocabulary is shared across corpora). However this is not supported in the low sharing case for CHE where we see increased performance from pooling (F1 31.3 to 38.7) when the target is C2 but decreased performance when the target is C1 (F1 29.5 to 20.0).

When we look at the pooling method (M3) and compare to the in-domain method (M1) no obvious size effect occurs for the number of entities in each class. To see this we can examine entity classes with an imbalanced number of instances in C1 and C2 such as CHE, GGP and PHE. Consider the following three cases: (1) Adding 147 instances of CHE from C2 to 44 instances from C1 is associated with CHE performance dropping from M1:29.5 to M3:20.0 when tested on C1; (2) Similarly adding 1430 instances of PHE from C2 to 507 instances from C1 is associated with PHE performance dropping from 46.0 in M1 to 39.7 in M3 when tested on C1; (3) But adding 1663 instances of GGP from C1 to 754 from C2 is associated with GGP rising from 57.2 in M1 to 61.1 in M3. If simply pooling more entities was important to improved f-score we would expect to see a clearer pattern of improvement but we do not.

The overall pooling loss for all classes on M3 is within 3% in both directions and within the

Model	Target	ANA	CHE	DIS	GGP	PHE	ORG	ALL
M1	C1	**57.1**	29.5	**80.4**	74.0	**46.0**	68.4	**69.9**
M2	C1	34.3	26.9	57.7	55.6	26.9	64.0	50.8
M3	C1	50.8	20.0	77.9	71.7	39.7	*72.2*	67.3
M4	C1	56.3	17.4	79.0	**74.1**	44.1	*70.8*	69.8
M5	C1	56.7	**29.6**	77.3	72.7	41.5	**72.8**	68.3
M6	C1	**57.1**	27.7	79.0	73.4	44.9	*69.9*	69.5
M1	C2	37.2	31.3	72.9	57.2	46.5	73.2	58.5
M2	C2	21.2	20.2	57.0	52.3	24.4	68.5	46.6
M3	C2	36.8	*38.7*	72.3	**61.1**	44.0	*77.4*	**59.7**
M4	C2	34.8	*34.4*	72.5	*57.5*	45.9	74.7	58.5
M5	C2	34.1	**41.6**	**73.6**	*58.9*	43.2	**78.5**	**59.6**
M6	C2	**39.9**	*35.0*	*73.3*	56.4	**46.6**	*75.0*	*59.1*

Table 4: Named entity recognition f-scores using Methods 1 to 6. All methods were tested using 100 iterations of Monte Carlo 10-fold cross validation. Figures in bold show best in class scores. Figures in italics show scores above the M1 baseline.

bounds observed by (Wang et al., 2009) and (Wagholikar et al., 2013) for their pooling of heterogeneous Medline corpora. Except for the ORG class which we higlighted above, we might cautiously quantify the loss of pooled entity mentions as being in the range up to 9.5% for CHE but more typically below 4%. The majority of the differences they observed - which are not present in our data - are most likely due to concept definition differences and annotation conventions.

In contrast to our expectations the M4 experiments showed very mild benefits for stacking and these were mixed across entity types. M4 tests on C2 showed no general improvement but some improvement in CHE and ORG. M4 tests on C1 resulted again in no overall improvement except for some gain for ORG, supporting our hypothesis that there is greater compatibility in ORG across domains.

The M5 approach of splitting the PHE labels for the two corpora resulted in a noticable improvement over M3 on the C1 test but unfortunately this was not sustained when testing on C2.

It is striking that in the M6 experiments the feature augmentation method only just meets the in-domain f-score on C1 and mildly exceeds it on C2. One explanation is that the corpora are so small that a richer feature set has only marginal effects on performance. Table 3 certainly indicates that many of the features have low predictive capacity (gain ratio values below 0.1) in an intra-corpus setting but this is not the case for others such as GENIA NE tags or HPO gazzetteer terms.

Overall when we average the f-scores across models for C1 and C2 we see that there is a marginal benefit to the M1, M4 and M6 strategies over M3 and M5 with M2 suffering the greatest loss in performance.

6 Conclusion

In this paper we have provided evidence that transference even to closely related domains in biomedical NER incurs a severe loss in f-score. We have demonstrated empirically that strategies that make use of multi-domain corpora such as stacking learners and feature augmentation mitigate the accuracy loss but do not necessarily result in superior performance except for selected classes such as organisms where there appears to be broad terminology consensus. Simple pooling of data across domains failed to exploit size effects especially for the complex class of phenotypes. The list of strategies employed has not been exhaustive and it is possible that others such as feature hierarchies (Arnold et al., 2008) might yield better results.

BioNER is complicated by various factors such as descriptive names, polysemous terms, conjuctions, nested constructions and a high quantity of abbreviations. We have shown that performance is also held back by not considering document level properties related to domain such as topicality. We can expect lower performance and higher annotation costs if we do not adequately allow for the distributional dissimilarities of domains during learning, even in closely related topical settings.

Acknowledgments

The authors gratefully acknowledge the many helpful comments from the anonymous reviewers of this paper. Nigel Collier's research is supported by the European Commission through the Marie Curie International Incoming Fellowship (IIF) programme (Project: Phenominer, Ref: 301806).

References

A. Arnold, N. Nallapati, and W. Cohen. 2008. Exploiting feature hierarchy for transfer learning in named entity recognition. In *Annual meeting of the Association for Computational Linguistics (ACL 2008)*, pages 245–253.

U. Braga-Neto and E. Dougherty. 2004. Is cross-validation valid for small-sample microarray classification? *Bioinformatics*, 20(3):374–380.

H. Daumé III. 2007. Frustratingly easy domain adaptation. In *Annual meeting of the Association for Computational Linguistics (ACL 2007)*, pages 256–263.

K. Degtyarenko, P. de Matos, M. Ennis, J. Hastings, M. Zbinden, A. McNaught, R. Alcántara, M. Darsow, M. Guedj, and M. Ashburner. 2008. ChEBI: a database and ontology for chemical entities of biological interest. *Nucleic acids research*, 36(suppl 1):D344–D350.

S. Doan, N. Collier, H. Xu, P. Duy, and T. Phuong. 2012. Recognition of medication information from discharge summaries using ensembles of classifiers. *BMC Medical Informatics and Decision Making*, 12(1):36.

A. Ekbal and S. Saha. 2013. Stacked ensemble coupled with feature selection for biomedical entity extraction. *Knowledge-Based Systems*.

S. Federhen. 2012. The NCBI taxonomy database. *Nucleic acids research*, 40(D1):D136–D143.

J. Finkel and C. Manning. 2009. Hierarchical bayesian domain adaptation. In *Proceedings of Human Language Technologies: The 2009 Annual Conference of the North American Chapter of the Association for Computational Linguistics*, pages 602–610.

G. Foster, C. Goutte, and R. Kuhn. 2010. Discrim inative instance weighting for domain adaptation in statistical machine translation. In *Proceedings of the 2010 Conference on Empirical Methods in Natural Language Processing (EMNLP 2010)*, pages 451–459.

Gene Ontology Consortium. 2000. Gene ontology: tool for the unification of biology. *Nature Genetics*, 25:19–29.

G. Gkoutos, E. Green, A. Mallon, J. Hancock, and D. Davidson. 2005. Using ontologies to describe mouse phenotypes. *Genome Biology*, 6:R8.

M. Gremse, A. Chang, I. Schomburg, A. Grote, M. Scheer, C. Ebeling, and D. Schomburg. 2011. The BRENDA tissue ontology (BTO): the first all-integrating ontology of all organisms for enzyme sources. *Nucleic Acids Research*, 39(suppl 1):D507–D513.

A. Hamosh, A. F. Scott, J. S. Amberger, and C. A. Bocchini. 2005. Online mendelian inheritance of man (OMIM), a knowledgebase of human genes and genetic disorders. *Nucleic Acids Research*, 33(suppl 1):D514–D517.

T. Hayamizu, M. Mangan, J. Corradi, J. Kadin, M. Ringwald, et al. 2005. The adult mouse anatomical dictionary: a tool for annotating and integrating data. *Genome Biol*, 6(3):R29.

K. Hettne, R. Stierum, M. Schuemie, P. Hendriksen, B. Schijvenaars, E. van Mulligen, J. Kleinjans, and J. Kors. 2009. A dictionary to identify small molecules and drugs in free text. *Bioinformatics*, 25(22):2983–2991.

J. Jiang and C. Zhai. 2007. Instance weighting for domain adaptation in NLP. In *Annual meeting of the Association for Computational Linguistics (ACL 2007)*, volume 2007, page 22.

J. D. Kim, T. Ohta, Y. Tateishi, and J. Tsujii. 2003. GENIA corpus - a semantically annotated corpus for bio-textmining. *Bioinformatics*, 19(Suppl.1):180–182.

J. Kim, T. Ohta, Y. Tsuruoka, Y. Tateisi, and N. Collier. 2004. Introduction to the bio-entity recognition task at JNLPBA. In N. Collier, P. Ruch, and A. Nazarenko, editors, *Proceedings of the International Joint Workshop on Natural Language Processing in Biomedicine and its Applications (JNLPBA), Geneva, Switzerland*, pages 70–75, August 28–29. held in conjunction with COLING'2004.

J. Lafferty, A. McCallum, and F. Pereira. 2001. Conditional random fields: probabilistic models for segmenting and labeling sequence data. In *Proceedings of the Eighteenth International Conference on Machine Learning, Massachusetts, USA*, pages 282–289, June 28th – July 1st.

Donald A.B. Lindberg, L. Humphreys, Betsy, and T. McCray, Alexa. 1993. The unified medical language system. *Methods of Information in Medicine*, 32:281–291.

Xiaohua Liu, Shaodian Zhang, Furu Wei, and Ming Zhou. 2011. Recognizing named entities in tweets. In *Annual meeting of the Association for Computational Linguistics (ACL 2011)*, pages 359–367.

A. McCallum and L. Wei. 2003. Early results for named entity recognition with conditional random fields, feature induction and web-enhanced lexicons. In *Proc. Seventh Conference on Natural language learning at HLT-NAACL 2003 - Volume 4*, CONLL '03, pages 188–191.

D. McClosky, E. Charniak, and M. Johnson. 2010. Automatic domain adaptation for parsing. In *Human Language Technologies: The 2010 Annual Conference of the North American Chapter of the Association for Computational Linguistics*, pages 28–36. Association for Computational Linguistics.

D. Natale, C. Arighi, W. Barker, J. Blake, C. Bult, M. Caudy, H. Drabkin, P. DEustachio, A. Evsikov, H. Huang, et al. 2011. The protein ontology: a structured representation of protein forms and complexes. *Nucleic acids research*, 39(suppl 1):D539–D545.

S. Pan and Q. Yang. 2010. A survey on transfer learning. *Knowledge and Data Engineering, IEEE Transactions on*, 22(10):1345–1359.

S. Pan, Z. Toh, and J. Su. 2013. Transfer joint embedding for cross-domain named entity recognition. *ACM Transactions on Information Systems (TOIS)*, 31(2):7.

S. Pyysalo, F. Ginter, J. Heimonen, J. Björne, J. Boberg, J. Järvinen, and T. Salakoski. 2007. Bioinfer: a corpus for information extraction in the biomedical domain. *BMC bioinformatics*, 8(1):50.

J. Quinlan. 1993. *C4. 5: programs for machine learning*, volume 1. Morgan kaufmann.

L. Ratinov and D. Roth. 2009. Design challenges and misconceptions in named entity recognition. In *Proceedings of the Thirteenth Conference on Computational Natural Language Learning (CoNLL)*, pages 147–155.

P. N. Robinson, S. Kohler, S. Bauer, D. Seelow, D. Horn, and S. Mundlos. 2008. The human phenotype ontology: a tool for annotating and analyzing human hereditary disease. *The American Journal of Human Genetics*, 83(5):610–615.

C. Rosse and J. L. V. Mejino. 2003. A reference ontology for bioinformatics: the Foundational Model of Anatomy. *Journal of Biomedical Informatics*, 36(6):478–500, December. PMID: 14759820.

K. Sagae and J. Tsujii. 2007. Dependency parsing and domain adaptation with lr models and parser ensembles. In *Conference on Empirical Methods in Natural Language Processing Conference on Computational Natural Language Learning (EMNLP-CoNLL)*, volume 2007, pages 1044–1050.

B. Settles. 2004. Biomedical named entity recognition using conditional random fields. In *Proceedings of the International Joint Workshop on Natural Language Processing in Biomedicine and its Applications (JNLPBA) at COLING'2004, Geneva, Switzerland*, pages 104–107, August 28–29.

C. L. Smith, C. W. Goldsmith, and J. T. Eppig. 2004. The mammalian phenotype ontology as a tool for annotating, analyzing and comparing phenotypic information. *Genome Biology*, 6:R7.

L. Tanabe, N. Xie, L. H. Thom, W. Matten, and W. J. Wilbur. 2005. GENETAG: a tagged corpus for gene/protein named entity recognition. *BMC Bioinformatics*, 6(Suppl 1):S3.

R. Tsai, S. Wu, W. Chou, Y. Lin, D. He, J. Hsiang, T. Sung, and W. Hsu. 2006. Various criteria in the evaluation of biomedical named entity recognition. *BMC bioinformatics*, 7(1):92.

K. Wagholikar, M. Torii, S. Jonnalagadda, H. Liu, et al. 2013. Pooling annotated corpora for clinical concept extraction. *J. Biomedical Semantics*, 4:3.

Y. Wang, J. Kim, R. Sætre, S. Pyysalo, and J. Tsujii. 2009. Investigating heterogeneous protein annotations toward cross-corpora utilization. *BMC bioinformatics*, 10(1):403.

Y. Wang, J. Kim, R. Sætre, S Pyysalo, T. Ohta, and J. Tsujii. 2010. Improving the inter-corpora compatibility for protein annotations. *Journal of bioinformatics and computational biology*, 8(05):901–916.

A. Yeh, A. Morgan, M. Colosimo, and L. Hirschman. 2005. Biocreative task 1a: gene mention finding evaluation. *BMC bioinformatics*, 6(Suppl 1):S2.

Domain Adaptation with Active Learning for Coreference Resolution

Shanheng Zhao
Elance
441 Logue Ave
Mountain View, CA 94043, USA
szhao@elance.com

Hwee Tou Ng
Department of Computer Science
National University of Singapore
13 Computing Drive, Singapore 117417
nght@comp.nus.edu.sg

Abstract

In the literature, most prior work on coreference resolution centered on the newswire domain. Although a coreference resolution system trained on the newswire domain performs well on newswire texts, there is a huge performance drop when it is applied to the biomedical domain. In this paper, we present an approach integrating domain adaptation with active learning to adapt coreference resolution from the newswire domain to the biomedical domain. We explore the effect of domain adaptation, active learning, and target domain instance weighting for coreference resolution. Experimental results show that domain adaptation with active learning and target domain instance weighting achieves performance on MEDLINE abstracts similar to a system trained on coreference annotation of only target domain training instances, but with a greatly reduced number of target domain training instances that we need to annotate.

1 Introduction

Coreference resolution is the task of determining whether two or more noun phrases (NPs) in a text refer to the same entity. Successful coreference resolution benefits many natural language processing (NLP) tasks, such as information extraction and question answering. In the literature, most prior work on coreference resolution recasts the problem as a two-class classification problem. Machine learning-based classifiers are applied to determine whether a candidate anaphor and a potential antecedent are coreferential (Soon et al., 2001; Ng and Cardie, 2002; Stoyanov et al., 2009; Zhao and Ng, 2010).

In recent years, with the advances in biological and life science research, there is a rapidly increasing number of biomedical texts, including research papers, patent documents, etc. This results in an increasing demand for applying natural language processing and information retrieval techniques to efficiently exploit information contained in these large amounts of texts. However, coreference resolution, one of the core tasks in NLP, has only a relatively small body of prior research in the biomedical domain (Kim et al., 2011a; Kim et al., 2011b).

A large body of prior research on coreference resolution focuses on texts in the newswire domain. Standardized data sets, such as MUC (DARPA Message Understanding Conference, (MUC-6, 1995; MUC-7, 1998)) and ACE (NIST Automatic Content Extraction Entity Detection and Tracking task, (NIST, 2002)) data sets are widely used in the study of coreference resolution.

Traditionally, in order to apply supervised machine learning approaches to an NLP task in a specific domain, one needs to collect a text corpus in the domain and annotate it to serve as training data. Compared to other NLP tasks, e.g., part-of-speech (POS) tagging or named entity (NE) tagging, the annotation for coreference resolution is much more challenging and time-consuming. The reason is that in tasks like POS tagging, an annotator only needs to focus on each markable (a word, in the case of POS tagging) and a small window of its neighboring words. In contrast, to annotate a coreferential relation, an annotator needs to first recognize whether a certain text span is a markable, and then scan through the text preceding the markable (a potential anaphor) to look for the antecedent. It also requires the annotator to understand the text in order to annotate coreferential relations, which are *semantic* in nature. If a markable is non-anaphoric, the annotator has to scan to the beginning of the text to realize that. Cohen et al. (2010) reported that it took an average of 20 hours to annotate coreferential relations in a single document with an average length of 6,155 words, while an annotator could annotate 3,000 words per hour in POS tag annotation (Marcus et al., 1993).

The simplest approach to avoid the time-consuming data annotation in a new domain is to train a coreference resolution system on a resource-rich domain and apply it to a different target domain without any additional data annotation. Although coreference resolution systems work well on test texts in the same domain as the training texts, there is a huge performance drop when they are tested on a different domain. This motivates the usage of domain adaptation techniques for coreference resolution: adapting a coreference resolution system from one source domain in which we have a large collection of annotated data, to a second target domain in which we need good performance. It is almost inevitable that we annotate *some* data in the target domain to achieve good coreference resolution performance. The question is how to minimize the amount of annotation needed. In the literature, active learning has been exploited to reduce the amount of annotation needed (Lewis and Gale, 1994). In contrast to annotating the entire data set, active learning selects only a subset of the data to annotate in an iterative process. How to apply active learning and integrate it with domain adaptation remains an open problem for coreference resolution.

In this paper, we explore domain adaptation for coreference resolution from the resource-rich newswire domain to the biomedical domain. Our approach comprises domain adaptation, active learning, and target domain instance weighting to leverage the existing annotated corpora from the newswire domain, so as to reduce the cost of developing a coreference resolution system in the biomedical domain. Our approach achieves comparable coreference resolution performance on MEDLINE abstracts, but with a large reduction in the number of training instances that we need to annotate. To the best of our knowledge, our work is the first to combine domain adaptation and active learning for coreference resolution.

The rest of this paper is organized as follows. We first review the related work in Section 2. Then we describe the coreference resolution system in Section 3, and the domain adaptation and active learning techniques in Section 4. Experimental results are presented in Section 5. Finally, we analyze the results in Section 6 and conclude in Section 7.

2 Related Work

Not only is there a relatively small body of prior research on coreference resolution in the biomedical domain, there are also fewer annotated corpora in this domain. Castaño et al. (2002) were among the first to annotate coreferential relations in the biomedical domain. Their annotation only concerned the pronominal and nominal anaphoric expressions in 46 biomedical abstracts. Gasperin and Briscoe (2007) annotated coreferential relations on 5 full articles in the biomedical domain, but only on noun phrases referring to bio-entities. Yang et al. (2004) annotated full NP coreferential relations on biomedical abstracts of the GENIA corpus. The ongoing project of the CRAFT corpus is expected to annotate all coreferential relations on full text of biomedical articles (Cohen et al., 2010).

Unlike the work of (Castaño et al., 2002), (Gasperin and Briscoe, 2008), and (Gasperin, 2009) that resolved coreferential relations on certain restricted entities in the biomedical domain, we resolve all NP coreferential relations. Although the GENIA corpus contains 1,999 biomedical abstracts, Yang et al. (2004) tested only on 200 abstracts under 5-fold cross validation. In contrast, we randomly selected 399 abstracts in the 1,999 MEDLINE abstracts of the GENIA-MEDCo corpus as the test set, and as such our evaluation was carried out on a larger scale.

Domain adaptation has been studied and successfully applied to many natural language processing tasks (Jiang and Zhai, 2007; Daume III, 2007; Dahlmeier and Ng, 2010; Yang et al., 2012). On the other hand, active learning has also been applied to NLP tasks to reduce the need of data annotation in the literature (Tang et al., 2002; Laws et al., 2012; Miller et al., 2012). Unlike the aforementioned work that applied only one of domain adaptation or active learning to NLP tasks, we combine both. There is relatively less research on combining domain adaptation and active learning together for NLP tasks (Chan and Ng, 2007; Zhong et al., 2008; Rai et al., 2010). Chan and Ng (2007) and Zhong et al. (2008) used *count merging* and *augment*, respectively, as their domain adaptation techniques whereas we apply and compare multiple state-of-the-art domain adaptation techniques. Rai et al. (2010) exploited a streaming active learning setting whereas ours is pool-based.

Dahlmeier and Ng (2010) evaluated the performance of three previously proposed domain adaptation algorithms for semantic role labeling. They evaluated the performance of domain adaptation with different sizes of target domain training data. In each of their experiments with a certain target domain training data size, the target domain training data were added all at once. In contrast, we add the target domain training instances selectively in an iterative process. Different from (Dahlmeier and Ng, 2010), we weight the target domain instances to further boost the performance of domain adaptation. Our work is the first systematic study of domain adaptation with active learning for coreference resolution. Although Gasperin (2009) tried to apply active learning for anaphora resolution, her results were negative: using active learning was not better than randomly selecting instances in her work. Miwa et al. (2012) incorporated a rule-based coreference resolution system for automatic biomedical event extraction, and showed that by adding training data from other domains as supplementary training data and using domain adaptation, one can achieve a higher F-measure in event extraction.

3 Coreference Resolution

The gold standard annotation and the output by a coreference resolution system are called the key and the response, respectively. In both the key and the response, a coreference chain is formed by a set of coreferential markables. A *markable* is a noun phrase which satisfies the markable definition in an individual corpus. Here is an example:

> When ***the same MTHC lines*** are exposed to TNF-alpha in combination with IFN-gamma, ***the cells*** instead become DC.

In the above sentence, ***the same MTHC lines*** and ***the cells*** are referring to the same entity and hence are coreferential. It is possible that more than two markables are coreferential in a text. The task of coreference resolution is to determine these relations in a given text.

To evaluate the performance of coreference resolution, we follow the MUC evaluation metric introduced by (Vilain et al., 1995). Let S_i be an equivalence class generated by the key (i.e., S_i is a coreference chain), and $p(S_i)$ be a partition of S_i relative to the response. Recall is the number of correctly identified links over the number of links in the key: $Recall = \frac{\sum(|S_i|-|p(S_i)|)}{\sum(|S_i|-1)}$. Precision, on the other hand, is defined in the opposite way by switching the role of key and response. F-measure is a trade-off between recall and precision: $F = \frac{2 \cdot Recall \cdot Precision}{Recall + Precision}$.

4 Domain Adaptation with Active Learning

4.1 Domain Adaptation

Domain adaptation is applicable when one has a large amount of annotated training data in the source domain and a small amount or none of the annotated training data in the target domain. We evaluate the AUGMENT technique introduced by (Daume III, 2007), as well as the INSTANCE WEIGHTING (IW) and the INSTANCE PRUNING (IP) techniques introduced by (Jiang and Zhai, 2007).

4.1.1 AUGMENT

Daume III (2007) introduced a simple domain adaptation technique by feature space augmentation. It maps the feature space of each instance into a feature space of higher dimension. Suppose x is the feature vector of an instance. Define Φ^s and Φ^t to be the mappings of an instance from the original feature space to an augmented feature space in the source and the target domain, respectively:

$$\Phi^s(x) = \langle x, x, \mathbf{0} \rangle \quad (1)$$

$$\Phi^t(x) = \langle x, \mathbf{0}, x \rangle \quad (2)$$

where $\mathbf{0} = \langle 0, 0, \ldots, 0 \rangle$ is a zero vector of length $|x|$. The mapping can be treated as taking each feature in the original feature space and making three versions of it: a general version, a source-specific version, and a target-specific version. The augmented source domain data will contain only the general and the source-specific versions, while the augmented target domain data will contain only the general and the target-specific versions.

4.1.2 INSTANCE WEIGHTING and INSTANCE PRUNING

Let x and y be the feature vector and the corresponding true label of an instance, respectively.

Jiang and Zhai (2007) pointed out that when applying a classifier trained on a source domain to a target domain, the joint probability $P_t(x, y)$ in the target domain may be different from the joint probability $P_s(x, y)$ in the source domain. They proposed a general framework to use $P_s(x, y)$ to estimate $P_t(x, y)$. The joint probability $P(x, y)$ can be factored into $P(x, y) = P(y|x)P(x)$. The adaptation of the first component is labeling adaptation, while the adaptation of the second component is instance adaptation. We explore only labeling adaptation.

To calibrate the conditional probability $P(y|x)$ from the source domain to the target domain, ideally each source domain training instance (x_i, y_i) should be given a weight $\frac{P_t(y_i^s|x_i^s)}{P_s(y_i^s|x_i^s)}$. Although $P_s(y_i^s|x_i^s)$ can be estimated from the source domain training data, the estimation of $P_t(y_i^s|x_i^s)$ is much harder. Jiang and Zhai(2007) proposed two methods to estimate $P_t(y_i^s|x_i^s)$: INSTANCE WEIGHTING and INSTANCE PRUNING. Both methods first train a classifier with a small amount of target domain training data. Then, INSTANCE WEIGHTING directly estimates $P_t(y_i^s|x_i^s)$ using the trained classifier. INSTANCE PRUNING, on the other hand, removes the top N source domain instances that are predicted wrongly, ranked by the prediction confidence.

4.1.3 Target Domain Instance Weighting

Both INSTANCE WEIGHTING and INSTANCE PRUNING set the weights of the source domain instances. In domain adaptation, there are typically many more source domain training instances than target domain training instances. Target domain instance weighting can effectively reduce the imbalance. Unlike INSTANCE WEIGHTING and INSTANCE PRUNING in which each source domain instance is weighted individually, we give all target domain instances the same weight. This target domain instance weighting scheme is not only complementary to INSTANCE WEIGHTING and INSTANCE PRUNING, but is also applicable to AUGMENT.

4.2 Active Learning

Active learning iteratively selects the most informative instances to label, adds them to the training data pool, and trains a new classifier with the enlarged data pool. We follow (Lewis and Gale, 1994) and use the uncertainty sampling strategy in our active learning setting.

```
D_s ← the set of source domain training instances
D_t ← the set of target domain training instances
D_a ← ∅
Γ ← coreference resolution system trained on D_s
T ← number of iterations
for i from 1 to T do
  for each d_i ∈ D_t do
    d̂_i ← prediction of d_i using Γ
    p_i ← prediction confidence of d̂_i
  end for
  D'_a ← top N instances with the lowest p_i
  D_a ← D_a + D'_a
  D_t ← D_t − D'_a
  provide correct labels to the unlabeled instances in D'_a
  Γ ← coreference resolution system trained on D_s and
  D_a using the chosen domain adaptation technique
end for
```

Figure 1: An algorithm for domain adaptation with active learning

4.3 Domain Adaptation with Active Learning

Combining domain adaptation and active learning together, the algorithm we use is shown in Figure 1.

In our domain adaptation setting, there is a parameter λ_t for target domain instance weighting. Because the number of target domain instances is different in each iteration, the weight should be adjusted in each iteration. We give all target domain training instances an equal weight of $\lambda_t = N_s/N_t$, where N_s and N_t are the numbers of instances in the source domain and the target domain in the current iteration, respectively. We set $N = 10$ to add 10 instances in each iteration to speed up the active learning process.

To provide the correct labels, the labeling process shows the text on the screen, highlights the two NPs, and asks the annotator to decide if they are coreferential. In our experiments, this is simulated by providing the gold standard coreferential information on this NP pair to the active learning process.

5 Experiments

5.1 The Corpora

We explore domain adaptation from the newswire domain to the biomedical domain. The newswire and biomedical domain data that we use are the ACE Phase-2 corpora and the GENIA-MEDCo corpus, respectively. The ACE corpora contain 422 and 92 training and test texts, respectively (NIST, 2002). The texts come from three newswire sources: BNEWS, NPAPER, and NWIRE. The GENIA-MEDCo corpus contains 1,999 MEDLINE abstracts[1]. We randomly split the GENIA corpus into a training set and a test set, containing 1,600 and 399 texts, respectively.

5.2 The Coreference Resolution System

In this study, we use Reconcile, a state-of-the-art coreference resolution system implemented by (Stoyanov et al., 2009). The input to the coreference resolution system is raw text, and we apply a sequence of preprocessing components to process it. Following Reconcile, the individual preprocessing steps include: 1) sentence segmentation (using the OpenNLP toolkit[2]); 2) tokenization (using the OpenNLP toolkit); 3) POS tagging (using the OpenNLP toolkit); 4) syntactic parsing (using the Berkeley Parser[3]); and 5) named entity recognition (using the Stanford NER[4]). Markables are extracted as defined in each individual corpus. All possible markable pairs in the training and test set are extracted to form training and test instances, respectively. The learning algorithm we use is maximum entropy modeling, implemented in the DALR package[5] (Jiang and Zhai, 2007). The coreference resolution system employs a comprehensive set of 62 features to represent each training and test instance, including lexical, proximity, grammatical, and semantic features (Stoyanov et al., 2009). We do not introduce additional features motivated from the biomedical domain, but use the same feature set for both the source and target domains.

5.3 Preprocessing

For the ACE corpora, all preprocessing components use the original models (provided by the OpenNLP toolkit, the Berkeley Parser, and the Stanford NER). For the GENIA corpus, since it is from a very different domain, the original models do not perform well. However, the GENIA corpus contains multiple layers of annotations. We use these annotations to re-train each of the preprocessing components (except tokenization) using the 1,600 training texts of the GENIA corpus[6]. We do not use any texts from the test set when training these models. Also, we do not use any NLP toolkits from the biomedical domain, but only use general toolkits trained with biomedical training data. These re-trained preprocessing components are then applied to process the entire GENIA corpus, including both the training and test sets.

	NPAPER TRAIN	NPAPER TEST	GENIA TRAIN	GENIA TEST
	Number of Docs			
	76	17	1,600	399
	Number of Words			
Total	68,463	17,350	391,380	95,405
Avg.	900.8	1,020.6	244.6	239.1
	Number of Markables			
Total	21,492	5,153	99,408	24,397
Avg.	282.8	303.1	62.1	61.1
	Number of Instances			
Total	3,365,680	871,314	3,335,640	798,844
Avg.	44,285.3	51,253.8	2,084.8	2,002.1

Table 1: Statistics of the NPAPER and GENIA data sets

Instead of using the entire ACE corpora, we choose the NPAPER portion of the ACE corpora as the source domain in the experiments, because it is the best performing one among the three portions. Under these preprocessing settings, the recall percentages of markable extraction on the training and test set of the NPAPER corpus are 94.5% and 95.5% respectively, while the recall percentages of markable extraction on the training and test of the GENIA corpus are 87.6% and 86.6% respectively. The statistics of the NPAPER and the GENIA corpora are listed in Table 1.

5.4 Baseline Results

Under our experimental settings, a coreference resolution system that is trained on the NPAPER training set and tested on the NPAPER test set achieves recall, precision, and F-measure of 59.0%, 70.6%, and 64.3%, respectively. This is comparable to the state-of-the-art performance (Stoyanov et al., 2009). Table 2 compares the performance of testing on the GENIA test set, but training with the GENIA training set or the NPAPER training set. Training with in-domain data achieves an F-measure that is 9.1% higher than training with out-of-domain data. Training with

[1] http://nlp.i2r.a-star.edu.sg/medco.html

[2] http://opennlp.sourceforge.net/

[3] http://code.google.com/p/berkeleyparser/

[4] http://nlp.stanford.edu/ner/

[5] http://www.mysmu.edu/faculty/jingjiang/software/DALR.html

[6] It turned out that the re-trained tokenization model gave poorer performance and produced many errors on punctuation symbols. Thus, we stuck to using the original tokenization model.

Training Set	Recall	Precision	F-measure
GENIA Training Set	37.7	71.9	49.5
NPAPER Training Set	30.3	60.7	40.4

Table 2: MUC F-measures on the GENIA test set

in-domain data is better than training with out-of-domain data for both recall and precision. This confirms the impact of domain difference between the newswire and the biomedical domain.

5.5 Domain Adaptation with Active Learning

In the experiments on domain adaptation with active learning for coreference resolution, we assume that the source domain training data are annotated. The target domain training data are *not* annotated but are used as a data pool for instance selection. The algorithm selects the instances in the data pool to annotate and add them to the training data to update the classifier. The target domain test set is strictly separated from this data pool, i.e., none of the target domain test data are used in the instance selection process of active learning.

From Table 1, one can see that both training sets in the NPAPER and the GENIA corpora contain large numbers of training instances. Instead of using the entire training sets in the experiments, we use a smaller subset due to several reasons. First, to train a coreference resolution classifier, we do not need so much training data (Soon et al., 2001). Second, a large number of training instances will slow the active learning process. Third, a smaller source domain training corpus suggests a more modest annotation effort even on the source domain. Lastly, a smaller target domain training corpus means that fewer words need to be read by human annotators to label the data.

We randomly choose 10 NPAPER texts as the source domain training set. A coreference resolution system that is trained on these 10 texts and tested on the entire NPAPER test set achieves recall, precision, and F-measure of 60.3%, 70.6%, and 65.0%, respectively. This is comparable to (actually slightly better than) a system trained on the entire NPAPER training set. As for the GENIA training set, we randomly choose 40 texts as the target domain training data. To avoid selection bias, we perform 5 random trials, i.e., choosing 5 sets, each containing 40 randomly selected GENIA training texts. In the rest of this paper, all performances of using *40 GENIA training texts* are the average scores over 5 runs, each of which uses a different set of 40 texts.

In the previous section, we have presented the domain adaptation techniques, the active learning algorithm, as well as the target domain instance weighting scheme. In the rest of this section, we present the experimental results to show how domain adaptation, active learning, and target domain instance weighting help coreference resolution in a new domain. We use *Augment*, *IW*, and *IP* to denote the three domain adaptation techniques: AUGMENT, INSTANCE WEIGHTING, and INSTANCE PRUNING, respectively. For a further comparison, we explore another baseline method, which is simply a concatenation of the source and target domain data together, called *Combine* in the rest of this paper. In all the experiments with active learning, we run 100 iterations, which result in the selection of 1,000 target domain instances.

The first experiment is to measure the effectiveness of target domain instance weighting. We fix on the use of uncertainty-based active learning, and compare weighting and without weighting of target domain instances (denoted as *Weighted* and *Unweighted*). The learning curves are shown in Figure 2. For *Combine*, *Augment*, and *IP*, it can be seen that *Weighted* is a clear winner. As for *IW*, at the beginning of active learning, *Unweighted* outperforms *Weighted*, though it is unstable. At the end of 100 iterations, *Weighted* outperforms *Unweighted*.

Since *Weighted* outperforms *Unweighted*, we fix on the use of *Weighted* and explore the effectiveness of active learning. For comparison, we try another iterative process that randomly selects 10 instances in each iteration. We found that selection of instances using active learning achieved better performance than random selection in all cases. This is because random selection may select instances that the classifier has very high confidence in, which will not help in improving the classifier.

In the third experiment, we fix on the use of *Weighted* and *Uncertainty* since they perform the best, and evaluate the effect of different domain adaptation techniques. The learning curves are shown in Figure 3. It can be seen that *Augment* is the best performing system. For a closer look, we tabulate the results in Table 3, with the statistical significance levels indicated. Statistical significance tests were conducted following (Chinchor, 2011).

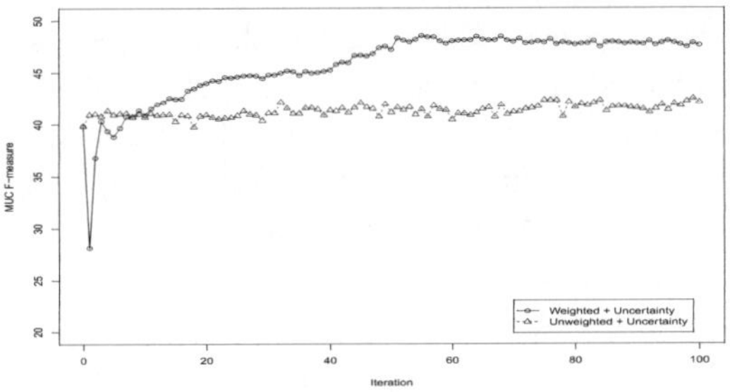

(a) Combine

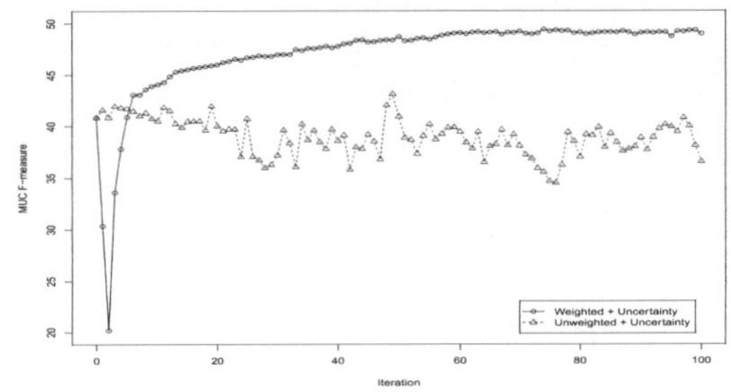

(b) Augment

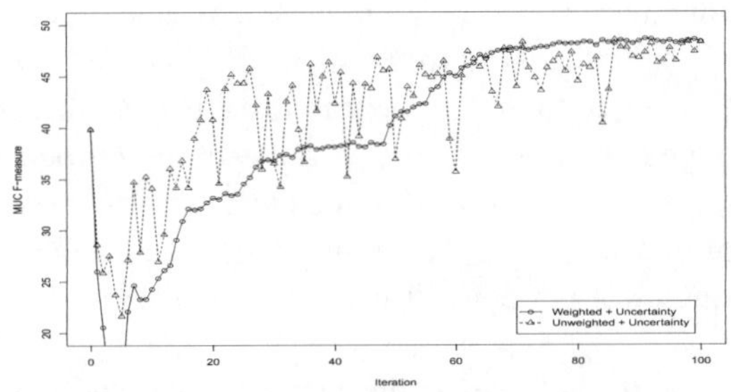

(c) IW

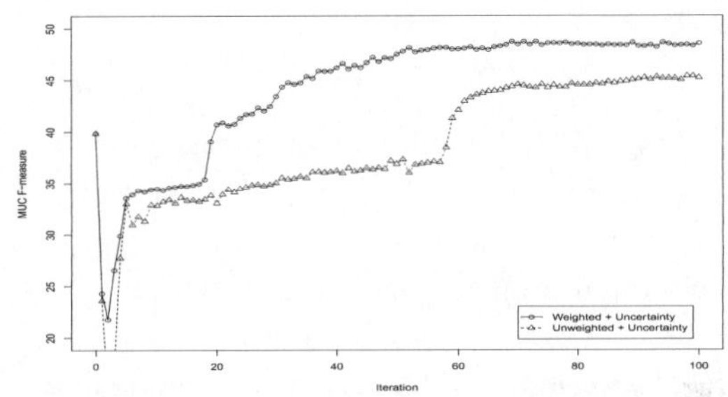

(d) IP

Figure 2: Learning curves of comparing target domain instances weighted vs. unweighted. All systems use uncertainty-based active learning.

Iteration	0	10	20	30	40	60	80	100
Combine+Unweighted	39.8	40.7	40.9	41.1	41.4	40.4	41.6	42.1
Combine+Weighted	39.8	40.9	44.0**	44.8**	45.2**	48.0**	47.7**	47.6**
Augment+Weighted	39.8	**44.1**††**	**46.0**††**	**47.0**††**	**47.8**††**	**49.1**††**	**49.1**††**	**49.0**††**
IW+Weighted	39.8	24.3	33.1	36.8	38.1	45.0**	48.2**††	48.3**††
IP+Weighted	39.8	34.4	40.7	43.4**	46.2**††	48.0**	48.5**††	48.5**††

Table 3: MUC F-measures of different active learning settings on the GENIA test set. All systems use *Uncertainty*. Statistical significance is compared against *Combine+Unweighted*, where * and ** stand for $p < 0.05$ and $p < 0.01$, respectively, and compared against *Combine+Weighted*, where †and ††stand for $p < 0.05$ and $p < 0.01$, respectively.

6 Analysis

Using only the source domain training data, a coreference resolution system achieves an F-measure of 39.8% on the GENIA test set (the column of "Iteration 0" in Table 3). From Figure 3 and Table 3, we can see that in the first few iterations of active learning, domain adaptation does not perform as well as using only the source domain training data. This is because when there are very limited target domain data, the estimation of the target domain is unreliable. Dahlmeier and Ng (2010) reported similar findings though they did not use active learning. With more iterations, i.e., more target domain training data, domain adaptation is clearly superior. Among the three domain adaptation techniques, *Augment* is better than *IW* and *IP*. It not only achieves a higher F-measure, but also a faster speed to adapt to a new domain in active learning. Also, similar to (Dahlmeier and Ng, 2010), we find that *IP* is generally better than *IW*. All systems (except *IW*) with *Weighted* performs much better than *Combine+Unweighted*. This shows the effectiveness of target domain instance weighting. The average recall, precision, and F-measure of our best model, *Augment+Weighted*, after 100 iterations are 37.3%, 71.5%, and 49.0%, respectively. Compared to training with only the NPAPER training data, not only the F-measure, but also both the recall and precision are greatly improved (cf Table 2).

Among all the target domain instances that were selected in *Augment+Weighted*, the average dis-

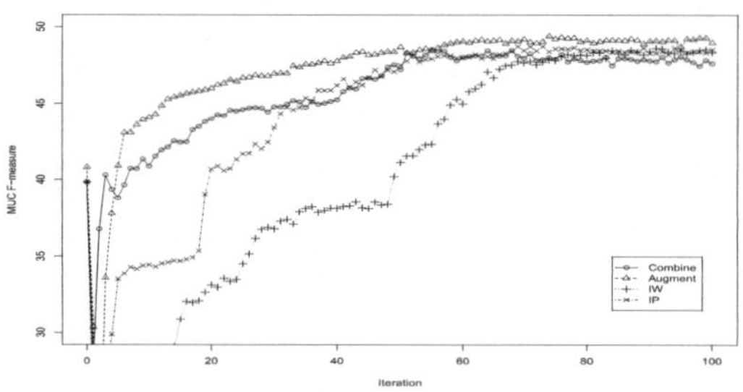

Figure 3: Learning curves of different domain adaptation methods. All systems use *Weighted* and *Uncertainty*.

tance of the two markables in an instance (measured in sentence) is 3.4 (averaged over the 5 runs), which means an annotator needs to read 4 sentences on average to annotate an instance.

We also investigate the difference of coreference resolution between the newswire domain and the biomedical domain, and the instances that were selected in active learning which represent this difference. One of the reasons that coreference resolution differs in the two domains is that scientific writing in biomedical texts frequently compares entities. For example,

> In Cushing's syndrome, the CR of GR was normal in spite of the fact that the CR of plasma cortisol was disturbed.

The two *CR*s refer to different entities and hence are not coreferential. However, a system trained on NPAPER predicts them as coreferential. In the newswire domain, comparisons are less likely, especially for named entities. For example, in the newswire domain, *London* in most cases is coreferential to other *London*s. However, in the biomedical domain, *DNA*s as in *DNA of human beings* and *DNA of monkeys* are different entities. A coreference resolution system trained on the newswire domain is unable to capture the difference between these two named entities, hence predicting them as coreferential. This also justifies the need for domain adaptation for coreference resolution. For the above sentence, after applying our method, the adapted coreference resolution system is able to predict the two *CR*s as non-coreferential.

Next, we show the effectiveness of our system using domain adaptation with active learning compared to a system trained with full coreference annotations. Averaged over 5 runs, a system trained on a single GENIA training text achieves an F-measure of 25.9%, which is significantly lower than that achieved by our method. With more GENIA training texts added, the F-measure increases. After 80 texts are used, the system trained on full annotations finally achieves an F-measure of 49.2%, which is 0.2% higher than *Augment+Weighted* after 100 iterations. However, after 100 iterations, only 1,000 target domain instances are annotated under our framework. Considering that one single text in the GENIA corpus contains an average of over 2,000 instances (cf Table 1), effectively we annotate only half of a text. Compared to the 80 training texts needed, this is a huge reduction. In order to achieve similar performance, we only need to annotate 1/160 or 0.63% of the complete set of training instances under our framework of domain adaptation with active learning.

Lastly, although in this paper we reported experimental results with the MUC evaluation metric, we also evaluated our approach with other evaluation metrics for coreference resolution, e.g., the B-CUBED metric, and obtained similar findings.

7 Conclusion

In this paper, we presented an approach using domain adaptation with active learning to adapt coreference resolution from the newswire domain to the biomedical domain. We explored the effect of domain adaptation, active learning, and target domain instance weighting for coreference resolution. Experimental results showed that domain adaptation with active learning and the target instance weighting scheme achieved a similar performance on MEDLINE abstracts but with a greatly reduced number of annotated training instances, compared to a system trained on full coreference annotations.

Acknowledgments

This research is supported by the Singapore National Research Foundation under its International Research Centre @ Singapore Funding Initiative and administered by the IDM Programme Office.

References

José Castaño, Jason Zhang, and James Pustejovsky. 2002. Anaphora resolution in biomedical literature. In *Proceedings of the International Symposium on Reference Resolution*.

Yee Seng Chan and Hwee Tou Ng. 2007. Domain adaptation with active learning for word sense disambiguation. In *Proceedings of the ACL2007*.

Nancy Chinchor. 2011. Statistical significance of MUC-6 results. In *Proceedings of the Sixth Message Understanding Conference*.

K. Bretonnel Cohen, Arrick Lanfranchi, William Corvey, William A. Baumgartner Jr., Christophe Roeder, Philip V. Ogren, Martha Palmer, and Lawrence Hunter. 2010. Annotation of all coreference in biomedical text: Guideline selection and adaptation. In *BioTxtM 2010*.

Daniel Dahlmeier and Hwee Tou Ng. 2010. Domain adaptation for semantic role labeling in the biomedical domain. *Bioinformatics*, 26(8):1098–1104.

Hal Daume III. 2007. Frustratingly easy domain adaptation. In *Proceedings of the ACL2007*.

Caroline Gasperin and Ted Briscoe. 2008. Statistical anaphora resolution in biomedical texts. In *Proceedings of the COLING2008*.

Caroline Gasperin, Nikiforos Karamanis, and Ruth Seal. 2007. Annotation of anaphoric relations in biomedical full-text articles using a domain-relevant scheme. In *Proceedings of the DAARC2007*.

Caroline Gasperin. 2009. Active learning for anaphora resolution. In *Proceedings of the NAACL-HLT2009 Workshop on Active Learning for Natural Language Processing*.

Jing Jiang and ChengXiang Zhai. 2007. Instance weighting for domain adaptation in NLP. In *Proceedings of the ACL2007*.

Jin-Dong Kim, Sampo Pyysalo, Tomoko Ohta, Robert Bossy, Ngan Nguyen, and Jun'ichi Tsujii. 2011a. Overview of BioNLP shared task 2011. In *Proceedings of BioNLP Shared Task 2011 Workshop*.

Youngjun Kim, Ellen Riloff, and Nathan Gilbert. 2011b. The taming of Reconcile as a biomedical coreference resolver. In *Proceedings of BioNLP Shared Task 2011 Workshop*.

Florian Laws, Florian Heimerl, and Hinrich Schütze. 2012. Active learning for coreference resolution. In *Proceedings of the NAACL2012*.

David D. Lewis and William A. Gale. 1994. A sequential algorithm for training text classifiers. In *Proceedings of the SIGIR1994*.

Mitchell P. Marcus, Beatrice Santorini, and Mary Ann Marcinkiewicz. 1993. Building a large annotated corpus of English: The Penn Treebank. *Computational Linguistics*, 19(2):313–330.

Timothy A. Miller, Dmitriy Dligach, and Guergana K. Savova. 2012. Active learning for coreference resolution. In *Proceedings of the BioNLP2012*.

Makoto Miwa, Paul Thompson, and Sophia Ananiadou. 2012. Boosting automatic event extraction from the literature using domain adaptation and coreference resolution. *Bioinformatics*, 28(13):1759–1765.

MUC-6. 1995. Coreference task definition (v2.3, 8 Sep 95). In *Proceedings of the Sixth Message Understanding Conference (MUC-6)*.

MUC-7. 1998. Coreference task definition (v3.0, 13 Jul 97). In *Proceedings of the Seventh Message Understanding Conference (MUC-7)*.

Vincent Ng and Claire Cardie. 2002. Improving machine learning approaches to coreference resolution. In *Proceedings of the ACL2002*.

NIST. 2002. The ACE 2002 evaluation plan. ftp://jaguar.ncsl.nist.gov/ace/doc/ACE-EvalPlan-2002-v06.pdf.

Piyush Rai, Avishek Saha, Hal Daume, and Suresh Venkatasubramanian. 2010. Domain adaptation meets active learning. In *Proceedings of the NAACL-HLT2010 Workshop on Active Learning for Natural Language Processing*.

Wee Meng Soon, Hwee Tou Ng, and Daniel Chung Yong Lim. 2001. A machine learning approach to coreference resolution of noun phrases. *Computational Linguistics*, 27(4):521–544.

Veselin Stoyanov, Nathan Gilbert, Claire Cardie, and Ellen Riloff. 2009. Conundrums in noun phrase coreference resolution: Making sense of the state-of-the-art. In *Proceedings of the ACL-IJCNLP2009*.

Min Tang, Xiaoqiang Luo, and Salim Roukos. 2002. Active learning for statistical natural language parsing. In *Proceedings of the ACL2002*.

Marc Vilain, John Burger, John Aberdeen, Dennis Connolly, and Lynette Hirschman. 1995. A model-theoretic coreference scoring scheme. In *Proceedings of the MUC-6*.

Xiaofeng Yang, Guodong Zhou, Jian Su, and Chew Lim Tan. 2004. Improving noun phrase coreference resolution by matching strings. In *Proceedings of the IJCNLP2004*.

Jian Bo Yang, Qi Mao, Qiao Liang Xiang, Ivor W. Tsang, Kian Ming A. Chai, and Hai Leong Chieu. 2012. Domain adaptation for coreference resolution: An adaptive ensemble approach. In *Proceedings of the EMNLP2012*.

Shanheng Zhao and Hwee Tou Ng. 2010. Maximum metric score training for coreference resolution. In *Proceedings of the COLING2010*.

Zhi Zhong, Hwee Tou Ng, and Yee Seng Chan. 2008. Word sense disambiguation using OntoNotes: An empirical study. In *Proceedings of the EMNLP2008*.

Towards Cross-Domain PDTB-Style Discourse Parsing

Evgeny A. Stepanov and **Giuseppe Riccardi**
Signals and Interactive Systems Lab
Department of Information Engineering and Computer Science
University of Trento, Trento, Italy
{stepanov,riccardi}@disi.unitn.it

Abstract

Discourse relation parsing is an important task with the goal of understanding text beyond the sentence boundaries. With the availability of annotated corpora (Penn Discourse Treebank) statistical discourse parsers were developed. In the literature it was shown that the discourse parsing subtasks of discourse connective detection and relation sense classification do not generalize well across domains. The biomedical domain is of particular interest due to the availability of Biomedical Discourse Relation Bank (BioDRB). In this paper we present cross-domain evaluation of PDTB trained discourse relation parser and evaluate feature-level domain adaptation techniques on the argument span extraction subtask. We demonstrate that the subtask generalizes well across domains.

1 Introduction

Discourse analysis is one of the most challenging tasks in Natural Language Processing that has applications in many language technology areas such as opinion mining, summarization, information extraction, etc. (see (Webber et al., 2011) and (Taboada and Mann, 2006) for detailed review). The release of the large discourse relation annotated corpora, such as Penn Discourse Treebank (PDTB) (Prasad et al., 2008), marked the development of statistical discourse parsers (Lin et al., 2012; Ghosh et al., 2011; Xu et al., 2012; Stepanov and Riccardi, 2013). Recently, PDTB-style discourse annotation was applied to biomedical domain and Biomedical Discourse Relation Bank (BioDRB) (Prasad et al., 2011) was released. This milestone marks the beginning of the research on cross-domain evaluation and domain adaptation of PDTB-style discourse parsers. In this paper we address the question of how well PDTB-trained discourse parser (news-wire domain) can extract argument spans of *explicit* discourse relations in BioDRB (biomedical domain).

The use cases of discourse parsing in biomedical domain are discussed in detail in (Prasad et al., 2011). Here, on the other hand, we provide very general connection between the two. The goal of Biomedical Text Mining (BioNLP) is to retrieve and organize biomedical knowledge from scientific publications; and detecting discourse relations such as contrast and causality is an important step towards this goal (Prasad et al., 2011). To illustrate this point consider a quote from (Brunner and Wirth, 2006), given below.

> *The addition of an anti-Oct2 antibody did not interfere with complex formation (Figure 3, lane 6),* since **HeLa cells do not express Oct2**. (Cause:Reason)

In the example, the discourse connective since signals a causal relation between the clauses it connects. That is, the reason why '*the addition of an anti-Oct2 antibody did not interfere with complex formation*' is '*HeLa cells' not expressing Oct2*'.

PDTB adopts non-hierarchical binary view on discourse relations: Argument 1 (*Arg1*) (in italics in the example) and Argument 2 (*Arg2*), which is syntactically attached to a discourse connective (in bold). Thus, a discourse relation is a triplet of a connective and its two arguments. In the literature (Lin et al., 2012; Stepanov and Riccardi, 2013) PDTB-style discourse parsing is partitioned into discourse relation detection, argument position classification, argument span extraction, and relation sense classification. For the *explicit* discourse relations (i.e. signaled by a connective), discourse relation detection is cast as classification of connectives as discourse and non-discourse. Argument position classification, on the other hand, involves detection of the location of *Arg1* with re-

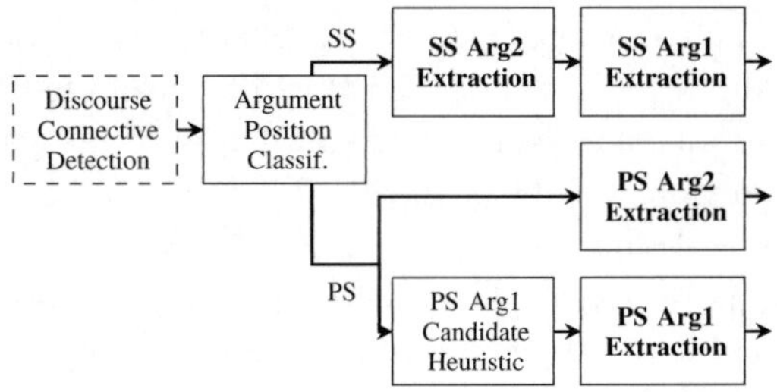

Figure 1: Discourse Parser Architecture. (CRF Argument Span Extraction models are in bold.)

spect to *Arg2*, that is to detect whether a relation is inter- or intra- sentential. Argument span extraction is the extraction (labeling) of text segments that belong to each of the arguments. Finally, relation sense classification is the annotation of relations with the senses from the sense hierarchy (PDTB or BioDRB).

To the best of our knowledge, the only subtasks that were addressed cross-domain are the detection of explicit discourse connectives (Ramesh and Yu, 2010; Ramesh et al., 2012; Faiz and Mercer, 2013) and relation sense classification (Prasad et al., 2011). While the discourse parser of Faiz and Mercer (2013)[1] provides models for both domains and does identification of argument head words in the style of Wellner and Pustejovsky (2007); there is no decision made on arguments spans. Moreover, there is no cross-domain evaluation available for each of the models. In this paper we address the task of cross-domain argument span extraction of *explicit* discourse relations. Additionally, we provide evaluation for cross-domain argument position classification as far as the data allows, since BioDRB lacks manual sentence segmentation.

The paper is structured as follows. In Section 2 we present the comparative analysis of PDTB and BioDRB corpora and the relevant works on cross-domain discourse parsing. In Section 3 we describe the PDTB discourse parser used for cross-domain experiments. In Section 4 we present the evaluation methodology and the experimental results. Section 5 provides concluding remarks.

2 PDTB vs. BioDRB Corpora Analysis and Related Cross-Domain Works

The two corpora used in our experiments are Penn Discourse Treebank (PDTB) (Prasad et al., 2008) and Biomedical Discourse Relation Bank (BioDRB) (Prasad et al., 2011). Both corpora follow the same discourse relation annotation style over different domain corpora: PDTB is annotated on top of *Wall Street Journal* (WSJ) corpus (financial news-wire domain); and it is aligned with Penn Treebank (PTB) syntactic tree annotation; BioDRB, on the other hand, is a corpus annotated over 24 open access full-text articles from the GENIA corpus (Kim et al., 2003) (biomedical domain), and, unlike PDTB, there is no reference tokenization or syntactic parse trees.

The detailed comparison of the corpora is out of the scope of this paper, and it is available in (Prasad et al., 2011). Similarly, the review of PDTB-style discourse parsing literature is not in its scope. Here, on the other hand, we focus on the corpus differences relevant for discourse parsing tasks and cross-domain application of discourse parsing subtasks.

Discourse relations in both corpora are binary: *Arg1* and *Arg2*, where *Arg2* is an argument syntactically attached to a discourse connective. With respect to *Arg2*, *Arg1* can appear in the same sentence (SS case), one or several of the preceding (PS case) or following (FS case) sentences. A discourse connective is a member of a well defined list of connectives and a relation expressed via such connective is an *Explicit* relation. There are other types of discourse and non-discourse relations annotated in the corpora; however, they are out of the scope of this paper. Discourse relations are annotated using a hierarchy of senses: even though the organization of senses and the number of levels are different between corpora, the most general top level senses are mapped to the PDTB top level senses: *Comparison*, *Contingency*, *Expansion*, and *Temporal* (Prasad et al., 2011).

The difference between the two corpora with respect to discourse connectives is that in case of PDTB the annotated connectives belong to one of the three syntactic classes: subordinating conjunctions (e.g. *because*), coordinating conjunctions (e.g. *but*), and discourse adverbials (e.g. *however*), while BioDRB is also annotated for a forth syntactic class – subordinators (e.g. *by*).

There are 100 unique connective types in PDTB (after connectives like *1 year after* are stemmed to *after*) in 18,459 explicit discourse relations. Whereas in BioDRB there are 123 unique connective types in 2,636 relations. According to

[1]Made available on `https://code.google.com/p/discourse-parser/`

the discourse connective analysis in (Ramesh et al., 2012), the subordinators comprise 33% of all connective types in BioDRB. Additionally, 11% of connective types in common syntactic classes that occur in BioDRB do not occur in PDTB; e.g. *In summary*, *as a consequence*. Thus, only 56% of connective types of BioDRB are common to both corpora. While in-domain discourse connective detection has good performance (Ramesh and Yu, 2010), this difference makes the cross-domain identification of discourse connectives a hard task, which is exemplified by experiments in (Ramesh and Yu, 2010) ($F_1 = 0.55$).

With respect to relation sense classification, the connective surface provides already high baselines (Prasad et al., 2011). However, cross-domain sense classification experiments indicate that there are significant differences in the semantic usage of connectives between two domains, since the performance of the classifier trained on PDTB does not generalize well to BioDRB ($F_1 = 0.57$).

To sum up, the corpora differences with respect to discourse connective usage affect the cross-domain generalization of connective detection and sense classification tasks negatively. The experiments in this paper are intended to evaluate the generalization of argument span extraction, assuming that the connective is already identified. In the following section, we present the PDTB-trained discourse parser optimized for in-domain performance.

3 PDTB-Style Discourse Parser

The discourse parser (see Figure 1) is a combination of argument position classification model for classifying discourse connectives as inter- or intra-sentential, and specific Conditional Random Fields argument extraction models for each of the arguments in these configurations. In the following subsections we provide descriptions for each of the components.

3.1 Argument Position Classification

Discourse connectives have a very strong preference on the location of the *Arg1* with respect to their syntactic category (Subordinating Conjunction, Coordinating Conjunction, and Discourse Adverbial) and position in the sentence (sentence initial or sentence medial); thus, classification of discourse connectives into inter-sentential or intra-sentential is an easy task yielding high supervised machine learning performance (Stepanov and Riccardi, 2013; Lin et al., 2012). With respect to the decision made in this step a specific argument span extraction model is applied.

For *Argument Position Classification* the unigram BoosTexter (Schapire and Singer, 2000) model with 100 iterations is trained on PDTB sections 02-22 and tested on sections 23-24. Similar to the previously published results, it has a high performace: $F1 = 98.12$. The features are connective surface string, POS-tags, and IOB-chains. The results obtained with automatic sentence splitting, tokenization, and syntactic parsing using Stanford Parser (Klein and Manning, 2003) are also high $F1 = 97.81$.

Since, unlike PTB for PDTB, for BioDRB there is no manual sentence splitting, tokenization, and syntactic tree annotation; the precise cross-domain evaluation of *Argument Span Extraction* step is not possible. However, in Section 4 we estimate the performance using automatic sentence splitting.

3.2 Argument Span Extraction

Argument span extraction is cast as token-level sequence labeling using Conditional Random Fields (CRF) (Lafferty et al., 2001). Previously, it was observed that in PDTB for inter-sentential discourse relations *Arg1* precedes *Arg2* in most of the cases. Thus, the CRF models are trained for the configurations where both of the arguments are in the same sentence (SS), and for *Arg1* in one of the previous sentences (PS); the following sentence *Arg1* case (FS) is ignored due to too few training instances being available (in PDTB 8 / 18,459). Consequently, there are 4 CRF models SS Arg1 and Arg2, and PS Arg1 and Arg2.

Same sentence case models are applied in a cascade, such that output of *Arg2* model is used as a feature for *Arg1* span extraction. For the case of *Arg1* in the previous sentences; based on the observation that in PDTB Arg2 span is fully located in the sentence containing the connective in 98.5% of instances; and Arg1 span is fully located in the sentence immediately preceding Arg2 in 71.7% of instances; the sentences in these positions are selected and CRF models are trained to label the spans.

The features used for training the models are presented in Table 1. The feature sets are optimized for each of the arguments in (Ghosh et al., 2011) (see the Table columns Arg1 and Arg2). Besides the features commonly used in NLP tasks such that token, lemma, inflectional affixes, and part-of-speech tag, the rest of the features are:

- *IOB-Chain* (*IOB*) is the path string of the syntactic tree nodes from the root node to the token, prefixed with the information whether a token is at the beginning (B-) or inside (I-) the constituent. The *chunklink* tool (Buchholz, 2000) is used to extract this feature from syntactic trees.

- *PDTB Level 1 Connective sense* (*CONN*) is the most general sense of a connective in PDTB sense hierarchy. It's general purpose is to label the discourse connective tokens, i.e. the value of the feature is '*NULL*' for all tokens except the discourse connective.

- *Boolean Main Verb* (*BMV*) is a boolean feature that indicates whether a token is a main verb of a sentence or not (Yamada and Matsumoto, 2003).

- *Arg2 Label* (*ARG2*) is an output of *Arg2* span extraction model, that is used as a feature for *Arg1* span extraction. *Arg2* span is easier to identify (Ghosh et al., 2011; Stepanov and Riccardi, 2013) since it is syntactically attached to the discourse connective. Thus, this feature serves to constrain the *Arg1* search space for intra-sentential argument span extraction. The value of the feature is either ARG2 suffixed for whether a token is Inside (I), Begin (B), or End (E) of the span, or 'O' if it does not belong to the *Arg2* span.

These features are expanded during training with n-grams (feature of CRF++[2]): tokens with 2-grams in the window of ± 1 tokens, and the rest of the features with 2 & 3-grams in the window of ± 2 tokens.

The in-domain performance of argument span extraction models is provided in the following section, after the description of the evaluation methodology.

4 Experiments and Results

In this Section we first describe the evaluation methodology and then the experiments on cross-domain evaluation of argument position classification and argument span extraction models.

[2]https://code.google.com/p/crfpp/

Feature	ABBR	Arg2	Arg1
Token	TOK	Y	Y
POS-Tag	POS		
Lemma	LEM	Y	Y
Inflection	INFL	Y	Y
IOB-Chain	IOB	Y	Y
Connective Sense	CONN	Y	Y
Boolean Main Verb	BMV		Y
Arg2 Label	ARG2		Y

Table 1: Feature sets for Arg2 and Arg1 argument span extraction.

The experimental settings for PDTB are the following: Sections 02-22 are used for training and Sections 23-24 for testing. For BioDRB, on the other hand, 12 fold cross-validation is used (2 documents in each fold, since in BioDRB there are 24 documents).

4.1 Evaluation Methodology

The performance of *Argument Span Extraction* is evaluated in terms of precision (*p*), recall (*r*), and F-measure (F_1) using the equations 1 – 3. An argument span is considered to be correct, if it exactly matches the reference string. Following (Ghosh et al., 2011) and (Lin et al., 2012), argument initial and final punctuation marks are removed .

$$p = \frac{\text{Exact Match}}{\text{Exact Match} + \text{No Match}} \quad (1)$$

$$r = \frac{\text{Exact Match}}{\text{References in Gold}} \quad (2)$$

$$F_1 = \frac{2 * p * r}{p + r} \quad (3)$$

In the equations, *Exact Match* is the count of correctly tagged argument spans; *No Match* is the count of argument spans that do not match the reference string exactly, i.e. even a single token difference is counted as an error; and *References in Gold* is the total number of arguments in the reference.

Since argument span extraction is applied after argument position classification, the classification error is propagated. Thus, for the evaluation of argument span extraction, misclassified instances are reflected in the counts of *Exact Matches* and *No Matches*. For example, misclassified same sentence relation results in that both its arguments are

	Arg2			Arg1		
	P	R	F1	P	R	F1
Gold						
SS	90.36	87.49	88.90	70.27	66.67	68.42
PS	79.01	77.10	78.04	46.23	36.61	40.86
ALL	85.93	83.45	84.67	61.94	54.98	58.25
Auto						
SS	86.83	85.14	85.98	64.26	63.01	63.63
PS	75.00	73.67	74.33	37.66	37.00	37.33
ALL	82.24	80.69	81.46	53.93	52.92	53.42

Table 2: In-domain performance of the PDTB-trained argument span extraction models on the test set with 'Gold' and 'Automatic' sentence splitting, tokenization, and syntactic features. The results are reported together with the error propagation from argument position classification for Same Sentence (SS), Previous Sentence (PS) models and joined results (ALL) as precision (P), recall (R) and F-measure (F1).

considered as not recalled for the SS, and for the PS they are considered as *No Match*.

However, we do not propagate error in cross-domain evaluation on BioDRB, since there is no reference information. Additionally, while *Arg1* span extraction models are trained on Gold *Arg2* features, for testing they are always automatic.

4.2 Cross-Domain Argument Position Classification

As it was mentioned above, there is no manual sentence splitting for BioDRB; thus, there is no references for whether a discourse relation has its *Arg1* in the same or different sentences. In order to evaluate cross-domain argument position classification we evaluate classifier decisions against automatic sentence splitting using Stanford Parser (Klein and Manning, 2003) on whole of BioDRB.

The BoosTexter model described in Section 3.1 has a high in-domain performance of 97.81. On BioDRB its performance is 95.26, which is still high. Thus, we can conclude that argument position classification generalizes well cross-domain, and that it is little affected by the presence of 'subordinators' that were not annotated in PDTB.

4.3 In-Domain Argument Span Extraction: PDTB

The in-domain performance of the argument span extraction models trained on PDTB sections 02-22 and tested on sections 23-24 is given on Table 2. The results are for 2 settings: 'Gold' and 'Auto'. In the 'Gold' settings the sentence splitting, tokenization and syntactic features are extracted from PTB, and in the 'Auto' they are extracted from automatic parse trees obtained using Stanford Parser (Klein and Manning, 2003).

The general trend in the literature, is that the argument span extraction for *Arg1* has lower performance than for *Arg2*, which is expected since *Arg2* position is signaled by a discourse connective. Additionally, Previous Sentence *Arg1* model performance is much lower than that of the other models due to the fact that it only considers immediately previous sentence; which, as was mentioned earlier, covers only 71.7% of the inter-sentential relations. In the next subsections, these models are evaluated on biomedical domain.

4.4 In-Domain Argument Span Extraction: BioDRB

In order to evaluate PDTB-BioDRB cross-domain performance we first evaluate the in-domain BioDRB argument span extraction. Since there is no gold sentence splitting, tokenization and syntactic parse trees, the models are trained using the features extracted from automatic parse trees. We use exactly the same feature sets as for PDTB models, which are optimized for PDTB. An important aspect is that in BioDRB the connective senses are different: there are 16 top level senses that are mapped to 4 top level PDTB senses. For the in-domain BioDRB models, the 16 senses were kept as is.

Since we do not have gold argument position information, we do not train in-domain argument classification model. Thus, the reported results are without error propagation. Later, this will allow us to assess cross-domain argument span extraction performance better.

The results reported in Table 3 are average precision, recall and f-measure of 12-fold cross-validation. With respect to automatic sentence splitting, there are 717 inter-sentential and 1,919 intra-sentential relations (27% to 73%). Thus, BioDRB is less affected by PS *Arg1* performance than PDTB models, where the ratio is 619 to 976 (39% to 61%). Additionally, BioDRB PS *Arg1* performance is generally higher than that of PDTB. Overall, in-domain BioDRB argument extraction model performance is in-line with the

	Arg2			Arg1		
	P	**R**	**F1**	**P**	**R**	**F1**
SS	80.94	79.88	80.41	66.51	61.82	64.07
PS	82.99	82.99	82.99	57.50	55.62	56.53
ALL	81.45	80.67	81.06	63.87	60.00	61.87

Table 3: In-domain performance of the BioDRB-trained argument span extraction models. Both training and testing are on automatic sentence splitting, tokenization, and syntactic features. The results are reported for Same Sentence (SS) and Previous Sentence (PS) models, and the joined results for each of the arguments (ALL) as average precision (P), recall (R), and F-measure (F1) of 12-fold cross-validation.

PDTB models, with the exception that previous sentence *Arg2* has higher performance than the same sentence one.

4.5 Cross-Domain Argument Span Extraction: PDTB - BioDRB

Similar to in-domain BioDRB argument span extraction, we perform 12 fold cross-validation for PDTB-BioDRB cross-domain argument span extraction. The cross-domain performance of the models described in Section 4.3 is given in the Table 4 under the 'Gold'. To make the cross-domain evaluation settings closer to the BioDRB in-domain evaluation, we additionally train PDTB models on the automatic features, i.e. features extracted from PDTB with automatic sentence splitting, tokenization and syntactic parsing. Similar to the in-domain BioDRB evaluation, results are reported without error propagation from argument position classification step.

The first observation from cross-domain evaluation is that argument span extraction generalizes to biomedical domain much better that the discourse parsing subtasks of discourse connective detection and relation sense classification. Unlike those subtasks, the difference between in-domain BioDRB argument span extraction models and the models trained on PDTB is much less: e.g. for discourse connective detection the in-domain and cross-domain difference for BioDRB is 14 points (f-measures 69 and 55 in (Ramesh and Yu, 2010)), and for argument span extraction 2 and 4 points for *Arg2* and *Arg1* respectively (see Tables 3 & 4).

The difference between the models trained on automatic and gold parse trees is also not high, and gold feature trained models perform better with

	Arg2			Arg1		
	P	**R**	**F1**	**P**	**R**	**F1**
Gold						
SS	80.37	76.58	78.42	60.82	56.40	58.52
PS	80.73	80.50	80.62	57.74	52.95	55.19
ALL	80.53	77.71	79.09	59.76	55.29	57.43
Auto						
SS	77.60	75.05	76.30	60.76	55.21	57.83
PS	81.39	81.23	81.31	57.71	51.72	54.47
ALL	78.72	76.80	77.74	59.60	54.12	56.71

Table 4: Cross-domain performance of the PDTB-trained argument span extraction models on BioDRB. For the 'Gold' setting the models from in-domain PDTB section are used. For 'Auto', the models are trained on automatic sentence splitting, tokenization, and syntactic features. The results are reported for Same Sentence (SS) and Previous Sentence (PS) models, and the joined results for each of the arguments (ALL) as average precision (P), recall (R), and F-measure (F1) of 12-fold cross-validation.

the exception of PS *Arg2*. Since training on automatic parse trees does not improve cross-domain performance, the rest of the experiments is using gold features for training.

4.6 Feature-Level Domain Adaptation

The two major differences between PDTB and BioDRB are vocabulary and connective senses. The out-of-vocabulary rate of PDTB on the whole BioDRB is 22.7% and of BioDRB on PDTB is 33.1%, which are very high. Thus, PDTB lexical features might not be very effective, and the models generalize well due to syntactic features. To test this hypothesis we train additional PDTB models on only syntactic features: POS-tags and IOB-chain and 'connective labels' – 'CONN' suffixed for the Beginning (B), Inside (I) or End (E) of the connective span, simulating discourse connective detection output. Moreover, we reduce the feature set to **unigrams** only (recall that features were enriched by 2 and 3 grams), such that the models become very general.

Even though BioDRB connective senses can be mapped to PDTB, in (Prasad et al., 2011) it was observed that relation sense classification does not generalize well. To reduce the dependency of argument span extraction models on relation sense classification, the connective sense feature in the

	Arg2			Arg1		
	P	R	F1	P	R	F1
Baseline						
SS	80.37	76.58	78.42	60.82	56.40	58.52
PS	80.73	80.50	80.62	57.74	52.95	55.19
ALL	80.53	77.71	79.09	59.76	55.29	57.43
Syntactic						
SS	82.00	75.03	78.33	61.07	51.80	56.01
PS	75.56	74.47	75.01	56.64	46.66	51.11
ALL	80.31	74.98	77.54	59.69	50.42	54.63
No Relation Sense						
SS	81.35	74.00	77.47	62.46	56.11	59.10
PS	80.35	80.13	80.24	57.58	52.25	54.74
ALL	81.16	75.67	78.30	60.86	54.87	57.69

Table 5: Cross-domain performance of the PDTB-trained argument span extraction models on BioDRB. For the 'Syntactic' setting the models are trained on only syntactic features (POS-tag + IOB-chain) and 'connective labels'. For 'No Relation Sense', the models are trained by replacing connective sense with 'connective labels'. The 'Baseline' is repeated from Table 4. The results are reported for Same Sentence (SS) and Previous Sentence (PS) models, and the joined results for each of the arguments (ALL) as average precision (P), recall (R), and F-measure (F1) of 12-fold cross-validation.

'Baseline' models (i.e. the models from Section 4.3) is also replaced by 'connective labels'. We train these models using gold features only, and, similar to previous experiments, do 12-fold cross-validation.

The performance of the adapted models is given in Table 5. The 'Syntactic' section gives the results of the models trained on syntactic features and the 'No Relation Sense' section gives the results for the models with 'connective labels' instead of connective senses, and the 'Baseline' repeats the performance of the PDTB-optimized models.

The PDTB-optimized baseline, outperforms the adapted models on *Arg2*; however, 'No Relation Sense' *Arg1* yields the best performance, and, though insignificantly, outperforms the baseline. Thus, the effect of replacing connective senses with 'connective labels' is negative for all cases except SS *Arg1*. Overall, the difference in performance between the 'Baseline' and 'No Relation Sense' models is an acceptable price to pay for the independence from relation sense classification.

	Arg2			Arg1		
	P	R	F1	P	R	F1
SS	81.72	76.14	78.82	61.53	56.36	58.82
PS	80.31	79.84	80.07	58.55	52.82	55.44
ALL	81.27	77.10	79.12	60.56	55.30	57.80

Table 6: Cross-domain performance of the PDTB-trained argument span extraction model on unigram and bigrams of token, POS-tag, IOB-chain and 'connective label'. The results are reported for Same Sentence (SS) and Previous Sentence (PS) models, and the joined results for each of the arguments (ALL) as average precision (P), recall (R), and F-measure (F1) of 12-fold cross-validation.

The most general models – unigrams of Part-of-Speech tags and IOB-chains together with 'connective labels' in the window of ± 2 tokens – all have the performance lower than the baseline, which is expected given its feature set. However, for the easiest case of intra-sentential *Arg2* it outperforms the model trained by replacing the connective sense in the baseline (i.e. 'No Relation Sense'). Degraded performance of *Arg1* models indicates that lexical features are helpful.

Introducing the tokens back into the 'Syntactic' model, and increasing the features to include also 2-grams, boosts the performance of the models to outperform the 'No Relation Sense' models in all but Previous Sentence *Arg2* category. However, the models now yield performance comparable to the PDTB optimized baseline (insignificantly better), while being unaffected by poor cross-domain generalization of relation sense classification (see Table 6).

The cross-domain argument extraction experiments indicate that models trained on PDTB-optimized feature set already have good generalization. However, they are dependent on relation sense classification task, which does not generalize well. By replacing connective senses with 'connective labels' we obtain models independent of this task while maintaining comparable performance. The in-domain trained BioDRB models, however, perform better, as expected.

5 Conclusion

In this paper we presented cross-domain discourse parser evaluation on subtasks of argument position classification and argument span extraction.

The observed cross-domain performances are indicative of good model generalization. However, since these models are applied later in the pipeline, they are affected by the cross-domain performance of the other tasks. Specifically, discourse connective detection, which was shown not to generalize well in the literature. Additionally, we have presented feature-level domain adaptation techniques to reduce the dependence of the cross-domain argument span extraction on other discourse parsing subtasks.

The syntactic parser (Stanford) that provides sentence splitting and tokenization is trained on Penn Treebank, i.e. it is in-domain for PDTB and out-of-domain for BioDRB; and it is known that domain-optimized tokenization improves performance on various NLP tasks. Thus, the future direction of this work is to evaluate argument span extraction using tools optimized for biomedical domain.

Acknowledgments

The research leading to these results has received funding from the European Union – Seventh Framework Programme (FP7/2007-2013) under grant agreement No. 610916 – SENSEI.

References

Cornelia Brunner and Thomas Wirth. 2006. Btk expression is controlled by oct and bob. 1/obf. 1. *Nucleic acids research*, 34(6):1807–1815.

Sabine Buchholz. 2000. Readme for perl script chunklink.pl.

Syeed Ibn Faiz and Robert E Mercer. 2013. Identifying explicit discourse connectives in text. In *Advances in Artificial Intelligence*, pages 64–76. Springer.

Sucheta Ghosh, Richard Johansson, Giuseppe Riccardi, and Sara Tonelli. 2011. Shallow discourse parsing with conditional random fields. In *Proceedings of the 5th International Joint Conference on Natural Language Processing (IJCNLP 2011)*.

J-D Kim, Tomoko Ohta, Yuka Tateisi, and Junichi Tsujii. 2003. Genia corpusa semantically annotated corpus for bio-textmining. *Bioinformatics*, 19(suppl 1):i180–i182.

Dan Klein and Christopher D. Manning. 2003. Fast exact inference with a factored model for natural language parsing. In *Advances in Neural Information Processing Systems 15 (NIPS 2002)*.

John Lafferty, Andrew McCallum, and Fernando C. N. Pereira. 2001. Conditional random fields: Probabilistic models for segmenting and labeling sequence data. In *Proceedings of 18th International Conference on Machine Learning*.

Ziheng Lin, Hwee Tou Ng, and Min-Yen Kan. 2012. A pdtb-styled end-to-end discourse parser. *Natural Language Engineering*, 1:1 – 35.

Rashmi Prasad, Nikhil Dinesh, Alan Lee, Eleni Miltsakaki, Livio Robaldo, Aravind Joshi, and Bonnie Webber. 2008. The penn discourse treebank 2.0. In *Proceedings of the 6th International Conference on Language Resources and Evaluation (LREC 2008)*.

Rashmi Prasad, Susan McRoy, Nadya Frid, Aravind Joshi, and Hong Yu. 2011. The biomedical discourse relation bank. *BMC Bioinformatics*, 12(1):188.

Balaji Polepalli Ramesh and Hong Yu. 2010. Identifying discourse connectives in biomedical text. *AMIA Annual Symposium Proceedings*, 2010:657.

Balaji Polepalli Ramesh, Rashmi Prasad, Tim Miller, Brian Harrington, and Hong Yu. 2012. Automatic discourse connective detection in biomedical text. *Journal of the American Medical Informatics Association*, 19(5):800–808.

Robert E. Schapire and Yoram Singer. 2000. Boostexter: A boosting-based system for text categorization. *Machine Learning*, 39(2/3):135–168.

Evgeny A. Stepanov and Giuseppe Riccardi. 2013. Comparative evaluation of argument extraction algorithms in discourse relation parsing. In *13th International Conference on Parsing Technologies (IWPT 2013)*, pages 36–44.

Maite Taboada and William C. Mann. 2006. Applications of rhetorical structure theory. *Discourse Studies*, (8):567–88.

Bonnie L. Webber, Markus Egg, and Valia Kordoni. 2011. Discourse structure and language technology. *Natural Language Engineering*, pages 1 – 54.

Ben Wellner and James Pustejovsky. 2007. Automatically identifying the arguments of discourse connectives. In *Proceedings of the 2007 Joint Conference on Empirical Methods in Natural Language Processing and Computational Natural Language Learning (EMNLP-CoNLL 2007)*.

Fan Xu, Qiao Ming Zhu, and Guo Dong Zhou. 2012. A unified framework for discourse argument identification via shallow semantic parsing. In *Proceedings of 24th International Conference on Computational Linguistics (COLING 2012): Posters*.

Hiroyasu Yamada and Yuji Matsumoto. 2003. Statistical dependency analysis with support vector machines. In *Proceedings of 8th International Workshop on Parsing Technologies*.

Translating SNOMED CT Terminology into a Minor Language

Olatz Perez-de-Viñaspre and Maite Oronoz
IXA NLP Group
University of the Basque Country UPV/EHU
Donostia
{olatz.perezdevinaspre, maite.oronoz}@ehu.es

Abstract

This paper presents the first attempt to semi-automatically translate SNOMED CT (*Systematized Nomenclature of Medicine – Clinical Terms*) terminology content to Basque, a less resourced language. Thus, it would be possible to build a new clinical healthcare terminology for Basque. We have designed the translation algorithm and the first two phases of the algorithm that feed the SNOMED CT's Terminology content, have been implemented (it is composed of four phases). The goal of the translation is twofold: the enforcement of the use of Basque in the bio-sanitary area and the access to a rich multilingual resource in our language.

1 Introduction

SNOMED Clinical Terms (SNOMED CT) (IHTSDO, 2014) is considered the most comprehensive, multilingual clinical healthcare terminology in the world. The use of a standard clinical terminology improves the quality and health care by enabling consistent representation of meaning in an electronic health record[1].

Osakidetza, the Basque Sanitary System ought to provide its service in the two co-official languages of the Basque Autonomous Community, in Spanish and in Basque. However, and being Basque a minority language in front of the powerful Spanish language, the use of Basque in the documentation services (for example in the Electronic Medical Records (EMR)) of Osakidetza, is almost zero. One of our goals in this work is to offer a medical terminology in Basque to the bio-medical personnel to try to enforce the use of Basque in the bio-sanitary area and in this way protect the linguistic rights of patients and doctors. Another objective in this work is to be able to access multilingual medical resources in Basque language. To try to reach the mentioned objectives, we want to semi-automatically translate the terminology content of SNOMED CT focusing in some of its main hierarchies.

To achieve our translation goal, we have defined an algorithm that is based on Natural Language Processing (NLP) techniques and that is composed of four phases. In this paper we show the systems and results obtained when developing the first two phases of the algorithm that, in this case, translates English terms into Basque. The first phase of the algorithm is based on the use of multilingual lexical resources, while the second one uses a finite-state approach to obtain Basque equivalent terms using medical affixes and also transcription rules.

In this paper we will leave aside explanations about i) the translation application, ii) the knowledge management and iii) the knowledge representation, and we will focus on term generation. The application framework that manages the terms has been already developed and it is in use. The knowledge representation schema has been designed and implemented and it is also being used (Perez-de-Viñaspre and Oronoz, 2013).

In the rest of the paper after motivating the work and connecting it to other SNOMED CT translations (sections 2 and 3), the algorithm and the material that are needed to implement the first two phases of the translation-algorithm are described (section 4). After that, results are shown and discussed (sections 5 and 6). Finally, some conclusions and future work are listed in the last section (section 7).

2 Background and significance

"Basque is the ancestral language of the Basque people, who inhabit the Basque Country, a region

[1] http://www.ihtsdo.org/snomed-ct/whysnomedct/snomedfeatures/

spanning an area in northeastern Spain and southwestern France. It is spoken by 27% of Basques in all territories (714,136 out of 2,648,998). Of these, 663,035 live in the Spanish part of the Basque country (Basque Country and Navarre) and the remaining 51,100 live in the French part (Pyrénées-Atlantiques)[2]". Basque is a minority language in its standardization process and persists between two powerful languages, Spanish and French. Although today Basque holds co-official language status in the Basque Autonomous Community, during centuries Basque was not an official language; it was out of educational systems, out of media, and out of industrial environments. Due to this features, the use of the Basque Language in the bio-sanitary system is low. One of the reasons for translating SNOMED CT is to try to increase the use of the Basque language in this area.

SNOMED CT is a multilingual resource as its concepts are linked to terms in different languages by means of a concept identifier. Thus, terms in our language will be linked to terms in all the languages in which SNOMED CT is released. Besides, as SNOMED CT is part of the Metathesaurus of UMLS (Unified Medical Language System (Bodenreider, 2004)), Basque speakers will have the possibility of accessing other lexical medical resources (RxNorm, MeSH) containing the concepts of SNOMED CT.

SNOMED CT has been already translated to other languages using different techniques. These translations were done either manually (this is the case of the Danish language (Petersen, 2011)), combining automatic translation with manual work (in Chinese, for example (Zhu et al., 2012)), or using exclusively an automatic translation helping system (that is the case of French (Abdoune et al., 2011)). In the design of the translation task, we have followed the guidelines for the translation of SNOMED CT (Høy, 2010) published by the IHTSDO as it is recommended.

3 SNOMED CT

SNOMED CT provides the core terminology for electronic health records and contains more than 296,000 active concepts with their descriptions organized into hierarchies. (Humphreys et al., 1997) shows that SNOMED CT has an acceptable coverage of the terminology needed to record patient conditions. Concepts are defined by means of description logic axioms and are used also to group terms with the same meaning. Those descriptions are more generally considered as terms.

There are three types of descriptions in SNOMED CT: Fully Specified Names (FSN), Preferred Terms (PT) and Synonyms. Fully Specified Names are the descriptions used to identify the concepts and they usually have a semantic tag in parenthesis that indicates its semantic type and, consequently, its hierarchy. Regarding what we sometimes refer to as "terms" we can distinguish between PTs and Synonyms.

There are 19 hierarchies to organize the content of SNOMED CT (plus 1 hierarchy for metadata). The concepts of SNOMED CT are grouped into hierarchies as *Clinical finding/disorder*, *Organism*, and so on. For translation purposes it is important to deeply analyze these hierarchies as some of them need to translate all the terms while others as *Organism* only admit the translation of the synonyms (the preferred term should be the taxonomic one). The guidelines for the translation of the hierarchies are given in (Høy, 2010). We want to remark that only the terms classified as PTs and synonyms in SNOMED CT have been taken into consideration for the translation purposes, as the structure (relationships, for example) is the ontological core of SNOMED CT.

Considering the lexical resources available in the bio-sanitary domain for Basque and the SNOMED CT language versions released, two source languages can be used for our translation task: English and Spanish. Basque is classified as a language isolate, and in consequence it is not related to English or Spanish and its linguistic characteristics are far away from both of them. For that reason, no English nor Spanish offers any advantage as translation source. Thus, we deeply analyzed both of them to choose the best option. Our starting point was the Release Format 2 (RF2), Snapshot distributions and the versions dated the 31-07-2012 for English and the 30-10-2012 for Spanish. It must be taken into consideration that the Spanish version of SNOMED CT is a manual translation of the English version.

To choose the source version of SNOMED CT that will be translated, we analyzed aspects as i) general numbers of FSNs, PTs and Synonyms, ii) length of the terms in each language and, ii) the lack of elements in each version. These data help

[2]http://en.wikipedia.org/wiki/Basque_language (January 23, 2014)

us to come to a decision:

1. The number of active concepts in both languages is the same (296,433) as the Spanish version uses the English concept file. Nevertheless, the number of terms in Spanish is significantly smaller. In Spanish 15,715 concepts lack of PTs and Synonyms.

2. Regarding the length of the PTs and synonyms, we counted the terms containing one token, two tokens, three tokens, four tokens and those with more than four tokens. In the English version the 6.76% of the terms has one token, the 23.28% two and the 20.70% three tokens. That is, quite simple terms compose the half of the synonyms in the lexicon. In the Spanish version, nevertheless, only the 33.79% of the synonyms has three tokens or less, and there are 66.21% synonyms with four tokens or more.

Considering these data, we can conclude that i) the English version is more complete and consistent than the Spanish one, and that ii) the terms in the English version are shorter in length and, in consequence, simpler to translate than the ones in the Spanish version. Thus, we decided to use the English version of SNOMED CT as the translation source as starting point.

We fix the priority between hierarchies for the translation taking into account the number of terms in each hierarchy. The most populated hierarchies are *Clinical finding/disorder* (139,643 concepts) and *Procedure* (75,078 concepts). The next most populated hierarchies are *Organism* (35,870 concepts) and *Body Structure* (26,960). The translation guidelines indicate that the PTs of the organisms should not be translated. For this reason and being conscious of our limitation to translate this huge terminology, we decided to prioritize the translation of the *Clinical finding/disorder*, the *Procedure* and the *Body Structure* hierarchies.

4 Translation Algorithm

We have defined a general algorithm that tries to achieve the translation with an incremental approach. Although the design is general and the algorithm could be used for any language pair, some linguistic resources for the source and objective languages are necessary. In our implementation, the algorithm takes a term in English as input and obtains one or more equivalent terms in Basque.

The mapping of SNOMED CT with ICD-10 works at concept level. Thus, before executing the implementation of the algorithm the mapping between them should be done (see section 5).

The algorithm is composed of four main phases. The first two phases are already developed and results regarding quantities are given in section 5. The last two phases will be undertaken in the very near future.

We want to remark that all the processes finish in the step numbered as 4 in the algorithm (see Figure 1). The Basque equivalents with their original English terms, and relative information (for instance, the SNOMED CT concept identifier) are stored in an XML document that follows the TermBase eXchange (TBX) (Melby, 2012) international standard (ISO 30042) as exposed in (Perez-de-Viñaspre and Oronoz, 2013). All the lexical resources are stored in another simpler TBX document called ItzulDB (see number 1 in Figure 1). This document is initialized with all the lexical resources available, such as specialized dictionaries and it is enriched with the new translation pairs generated that overcome a confidence threshold with the intention of using them to translate new terms. In this way we achieve feedback.

Let us describe the main phases:

1. *Lexical knowledge*. In this phase of the algorithm (see numbers 1-2-4 in Figure 1), some specialized dictionaries and the English, Spanish and Basque versions of the International Statistical Classification of Diseases and Related Health in its 10th version (ICD-10) are used. ItzulDB is initialized with all the translation pairs (English-Basque) extracted from different dictionaries of the bio-medical domain and the pairs extracted from the ICD-10. For example the input term "abortus" will be stored with all its Basque equivalents *"abortu"*, *"abortatze"* and *"hilaurtze"*. This XML database is enriched with the new elements that are generated when the algorithm is applied (number 4 in Figure 1). Figure 2 shows an example of some translations obtained using *ItzulDB*.

2. *Morphosemantics*. When a simple term (term with a unique token) is not found in *ItzulDB* (number 3 in Figure 1) it is analyzed at word-level, and some generation-rules are used to

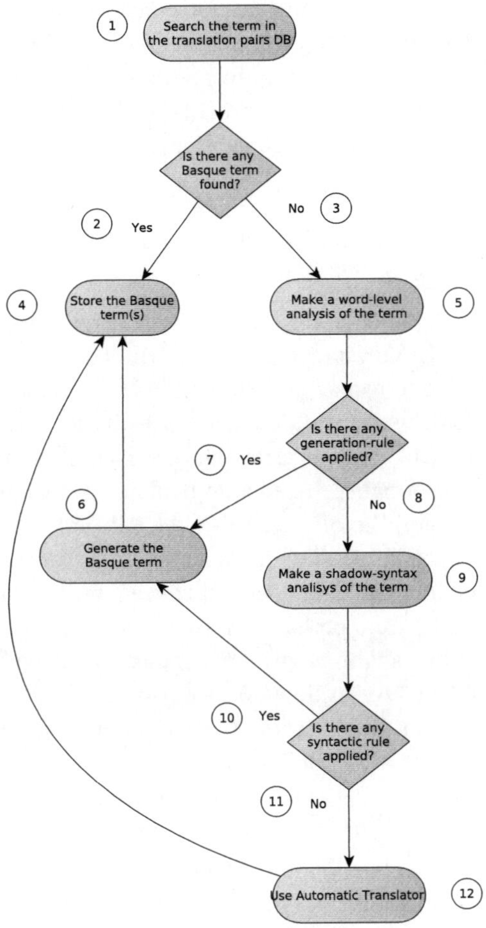

Figure 1: Schema of the Algorithm.

Input term: Deoxyribonuclic acid
Steps in Figure 1 number: 1,2,4
Translation: *Azido desoxirribonukleiko, ADN, DNA*

Figure 2: Terms obtained from *ItzulDB*.

create the translation. We apply medical suffix and prefix equivalences and morphotactic rules, as well as some transcription rules, for this purpose. This is the case in Figure 3.

Input term: Photodermatitis
Steps in Figure 1 number: 3,5,7,6,4
Applied rules:
Identified parts: photo+dermat+itis
Translated parts: foto+dermat+itis
Translation: *Fotodermatitis*

Figure 3: Terms obtained using generation-rules.

3. *Shallow Syntax.* In the case that the input term does not appear in *ItzulDB* and it can not be generated by word-level rules (number 8 in the algorithm), chunk-level generation rules are used. Our hypothesis is that some chunks of the term will appear in *ItzulDB* with their translation. The application should generate the entire term using the translated components (see example in Figure 4).

Input term: Deoxyribonucleic acid sample
Steps in Figure 1 number: 8, 9, 10, 6, 4
Chunks in *ItzulDB*:
1st chunk: Deoxyribonucleic acid
Basque: *azido desoxirribonukleiko, ADN, DNA*
2nd chunk: sample
Basque: *lagin*
Translation: *Azido desoxirribonukleikoaren lagin, ADN lagin, DNA lagin*

Figure 4: Terms obtained using chunk-level generation rules.

4. *Machine Translation.* In the last phase, our aim is to use a rule-based automatic translation system called *Matxin* (Mayor et al., 2011) that we want to adapt to the medical domain. Figure 5 shows an attempt of translation with the non adapted translator. For example, *Matxin* translates "colon" as the punctuation mark (*"bi puntu"* or ":") because it lacks the anatomical meaning.

Input term: Partial excision of oesophagus and interposition of colon
Steps in Figure 1 number: 12, 4
Translation: *Esofagoaren zati baten excisiona eta interpositiona bi puntua*

Figure 5: Terms obtained using *Matxin*.

The IHTSDO organization releases a semi-automatic mapping between SNOMED CT and the ICD-10. By identifying the sense of a concept in SNOMED CT, the best semantic space in the ICD-10 for this concept is searched obtaining linked codes. In this way we can obtain the corresponding Basque term for some of the SNOMED CT concepts through ICD-10. Considering that the structures of SNOMED CT and the ICD-10 are quite different, and that the mapping sometimes has "mapping conditions", the use of this resource has been complex, but fruitful for very specialised terms. Although as we said this mapping is the unique source for obtaining very specialised terms, it should be used carefully as the objectives of SNOMED CT and ICD-10 are different. ICD-10 has classification purposes while SNOMED CT has representation purposes.

A brief description of the first two phases of the algorithm is done in the next subsections (subsections 4.1 and 4.2):

4.1 Phase 1: Lexical Resources

The multilingual specialized dictionaries with English and Basque equivalences that have been used to enrich *ItzulDB* in the first phase of the algorithm are:

- *ZT Dictionary*[3]: This is a dictionary about science and technology that contains areas as medicine, biochemistry, biology... It contains 13,764 English-Basque equivalences.
- *Nursing Dictionary*[4]: It has 5,393 entries in the English-Basque chapter.
- *Glossary of Anatomy*: It contains anatomical terminology (2,578 useful entries) used by University experts in their lectures.
- *ICD-10*[5]: This classification of diseases was translated into Basque in 1996. It is also available in English and in Spanish. The mapping between the different language editions conforming a little dictionary, allowed us to obtain 7,061 equivalences between English and Basque.
- *EuskalTerm*[6]: This terminology bank contains 75,860 entries from wich 26,597 term equivalences are labeled as from the biomedical domain.
- *Elhuyar Dictionary*[7]: This English-Basque dictionary, is a general dictionary that contains 39,164 equivalences from English to Basque.

All these quite different dictionaries have been preprocessed in order to initialize *ItzulDB*. *Elhuyar Dictionary* is a general dictionary that has both not domains pairs but also contains some specialized terminology. This general dictionary will help i) in the translation of not domain terms and ii) also in the translation of the chunks in Phase 3, and thus, on the generation of new terms in Basque.

4.2 Phase 2: Finite State Transducers and Biomedical Affixes

A first approach to this work is presented in (Perez-de-Viñaspre et al., 2013). In that work, finite state transducers described in Foma (Hulden, 2009) are used to automatically identify the affixes in English Medical terms and by means of affix translation pairs, to generate the equivalent terms in Basque. We observed that the behavior of the roots in this type of words is similar to prefixes, so, we will not make distinction between them and we will name them prefixes. A list of 826 prefixes and 143 suffixes with medical meanings was manually translated. An evaluation of the system was performed in a Gold Standard of 885 English-Basque pairs. The Gold Standard was composed of the simple terms that were previously translated in the first phase of the algorithm. A precision of 93% and a recall of 41% were obtained.

In that occasion, only SNOMED CT terms for which all the prefixes and suffixes were identified were translated. For example, terms with the prefix "phat" were not translated as this affix does not appear in the prefixes and suffixes list. For instance, the "hypophosphatemia" term was not translated even though the "hypo", "phos" and "emia" affixes were identified.

We have improved this work by increasing the number of affixes and implementing transcription rules from English/Latin/Greek to Basque.

Figure 6 will help us to get a wider view of the work exposed. The input term "symphysiolysis" is split into the possible affix combination in the first step ("sym+physio+lysis" or "sym+physi+o+lysis"). Then, those affixes are translated by means of its equivalents in Basque ("sim+fisio+lisi" or "sim+fisi+o+lisi"). And finally, by means of morphotactic rules, the well-formed Basque term is composed (in both cases "sinfisiolisi" is generated).

5 Results

Considering the huge size of the descriptions in SNOMED CT and to make the translation pro-

[3]http://zthiztegia.elhuyar.org

[4]http://www.ehu.es/euskalosasuna/Erizaintza2.pdf

[5]http://www.ehu.es/PAT/Glosarios/GNS10.txt

[6]http://www.euskadi.net/euskalterm

[7]http://hiztegiak.elhuyar.org/en

Table 1: Results of the translation.

	Disorder		Finding		Body Structure		Procedure	
	#Synonyms	#Matches	#Synonyms	#Matches	#Synonyms	#Matches	#Synonyms	#Matches
ICD-10 mapping	11,227	-	1,878	-	0	-	0	-
In dictionaries	4,804	3,488	1,836	915	5,896	2,992	778	473
ZT Dictionary	1,104	883	367	311	1,812	1,212	293	253
Nursing Dictionary	437	350	340	245	978	725	199	157
Glossary of Anatomy	3	3	10	8	1,982	1,431	2	2
ICD-10	2,434	2,308	216	195	410	370	5	4
EuskalTerm	906	596	442	306	2,346	1,423	202	155
Elhuyar	299	135	956	300	1,090	367	270	91
Morphosemantics	2,620	2,184	705	578	970	779	1,551	1,362
Total	**17,627**	**5,672**	**4,419**	**1,493**	**6,866**	**3,771**	**2,329**	**1,835**

Input term: symphysiolysis
Identified affixes: sym+physio+lysis, sym+physi+o+lysis
Translation of the affixes: sim+fisio+lisi, sim+fisi+o+lisi
Morphotactics output term: *sinfisiolisi*

Figure 6: Term translated by means of affix equivalences.

cess easy to handle, we have divided it into hierarchies. The *Clinical finding/disorder* hierarchy is specially populated so we have split it considering its semantic tags: *disorders* and *findings*. In addition, the terms from the *Procedure* and *Body Structure* hierarchies have been evaluated too.

Before showing the results, we want to remark some aspects of the evaluation:

- Phase 1: the evaluation has been performed in terms of *quantity*, not of *quality* of the equivalent terms obtained. As the used resources are dictionaries manually generated by lexicographers and domain experts, the quality of the Basque terms is assumed. In any case, and due to the fact that Basque is in its standardization process, the orthographic correctness of the descriptions (see section 6) will be manually checked in the near future.

- Phase 2: the quality of the generated terms could be measured extrapolating the results in the evaluation of the baseline system described in subsection 4.2. That is, 93% precision and 41% recall. The quantity results are shown considering the improvements described in the same subsection.

Table 1 shows the results for the mentioned hierarchies and semantic tags when the translation is performed using both methods: dictionary matching and morphosemantics. Remind that in a previous phase a concept level mapping is completed between SNOMED CT and ICD-10. The first row in Table 1 labeled as "ICD-10 mapping" shows that it is relevant only for the *Clinical disorders and findings* hierarchy, being the *disorder* semantic tag the most benefited one with 11,228 equivalences. The remainder of the results is given at term level.

We made a distinction between the number of obtained Basque terms (1st column, labeled as "#Synonyms") and the number of English terms translated (2nd column, labeled as "#Matches"). Let us see the difference between those two columns looking at the numbers in Table 1. For example, in the *disorder* semantic tag there are 3,488 matches (3,488 original English terms translated), but the number of obtained Basque terms is 4,804 (adding the number of equivalents of all the dictionaries). The reason is that the same input term may have synonyms or even the same equivalent term given by different dictionaries. For example, for the term "allopathy", the same term "alopatia" is obtained in the ZT and Nursing dictionaries (this equivalence will be counted in both ZT and Nursing dictionaries rows).

Table 2 shows the number of tokens in the original English terms. This table refers not to the concepts, but to the terms in the source SNOMED CT in English. The first row shows the number of English terms to which we obtained a Basque equivalent or synonym, the second one the total of English terms and finally, the last row the percentage of translated terms.

Table 3 gives the overall numbers of the translated concepts, in order to take a wide view of the process done.

Let us see the highlights of the results for each

Table 2: Results of the translation regarding the number of tokens of the original term.

		1 token	2 tokens	3 tokens	4 tokens	> 4 tokens	Total
Disorder	**Translated Terms**	3,315	1,114	538	279	426	5,672
	Terms in total	4,066	22,023	24,036	20,005	37,316	107,446
	Percentage	81.53%	5.06%	2.24%	1.40%	1.14%	5.27%
Finding	**Translated Terms**	1,222	158	39	20	54	1,493
	Terms in total	1,830	8,837	10,980	9,814	19,106	50,567
	Percentage	66.78%	1.79%	0.36%	0.20%	0.28%	2.95%
Body Structure	**Translated Terms**	1,942	1,416	334	66	13	3,771
	Terms in total	2,692	11,519	12,575	10,903	21,631	59,320
	Percentage	72.14%	12.29%	2.66%	0.61%	0.06%	6.36%
Procedure	**Translated Terms**	1,741	80	11	2	1	1,835
	Terms in total	1,982	9,966	15,848	16,578	37,695	82,069
	Percentage	87.84%	0.80%	0.07%	0.01%	0.003%	2.24%

Table 3: Overall results.

	Disorder	Finding	Body Structure	Procedure
Translated Concepts	14,125	2,777	3,231	1,502
Concepts in total	65,386	33,204	31,105	82,069
Percentage	21.60%	8.36%	10.39%	1.83%

hierarchy or semantic tag:

- 21.60% of the *disorders* has been translated (see Table 3). This can be considered a very good result. The ICD-10 mapping produces the majority of the translations as it could be expected in this hierarchy (11,227 synonyms obtained). In Table 2 the strength of the morphosemantics phase is evident as the 81.53% of the simple terms is translated.

- The *finding* semantic tag is the most balanced, as no one of the algorithm phase's contribution outlines. The translation of the 8.36% of the concepts is achieved.

- Regarding the results of the *Body Structure* hierarchy, Table 1 shows that the Glossary of Anatomy only contributes in this area. The 10.39% of the concepts get a Basque equivalent.

- In the translation of the *Procedure* hierarchy the dictionaries do not help much as shown in Table 1. In contrast, the mophosemantics contribution allows to translate the 87.84% of the simple terms (see Table 2).

6 Discussion

Some general dictionaries as the ZT dictionary usually contribute in the translation of most of the terms, while more specialized dictionaries only provide translations in the terms related to their domain. For example, both dictionaries, the ZT dictionary and the Nursing dictionary, obtained the Basque terms "mikrozefalia" for "microcephaly" and "metatartso" for "metatarsus". The ICD-10 mapping contributed mainly in the translation of the disorders, and the Glossary of Anatomy in the translation of terms from the Body Structure hierarchy. Sometimes more than an equivalent in Basque is obtained in the translation. For example, for the term "leprosy" we got the equivalents "legen beltz", "legen" and "legenar". Some problems were detected in the Basque terms regarding the standard orthography (the ICD-10 was translated in 1996 and the spelling rules have changed since then) and the form of the word (some obtain the word in finite forms, i.e. "abdomena" for "abdomen" and other in non finite form, "abdomen").

To which the terms generated by finite-state transducers concern, we detected many new affixes from the SNOMED CT terms that do not appear in our lexicon. Even most of those affixes will be correctly transcripted by our transducers, experts insist on enriching the lexicon with new pairs.

7 Conclusions

We have designed a translation algorithm for the multilingual terminology content of SNOMED CT and we have implemented the first two phases. On the one hand, lexical resources feed our database, and on the other hand, Basque equivalents are generated using transducers and medical and biological affixes.

Dictionaries provide Basque equivalents of any term length (i.e. unique and multitoken terms) while transducers get as input unique token terms.

In both translation methods results for the most populated hierarchies are shown even though they are applied for all the hierarchies in SNOMED CT. When using lexical resources, results are promising and the contribution of the ICD-10 mapping is remarkable. We obtained the equivalents in Basque of 21.60% of the disorders.

In any case, as we said before, our objective in the future is that specialist in medical terminology can check the quality of the obtained terms and correct them with the help of a domain corpus in Basque. A platform is being developed for this purpose. After the evaluation, and only if it reaches high quality results, our aim is to contact SNOMED CT providers to offer them the result of our work, that at the moment only pertains to the research area.

Regarding the developed systems evaluation, the system used in the first phase extracts English-Basque pairs from dictionaries, so being quite a simple system, does not need of a deep evaluation. A first evaluation of the system that generates terms using medical affixes has been presented. At present, we are evaluating the improvements of this second system with promising results.

In a near future, we want to implement the remainder of the phases in the algorithm: the use of syntax rules for term generation, and the adaptation of the machine translation tool. The promising results in this first approximation encourage us in the way to semi-automatically generate a version in Basque of SNOMED CT.

Acknowledgments

The authors would like to thank Mikel Lersundi for his help. This work was partially supported by the European Commission (325099), the Spanish Ministry of Science and Innovation (TIN2012-38584-C06-02) and the Basque Government (IT344-10 and IE12-333). Olatz Perez-de-Viñaspre's work is funded by a PhD grant from the Basque Governement (BFI-2011-389).

References

Hocine Abdoune, Tayeb Merabti, Stéfan J. Darmoni, and Michel Joubert. 2011. Assisting the Translation of the CORE Subset of SNOMED CT Into French. In Anne Moen, Stig Kjær Andersen, Jos Aarts, and Petter Hurlen, editors, *Studies in Health Technology and Informatics*, volume 169, pages 819–823.

Olivier Bodenreider. 2004. The Unified Medical Language System (UMLS): Integrating Biomedical Terminology. *Nucleic acids research*, 32(suppl 1):D267–D270.

Asta Høy. 2010. Guidelines for Translation of SNOMED CT. Technical Report version 2.0, International Health Terminology Standards Development Organization IHTSDO.

M. Hulden. 2009. Foma: a Finite-State Compiler and Library. In *Proceedings of EACL 2009*, pages 29–32, Stroudsburg, PA, USA.

Betsy L Humphreys, Alexa T McCray, and May L Cheh. 1997. Evaluating the coverage of controlled health data terminologies: report on the results of the NLM/AHCPR large scale vocabulary test. *Journal of the American Medical Informatics Association*, 4(6):484–500.

International Health Terminology Standards Development Organisation IHTSDO. 2014. SNOMED CT Starter Guide. February 2014. Technical report, International Health Terminology Standards Development Organisation.

Aingeru Mayor, Iñaki Alegria, Arantza Diaz de Ilarraza, Gorka Labaka, Mikel Lersundi, and Kepa Sarasola. 2011. Matxin, an Open-source Rule-based Machine Translation System for Basque. *Machine Translation*, 25:53–82. 10.1007/s10590-011-9092-y.

Alan K. Melby. 2012. Terminology in the Age of Multilingual Corpora. *The Journal of Specialised Translation*, 18:7–29, July.

Olatz Perez-de-Viñaspre and Maite Oronoz. 2013. An XML Based TBX Framework to Represent Multilingual SNOMED CT for Translation. In *Advances in Artificial Intelligence and Its Applications*, pages 419–429. Springer.

Olatz Perez-de-Viñaspre, Maite Oronoz, Manex Agirrezabal, and Mikel Lersundi. 2013. A Finite-State Approach to Translate SNOMED CT Terms into Basque Using Medical Prefixes and Suffixes. *Finite State Methods and Natural Language Processing*, page 99.

Palle G. Petersen. 2011. How to Manage the Translation of a Terminology. Presentation at the IHTSDO October 2011 Conference and Showcase, October.

Yanhui Zhu, Huiting Pan, Lei Zhou, Wei Zhao, Ana Chen, Ulrich Andersen, Shuxiang Pan, Lixin Tian, and Jianbo Lei. 2012. Translation and Localization of SNOMED CT in China: A pilot study. *Artificial Intelligence in Medicine*, 54(2):147–149.

A System for Building FrameNet-like Corpus for the Biomedical Domain

He Tan
School of Engineering
Jönköping University, Sweden
he.tan@jth.hj.se

Abstract

Semantic Role Labeling (SRL) plays an important role in different text mining tasks. The development of SRL systems for the biomedical area is frustrated by the lack of large-scale domain specific corpora that are annotated with semantic roles. In our previous work, we proposed a method for building FramenNet-like corpus for the area using domain knowledge provided by ontologies. In this paper, we present a framework for supporting the method and the system which we developed based on the framework. In the system we have developed the algorithms for selecting appropriate concepts to be translated into semantic frames, for capturing the information that describes frames from ontology terms, and for collecting example sentence using ontological knowledge.

1 Introduction

Semantic Role Labeling (SRL) is a process that, for each predicate in a sentence, indicates what semantic relations hold among the predicate and its associated sentence constituents. The associated constituents are identified and their semantic role labels are assigned, as in: $[_{Transporter}$CBG$]$ **delivers** $[_{Entity}$cortisol$]$ $[_{Destination}$to target cells$]$. SRL could play an important role in text mining tasks such as information extraction, question answering and text summarization. With the advent of large resources like FrameNet (Fillmore et al., 2001) and PropBank (Palmer et al., 2005), SRL has become a well-defined task with a substantial body of work and comparative evaluation. Much of this work has focused on the arguments of verbs, and has been trained and evaluated on newswire text.

Recently, work has turned to bring SRL to the biomedical area (Wattarujeekrit et al., 2004; Tsai et al., 2006; Dolbey et al., 2006; Bethard et al., 2008). Biomedical text considerably differs from the PropBank and FrameNet data, both in the style of the written text and the predicates involved. Predicates in the data are typically verbs, biomedical text often prefers nominalizations, gerunds and relational nouns (Cohen et al., 2008; Kilicoglu et al., 2010). Predicates like *endocytosis* and *translocate*, though common in biomedical text, are absent from both the FrameNet and PropBank data (Wattarujeekrit et al., 2004; Bethard et al., 2008; Tan, 2010). Predicates like *block*, *generate* and *transform*, have been used in biomedical documents with different semantic senses and require different number of semantic roles compared to FrameNet (Tan, 2010) and PropBank data (Wattarujeekrit et al., 2004).

The projects, such as PASBio (Wattarujeekrit et al., 2004), BioProp (Tsai et al., 2006) and BioFrameNet (Dolbey et al., 2006), have made efforts on building resources for training SRL systems in the biomedical domain. PASBio annotated the semantic roles for 31 predicates (distributed 29 verbs) in style of PropBank. It used a model for a hypothetical signal transduction pathway of an idealized cell, to motivate verb choices. BioProp, also a PropBank-like corpus, annotated the semantic roles of 30 frequent biomedical verbs found in the GENIA corpus. BioFrameNet built a FrameNet-like corpus having 32 verbs and nouns annotated with the semantic roles. It considers a collection of GeneRIF (Gene References in Function) texts that are annotated by the protein transport classes in the Hunter Lab knowledge base. Up until recently, these corpora are relatively small.

One of obstacles to building FrameNet-like resources is to manually construct large, coherent and consistent frame sets for the domain. In (Tan et al., 2012) we argue that we can build large-scale FrameNet-like resources using domain knowledge from ontologies. A large number of ontologies have been developed in biomedical area, such as OBO ontologies (Smith et al., 2007). Many of them represent the knowledge of domain-specific events (any activities, processes and states). Although most of the ontologies are controlled vocabularies and do not explicitly describe the attributes of events, this information is implicitly contained in ontology terms. Together with the knowledge explicitly represented in the data models of ontologies the information can guide us in constructing large, coherent and consistent frame sets and also ease the task of collecting example sentences. In next section we describe the background knowledge and then present how the ontological knowledge can be used to build frame-semantic descriptions. Section 3 describes a general framework that supports this ontology-driven construction of frame-semantic descriptions and the current system we have developed based on the framework. Related work is given in section 4. Then we conclude the paper with a conclusion and the discussion of future work.

2 Ontology and Frame Semantics

Ontology is a formal representation of knowledge of a domain of interest. An ontology includes concepts that represent classes of entities within a domain, and defines different types of relations among concepts, as well as the rules for combining these concepts and relations. Most currently widely used ontologies in the biomedical domain are controlled vocabularies. The data models essentially contain lists of concepts, and organize them in an *is-a* and *part-of* hierarchy.

In practice, a concept contains one or more terms that are chosen for naming the concept. A preferred term is assigned as the name of the concept, and others could become synonyms. Terms are carefully chosen to clearly and precisely capture the intended meaning of the entities the concept refer to. The terms are noun or noun phrases. As showed in the results of the survey of naming conventions in OBO ontologies (Schober et al., 2009), multi-word terms are constructed in a consistent manner. They are created by re-using strings that appear in the terms already defined in this or in other ontologies. Although attributes of the entities belonging to concepts are not explicitly described in the data model, they remain implicit in the terms (Stevens et al., 2000). The constituents of the terms might contain the information.

Table 1: Protein Transport Concepts

GO:0009306 protein **secretion**
GO:0017038 protein **import**
GO:0071693 protein **transport** *within* extracellular region
GO:0072322 protein **transport** *across* periplasmic space
GO:0072323 chaperone-mediated protein **transport** *across* periplasmic space
GO:0042000 **translocation** *of* peptides or proteins *into* host
GO:0051844 **translocation** *of* peptides or proteins *into* symbiont
GO:0051808 **translocation** *of* peptides or proteins *into* other organism *involved in* symbiotic interaction

The Gene Ontology (GO) (The Gene Ontology Consortium, 2000) is the most widely used controlled vocabulary in the area. It provides the terms for declaring molecular functions, biological processes and cellular components of gene and gene products. Table 1 lists the names of 8 subclasses of `GO:0015031 protein transport` in the *is-a* hierarchy. The head of a phrase determines the semantic category of object or situation which the phrase refer to. Therefore, the head words of the terms, `translocation`, `import`, `secretion` and `transport`, refer to a "protein transport" category, since the concepts represent different kinds of "protein transport". Other constituents of the terms express the attributes or properties of the event. For example, `translocation of peptides or proteins into other organism involved in symbiotic interaction (GO:0051808)`, express the entity (`peptides or proteins`), the destination (`into other organism`) and the condition (`involved in symbiotic interaction`) of a protein transport event. These information are not represented in the model of the ontology.

Frame Semantics (Fillmore, 1985) is the study of how the words evoke or activate frame knowledge, and how the frames thus activated can be used to understand the text that contains the words. Frame semantics assumes that in order to understand the meanings of the words in a language, we must first have knowledge of the background and motivation for their existence in the language and for their use in discourse. The knowledge is defined in the conceptual structures (frames). In the FrameNet, the lexicographic application of the theory, a semantic frame describes an event, a situation or an object, together with the frame elements (FE) that represent the aspects and components of the frame. Lexical units (LU) that belong to the frame, are the words that evoke the frame. Each frame is associated with example sentences within which LUs and FEs are marked. The FrameNet builds frames by collecting and analysing the attestations of words with semantic overlap from the British National Corpus (BNC).

We propose that the domain knowledge contained in ontologies can instruct us in building a FrameNet-like corpus, without having an existing large scale domain corpus like BNC. The construction starts with creating large coherent and consistent frame sets and then collecting associated example sentences. The information implicitly contained in ontology terms together with the knowledge represented in the models of ontologies provide the background knowledge that is required to building the frame-semantic descriptions. After the frames are created, associated example sentences can be collected using knowledge based search engines for biomedical text, and then be annotated.

For example, a frame Protein Transport can be characterized based on the concept `GO:0015031 protein transport`. In the frame, by studying the terms of the subclasses and descendants of the concept (such as those in table 1), the aspects and components of the frame (such as entity, destination and condition), and the domain-specific words evoking the frame (like translocation, import, secretion and transport) are captured. Furthermore, we can identify a *inheritance* relation between this frame and the frame `Transport` built based on the concept `GO:0006810 transport`, since there is the *is-a* relation between `GO:0006810 transport` and `GO:0015031 protein transport` in the GO. Now a complete frame-semantic description for Protein Transport, including FEs, LUs, and relations to other frames, is obtained after all the related concepts and relations are studied.

3 The System

In this section we present a framework that supports this ontology-driven construction of FrameNet-like corpus and describe the current system we have developed based on the framework.

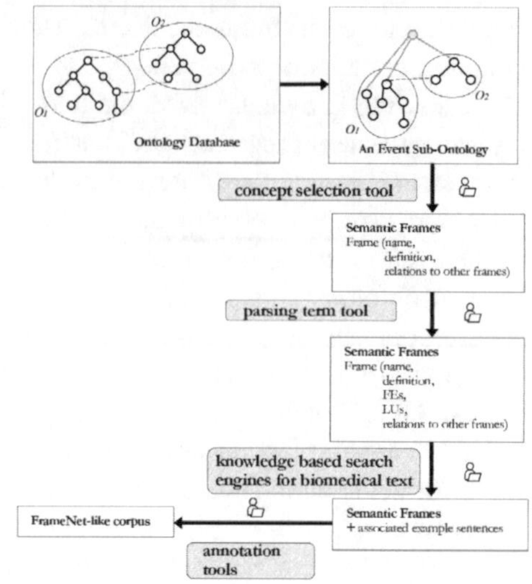

Figure 1: A Framework of Ontology-driven Building Corpus

3.1 Framework

In Fig 1 we propose the framework for supporting the ontology-driven construction of domain corpus with frame-semantics annotations. Before starting the building process, a sub-ontology of biomedical events is extracted from an ontology or an ontology database in which relations between ontology terms are identified. Firstly, concepts representing biomedical events, are gathered. A concept represents a biomedical event if it is a concept that is classified to a type of event in top-domain ontology (like the semantic type `T038 Biologic Function` in UMLS semantic network (Bodenreider, 2004)), or is a subclass or descendant of a concept that has been identified as a representation of biomedical event, or can be defined as a concept describing event based on its definition. After the concepts are identified, an event sub-ontology, including the concepts and the relations between them in original ontologies, is extracted. A root is assigned to the sub-ontology if the concepts are from more than one sub-trees in original ontologies.

The concept selection tool suggests the appropriate concepts that will be translated into frames. The algorithm may consider the characteristics that indicate the generalness of a concept as the selection criteria, such as the location of the concept in the hierarchy and the number of subclasses and descendants the concept has. Further, the concept could be manually identified by domain experts. After a concept is selected, the frame describing the event represented by the concept, is created. Relations between frames are decided according to the relations between the corresponding concepts. The name and definition of a frame is edited by domain experts based on the definition of the concept.

The frame description is accomplished by studying the sub-tree under the concept. After collecting the terms in the sub-tree, the parsing term tool analyses the compositional structure of the term, which elucidate the meaning of a term. The tool may derive the compositional structure of a term based a syntax parse of the term. LUs and FEs then are suggested based on the compositional structures. A final frame-semantic description is decided with interactions to domain experts.

The associated example sentences of a frame could be collected using semantic search engines for biomedical text, like GoPubMed (Doms and Schroeder, 2005). Such search engines annotate documents with concepts of domain ontologies by mapping phrases in text of documents to concepts. Based on this underlying domain knowledge search engines are able to maximize precision and recall of the documents that the user is interested to collect specific information. Therefore, example sentences can be collected from the documents annotated by the concepts in the sub-tree used to characterize the associated frame. In the end annotating example sentences with LUs and FEs of the associated frame is completed by domain experts under the assistance of annotation tools.

3.2 The System

We have developed a system based on the framework for building FrameNet-like corpus using domain ontologies.

An Event Sub-Ontology

In the current system we experimented with the GO biological process ontology (data-version: 2012-10-27). In UMLS semantic network the root node of the ontology `biological process (GO:0008150)` is classified into the semantic type `T038 Biologic Function` . The ontology contains 24,181 concepts and 65,988 terms. The terms include the names of the concepts and their *exact* synonyms. Other synonyms (*broad*, *narrow* and *related* synonyms) are not included, since only terms intending to precisely capture the meaning of a concept are considered. For example, `fat body metabolism`, a *broad* synonym of `GO:0015032 storage protein import into fat body`, describes a much broader activity than that belongs to the concept.

Method for Concept Selection

Different types of frames are used to describe different situations. Frames can range from highly abstract to very specific. To assist the user in selecting appropriate concepts to be translated into frames, the system provides the structure information of the ontology, and the definitions of the concepts and their locations in the ontology.

The event ontology O can be represented as a directed graph G. Graph elements are considered to calculate the structure information of O and the location of the concepts in G including,

- the $root$, the node having no outgoing *is-a* arcs. The graph G has one root.
- a $leaf$ node , a node having no ingoing *is-a* arcs in the graph.
- $sibling$ nodes, nodes connected to the same node through *is-a* arcs.
- $descendant$ nodes of a node n_i, nodes in the sub-tree rooted at n_i.
- a path p_{ij}, any sequence of directed edges from the node n_i to the node n_j.
- a generation g_i, the set of all sibling nodes connected to the node n_i.
- $depth$, the cardinality of a path
- $breadth$, the cardinality of a generation.

As the structure information of O we calculate the number of nodes in G, the average and maximal shortest paths from the root to leaves, the average and maximal breadth of the generations having different distances from the root. To show the location of a concept in G, we calculate the shortest path from the concept to the root, and the number of its descendants and siblings.

The user selects appropriate concepts based on the above information, and may also using their own domain knowledge. For example, a frame could be constructed based on the concept `GO:0006810 transport`. The structural information as showed in table 2 suggests that the concept is richly described in the ontology and it covers a large set of related events. Further, the user (a domain expert) himself/herself could be aware that transport events have been studied in the area over

	#node	depth of shortest path to root (SPR)	#sibling	avg. depth of SPR from leaves	max. depth of SPR from leaves	avg. breadth	max. breadth.	#leaf
biological_process	24181	-	-	6.5	14	3.7	413	12871
transport	1210	2	5	5.9	14	3.5	41	754
protein transport	182	3	41	5.7	9	4.2	40	132

Table 2: The structural information of GO biological process ontology (data-version: 2012-10-27) and the sub-trees under the concept `GO:0006810 transport` and `GO:0015031 protein transport`.

the last 30 years. Most cellular processes are accompanied by transport events. For understanding biomedical texts, transport events are among the most important things to know about.

Method for Parsing Terms

After a concept is selected, the terms in the subtree rooted at the concept are collected to be analysed for building frame description. In the current system the analysis is separated into three steps.

Terms are noun phrases (NP). The first step is to tokenize phrase string into an ordered sequence of an atomic (non-decomposable) token. The phrase string is split on white-space characters and non-alphanumeric characters. White-space character are discarded, but non-alphanumeric characters are preserved and treated as special word tokens. For example, "`alpha-glucoside transport` " (`GO:0000017`) is tokenized into {alpha, -, glucoside, transport}

The second step is to identify the head word of NP. We assume that the head of a phrase is composed of only one token. A naive Bayes classifier classifies a token as the head of a phrase, if the highest value for the posterior probability of being the head word given the token is obtained among all the tokens in the phrase. The posterior probability of being the head word w given token t is estimated using Bayes rule (Mitchell, 1997):

$$P(w|t) = \frac{P(w)P(t|w)}{P(t)}$$

As $P(t)$ is independent of w being the head, it can be ignored. This gives: $P(w|t) = P(w)P(t|w)$.

A token is either the head word or not the head work of a phrase, so $P(w)$ is a constant. $P(t|w)$ is estimated by the feature probabilities of token t. Assuming that the features x_i are all conditionally independent of one another, we have

$$P(t|w) = \prod_{i=1}^{n} P(x_i = a_{ik}|w)$$

$P(x_i = a_{ik}|w)$ is estimated using the maximum likelihood estimation method. Let $n(x_i = a_{ik}, t)$ be the number of occurrences of token t where attribute x_i is a_{ik} and t is a head word, and $n(w)$ be the number of occurrences of the token t where t is a head word. Then $P(x_i = a_{ik}|w)$ is estimated by

$$P(x_i = a_{ik}|w) = \frac{n(x_i = a_{ik}, w) + \lambda}{n(w) + \lambda|V|}$$

where λ is the earlier defined Laplace smoothing parameter, and $|V|$ is the number of distinct values of the attribute x_i.

Attributes of a token t in a phrase p include,

- token string,
- the part-of-speech (POS) of t in p, (the POS of t in p is assigned using MedPost POS Tagger (Smith et al., 2004)),
- the POS of the tokens before and after t in p,
- the length of p (the number of tokens in p),
- the position of t in p.

We have evaluated the method on identifying the heads of terms in GO biological process ontology. The length of terms in the ontology ranges from 1 to 39. For each length, 10% of terms are randomly selected as training data if it is applicable. The result of 10-fold cross validation showed that 93.9% of the heads are correctly identified on average.

A term, a NP, has a noun as its head. The system collects other forms (such as verb, objective, etc.) having the same meaning as the head by looking up the SPECIALIST Lexicon (Bodenreider, 2004), a general English lexicon including many biomedical term. Words in different forms are all suggested as predicates for frame.

The last step is to capture the information hidden in modifiers in phrases. Modifiers describe the head word of a phrase and makes its meaning more specific. They modify phrases by adding information about "where", "when", or "how" something

Table 3: Major Modifier Types in Ontology Terms

Pre-modifiers	head	Post-modifiers
attributive adjective	noun	prepositional phrase
ed-participial adjective		ed-clause
ing-participial adjective		ing-clause
noun		to-clause
		appositive noun phrase

is done. The information gives the suggestions on what FEs to be defined for a frame. In a NP, the head word is preceded by a determiner or one or more pre-modifiers, and may also be followed by one or more post-modifiers. The major structural types of pre-modifiers and post-modifiers are given in table 3. We observed that determiners and relative clauses rarely appear in ontology terms.

The number of FEs is limited in a frame. The information about the major attributes of event appears frequently in the terms. For example, in the sub-tree under `GO:0006810 transport`, 92.6% terms contain the entity undergoing the "transport" event, and 19.3% terms describe the destination (see Table 4). Therefore, although there maybe a large number of terms in a sub-tree, a very small number of the terms can be used to capture the major attributes of the event.

To facilitate the user in identifying the FEs, the system collects a smallest set of terms covering all the attributes of the event that have been described in the sub-tree. The attributes of the event reside in different modifier types appearing in the terms. Further, prepositional phrase modifiers starting with different prepositions may describe different properties. The algorithm for collecting the term set is given as follows,

T ={the set of terms in the sub-tree} ;
M={the set of modifier types m} ;
$P, L = \emptyset$;
repeat
    l = the longest $t \in T$;
    foreach m *in* l **do**
        if (*m is a prepositional phrase* **and** *m starts with a preposition $p \notin P$*) **or** $m \notin P$
        then
            add l to L ;
            foreach m,p *in* l **do**
                if $m, p \notin P$ **then**
                    add m, p to P ;
            end
            break ;
    end
    remove l from T ;
until $T = \emptyset$ **or** $length(l) = 1$;
return L

Method for Collecting Example Sentences

The example sentences are retrieved from the PubMed/MEDLINE database by using the GoPubMed. The sentences to be annotated, are always the most relevant and from the latest publications. For a LU, we acquired sentences by using the GO terms with the head from which the LU is derived. The query starts from using the most general GO terms. In cases when only specific GO terms are available and the number of query results is too small, the query term is generalized by removing modifiers from terms. For example, the lexical units, `release.n` and `release.v`, are derived and only derived from `renin release into blood stream` (a synonym of `GO:0002001 renin secretion into blood stream`). No query result returns for the GO term (AND operator is used to combine the tokens in the term in the query). The general term "protein release" is used as the query term instead.

Annotation Tool

The current system contains a tool that supports manual annotation following the FrameNet's guidelines described in (Ruppenhofer et al., 2005).

File Format

The corpus is stored in XML files using the same format as the FrameNet. The correspondences between frames and ontology concepts are stored in a RDF file. Such relations could benefit integrations of different lexical resources and/or knowledge bases in the future. A correspondence is encoded as follows:

```
<correspondence id="1">
 <concept rdf:about=
   "http://www.geneontology.org/go#GO:0006810"/>
 <frame rdf:about=
   "http://hj.se/ontobiofn/frames#0000001"/>
 <comment/>
</correspondence>
```

It provides the features: concept (the URI of some concept of an ontology); frame (the URI of the frame translated from the concept); comment (the comment on this correspondence given by the user); and an id assigned to this correspondence.

3.3 Evaluation of the System

We have successfully built a FrameNet-like corpus using the method of ontology-driven construction (Tan et al., 2012). The construction is done manually by 2 master students with biology background. The corpus covers transport events in the domain. The GO is used as the source ontology for domain knowledge. The corpus contains 2 frames.

	TE	TO	TDS	TC	TL	TP	TT	TDR	TA	TPL
Protein Transport (581 terms)	99.5% (578)	8.6% (50)	37.4% (159)	16.4% (95)	7.1% (41)	4.6% (27)	1.0% (6)	0.3% (2)	0.2% (1)	0% (0)
Transport (2235 terms)	92.6% (2070)	12.2% (272)	19.3% (432)	9.9% (221)	5.7% (127)	7.3% (164)	1.9% (43)	1.5% (34)	1.8% (40)	0.36% (8)

Table 4: The percentage of the GO terms that indicate the FEs (the number of GO terms). FEs are Transport_Entity (TE), Transport_Origin (TO), Transport_Destination (TDS), Transport_Condition (TC), Transport_Location (TL), Transport_Path (TP), Transport_Transporter (TT),Transport_Direction (TDR), Transport_Attribute (TA), Transport_Place (TPL).

Table 5: Time for Building the Corpus

	using system	manual
construct frames	2 days	2 weeks
gather and annotate example sentences	2.5 weeks	3 weeks

The Transport frame follows the definition of the GO concept, `GO:0006810 transport` (Tan et al., 2012). It has a sub-frame Protein Transport, which characterizes transport events of proteins (Tan et al., 2011). It follows the definition of `GO:0015031 protein transport`. To accomplish the description of the two frames, 2235 terms and 581 terms, respectively, were collected and analysed from the GO. Based on the background knowledge implicitly described in the terms, 10 FEs are identified for the frame Transport (inherited by the frame Protein Transport), and 129 LUs are collected. Maximally for each LU 10 annotated sentences are gathered. Totally, 955 example sentences were retrieved from PubMed and annotated.

We evaluate the effectiveness and efficiency of the system. 2 different master students are asked to build a FrameNet-like corpus covering transport and protein transport events using the method. The GO is also provided as the source ontology. The 2 students have biology background and have the knowledge of the FrameNet and ontology. Both students correctly complete the task using the system in the evaluation. They build the 2 frames Transport and Protein Transport, and construct the same frame descriptions using the domain knowledge from the GO. They are also required to maximally collect and annotate 10 sentences for each LU. The set of the example sentences are not exactly the same set of sentences chosen in the previous corpus. Table 5 shows the time they use on average and the time spent in the manual construction.

4 Related Work

Interfacing ontologies and lexical resources has been initiated in several work (Guarino, 1998; Gangemi et al., 2003; Niles and Pease, 2003). The work in (Gangemi et al., 2003; Niles and Pease, 2003) has attempted to reorganize WordNet's top-level synset taxonomy using ontology concepts. More recently, the FrameNet project links FrameNet's semantic types to ontology concepts, to constrain the filler types of frame elements for specific domains (Scheffczyk et al., 2006). It is the first step of their work aiming at improving FrameNet capability for deductive reasoning with natural language. The authors suggest that the alignment between lexicons and ontologies could restructure the lexicon on the basis of ontological-driven principles, and enables ontologies to be used automatically by natural language processing (NLP) applications.

5 Conclusion

In this paper we present our method for building FrameNet-like corpus for biomedical area starting with use of ontological domain knowledge. Ontological knowledge can lead to well-defined semantics exposed on the corpus, which can be very valuable in NLP and text mining applications. We have developed a framework of supporting the method and implemented a system based on the framework. In the current system we developed the algorithms for selecting appropriate concepts to be translated into semantic frames, for capturing the information that describes aspects and components of frames from ontology terms, and for collecting example sentence using ontology concepts.

In the future we will continue to extend the corpus using ontological knowledge. The event ontology to be used as domain knowledge will include terms from different ontologies. We will evaluate our system when it deals with different ontologies and their terms. Another direction of the future work is to investigate how the ontological knowledge bundled with the corpus are used by NLP and text mining applications.

References

Steven Bethard, Zhiyong Lu, James H Martin, and Lawrence Hunter. 2008. Semantic role labeling for protein transport predicates. *BMC Bioinformatics*, 9:277.

Olivier Bodenreider. 2004. The unified medical language system (umls): integrating biomedical terminology. *Nucleic Acids Research*, pages D267–D270.

K. Bretonnel Cohen, Martha Palmer, and Lawrence Hunter. 2008. Nominalization and alternations in biomedical language. *PLoS ONE*, 3(9).

Andrew Dolbey, Michael Ellsworth, and Jan Scheffczyk. 2006. Bioframenet: A domain-specific framenet extension with links to biomedical ontologies. In *Proceedings of KR-MED*, pages 87–94.

Adress Doms and Michael Schroeder. 2005. Gopubmed: exploring pubmed with the gene ontology. *Nucleic Acids Research*, 33:W783–786.

Charles J. Fillmore, Charles Wooters, and Collin F. Baker. 2001. Building a large lexical databank which provides deep semantics. In *Proceedings of the PACLIC*.

Charles J. Fillmore. 1985. Frames and the semantics of understanding. *Quaderni di Semantica*, 6(2):222–254.

Aldo Gangemi, Nicola Guarino, Claudio Masolo, and Alessandro Oltramari. 2003. Sweetening wordnet with dolce. *AI Magazine*, 3(24):13–24.

Nicola Guarino. 1998. Some ontological principles for designing upper level lexical resources. In *Proceedings of First International Conference on Language Resources and Evaluation*, pages 527–534.

Halil Kilicoglu, Marcelo Fiszman, Graciela Rosemblat, Sean Marimpietri, and Thomas C. Rindflesch. 2010. Arguments of nominals in semantic interpretation of biomedical text. In *Proceedings of the 2010 Workshop on BioNLP*.

Tom Mitchell. 1997. *Machine Learning*. McGraw-Hill.

Ian Niles and Adam Pease. 2003. Linking lexicons and ontologies: Mapping wordnet to the suggested upper merged ontology. In *Proceedings of the IEEE International Conference on Information and Knowledge Engineering*.

Martha Palmer, Daniel Gildea, and Paul Kingsbury. 2005. The proposition bank: an annotated corpus of semantic roles. *Computational Linguistics*, 31:71–105.

Josef Ruppenhofer, Michael Ellsworth, Miriam R. L. Petruck, Christopher R. Johnson, and Jan Scheffczyk. 2005. FrameNet II: Extended theory and practice. Technical report, ICSI.

Jan Scheffczyk, Adam Pease, and Michael Ellsworth. 2006. Linking framenet to the sumo ontology. In *International Conference on Formal Ontology in Information Systems*.

Daniel Schober, Barry Smith, Suzanna Lewis, Waclaw Kusnierczyk, Jane Lomax, Chris Mungall, Chris Taylor, Philippe Rocca-Serra, and Susanna-Assunta Sansone. 2009. Survey-based naming conventions for use in obo foundry ontology development. *BMC Bioinformatics*, 10(1):125.

L. Smith, T. Rindflesch, and W. J. Wilbur. 2004. MedPost: a part-of-speech tagger for bioMedical text. *Bioinformatics*, 20(14):2320–2321.

Barry Smith, Michael Ashburner, and et al. 2007. The obo foundry: coordinated evolution of ontologies to support biomedical data integration. *Nature Biotechnology*, 25(11):1251–1255.

Robert Stevens, Carole A. Goble, and Sean Bechhofer. 2000. Ontology-based knowledge representation for bioinformatics. *Briefings in Bioinformatics*, 1:398–414.

He Tan, Rajaram Kaliyaperumal, and Nirupama Benis. 2011. Building frame-based corpus on the basis of ontological domain knowledge. In *Proceedings of the 2011 Workshop on BioNLP*, pages 74–82.

He Tan, Rajaram Kaliyaperumal, and Nirupama Benis. 2012. Ontology-driven construction of corpus with frame semantics annotations. In *CICLing 2012, Part I, LNCS 7181*, pages 54–65.

He Tan. 2010. A study on the relation between linguistics-oriented and domain-specific semantics. In *Proceedings of the 3rd International Workshop on SWAT4LS*.

The Gene Ontology Consortium. 2000. Gene ontology: tool for the unification of biology. *Nature Genetics*, 25:25–29.

Richard Tzong-Han Tsai, Wen-Chi Chou, Ying-Shan Su, Yu-Chun Lin, Cheng-Lung Sung, Hong-Jie Dai, Irene Tzu-Hsuan Yeh, Wei Ku, Ting-Yi Sung, and Wen-Lian Hsu. 2006. Biosmile: adapting semantic role labeling for biomedical verbs: an exponential model coupled with automatically generated template features. In *Proceedings of the 2005 Workshop on BioNLP*.

Tuangthong Wattarujeekrit, Parantu K Shah, and Nigel Collier. 2004. Pasbio: predicate-argument structures for event extraction in molecular biology. *BMC Bioinformatics*, 5:155.

Gene–disease association extraction by text mining and network analysis

Changqin Quan
AnHui Province Key Laboratory of Affective Computing and Advanced Intelligent Machine,
School of Computer and Information,
HeFei University of Technology
quanchqin@gmail.com

Fuji Ren
Faculty of Engineering,
University of Tokushima,
ren@is.tokushima-u.ac.jp

Abstract

Biomedical relations play an important role in biological processes. In this work, we combine information filtering, grammar parsing and network analysis for gene-disease association extraction. The proposed method first extracts sentences potentially containing information about gene-diseases interactions based on maximum entropy classifier with topic features. And then Probabilistic Context–Free Grammars is applied for gene-disease association extraction. The network of genes and the disease is constituted by the extracted interactions, network centrality metrics are used for calculating the importance of each gene. We used breast cancer as testing disease for system evaluation. The 31 top ranked genes and diseases by the weighted degree, betweenness, and closeness centralities have been checked relevance with breast cancer through NCBI database. The evaluation showed 83.9% accuracy for the testing genes and diseases, 74.2% accuracy for the testing genes.

1 Introduction

Since the start of Human Genome Project in 1990, over 40 kinds of organism genome have been sequenced. Biological databases expand rapidly with the exponential growth of biological data. For instance, until now, over 260,000 named organisms have their nucleotide sequences in the GenBank (Benson et al. 2008) which integrates data from the major DNA and protein sequence. However, data is not information. Compared with situations before 2003, the key problem today has turned to methods of knowledge extraction. Understanding the role of genetics in diseases is one of the major goals of the post-genome era. The expanding rate of knowledge in gene–disease associations can hardly match up with the growth of biological data. It takes time before new discoveries are included in the databases such as Online Mendelian Inheritance in Man (OMIM), and most of the information represented in these databases is manually collected from literature.

To address this challenge, we proposed an automatic gene-disease association extraction approach based on text mining and network analysis. We combine information filtering, grammar parsing and network analysis. We started by calculating main topics of each sentences in the corpus based on supervised Latent Dirichlet Allocation (sLDA) model (Blei and McAuliffe 2007). The most probable topics derived from sLDA model for each sentence are used as features for training maximum entropy (MaxEnt) (Manning and Schutze, 1999) classifier, which extracts sentences potentially containing information about gene-diseases interactions. After that, Probabilistic Context–Free Grammars (PCFGs) (Klein and Christopher 2003) is applied for sentence grammar parsing. Based on the syntactic tree of each sentence, we extract paths between specific entities such as diseases or genes. The network of all candidate genes and the disease is constituted by the interactions extracted from the sentences in the corpus. Our main hypothesis in network analysis is that the most important and the most central genes in an interaction network are most likely to be related to the disease. Last, network centrality metrics are used for calculating the importance of each gene.

The rest of this paper is organized as follows. Section 2 surveys related work. In Section 3, we introduce the proposed approach of extracting interactions from literature. Section 4 presents gene-disease interaction network analysis. And then Section 5 presents and discusses the experimental results. Lastly we conclude this paper and discuss future work in Section 6.

2 Related Work

Much effort is currently spent on extracting gene–disease associations (Özgür et al. 2008; Chun et al. 2006). Biomedical relation extraction techniques basically include two branches: interaction database based methods and text mining methods. Interaction database based methods rely on the availability of interaction databases, such as OMIM, MINT (Zanzoni et al. 2002), IntAct (Kerrien et al. 2012), BIND (Bader et al. 2003), which predict interactions between entities using sequence, structural, or evolutionary information (Krallinger, Leitner, and Valencia 2010). Although these databases host a large collection of manually extracted interactions from the literature, manually curated databases require considerable effort and time with the rapid increasing of biomedical literature.

Since most biological facts are available in the free text of biomedical articles, the wealth of interaction information provided in biomedical articles motivated the implementation of text mining approaches to automatically extract biomedical relations. Text mining approaches to gene–disease association extraction have shown an evolution from simple systems that rely solely on co-occurrence statistics (Adamic et al. 2002; Al-Mubaid and Singh 2005) to complex systems utilizing natural language processing techniques and machine learning algorithms (Freudenberg and Propping 2002; Glenisson et al. 2004; Özgür et al. 2008). Well-known tools for discovering gene–disease associations include DAVID (Huang et al. 2009), GSEA (Subramanian et al. 2005), GOToolBox (Martin et al. 2004), rcNet (Huang et al. 2011) and many others. However, in many cases, since the existing annotations of disease-causative genes is far from complete (McKusick 2007), and a gene set might only contain a short list of poorly annotated genes, existing approaches often fail to reveal the associations between gene sets and disease phenotypes (Huang et al. 2011).

Network-based approaches (Wuchty, Oltvai, and Barabási, 2003; Schwikowski et al. 2000; Chen et al. 2006) is performed by assessing how much genes interact together and are close to known disease genes in protein networks. Relation extraction among genes is the fundamental step for gene-interaction network creation. Recently, syntactic analysis has been considered for relation extraction, and different parsing grammars have been applied. Temkin and Gilder (2003) used a full parser with a lexical analyzer and a context free grammar (CFG) to extract protein-protein interactions. In Yakushiji et al. (2005)'s work, they proposed a protein-protein interaction extraction system based on head-driven phrase structure grammar (HPSG). Although the pattern generation is complicated, the performance is not satisfactory. In addition, dependency grammar is used frequently in this domain. Erkan et al. (2007) proposed a semi-supervised classification for extracting protein interaction sentences using dependency parsing. Katrin et al. (2007) defined some rules based on dependency parse tree for relation extraction. The problem of those systems using dependency parse is that they cannot treat non-local dependencies, and thus rules acquired from the constructions are partial (Yakushiji et al. 2005). Differently, in this work, we apply sentence filtering based on topics and phrase structure parsing for relation extraction. The extracted sentences potentially contain information about gene-diseases interactions. Phrase structure grammars are based on the constituency relation, as opposed to the dependency relation associated with dependency grammars. Phrase structure parsing is full parsing, which takes into account the full sentence structure.

In addition, many researches (Aerts et al. 2005; Chen et al. 2009; Ma et al. 2007; Hutz et al. 2008; Morrison et al. 2005; Özgür et al. 2008) used an initial list of seed genes to build a disease-specific gene-interaction network, and thus they are biased in favor of the seed genes, consequently the results also depend on the pickup seed genes.

3 Extracting interactions from literature

3.1 The Corpus

We used 44,064 articles from PubMed Central (PMC) Open Access which is a free full-text archive of biomedical and life sciences journal literature. All articles were extracted by querying the keyword of "breast cancer". We applied a segmentation tool Splitta for segmenting articles into sentences which includes proper tokenization and models for high accuracy sentence boundary detection with reported error rates near 0.25% coded by Gillick (2009).

A gene name dictionary was built from OMIM database. The disease name dictionary was built based on Genetic Association Database (GAD) which is an archive of human genetic association studies of complex diseases and disorders.

3.2 Key sentences extraction

We applied MaxEnt classifier with topic features for key sentences extraction. The extracted sentences potentially contain information about genes and breast cancer interactions.

A Latent Dirichlet Allocation (LDA) model was used to infer topics of sentences. Three most probable topics of each sentence were put into trained MaxEnt classifier as features for extracting sentences that potentially contain interaction relationship between genes and diseases.

3.2.1 Key words annotation

We assume that each sentence indicating interactions should contain at least one gene and target disease name. Key words are the words increasing possibility of sentence containing interaction relationships, such as genes and diseases. As mentioned above, we built the gene name dictionary with data from OMIM database and disease name dictionary from Genetic Association Database (GAD). All gene names and disease names were considered as key words.

3.2.2 Topic model based on Gibbs Sampling

Latent Dirichlet Allocation (LDA) was applied based on Gibbs Sampling method in our system. Compared with algorithm obtaining approximate maximum-likelihood estimates for topics-words distribution and the hyperparameters of the prior on documents-topics distribution given by Blei, Ng and Jordan (2002), Gibbs Sampling method doesn't need to explicitly represent the model parameters which effect on the final results (Griffiths, 2002).

For a word w in a specific article, the possibility it belongs to topic j can be given by :

$$P(z_i = j \mid z_{-i}, w) \propto P(w_i \mid z_i = j, z_{-i}, w_{-i}) P(z_i = j \mid z_{-i}) \quad (1)$$

where z_i represents current topic, z_{-i} represents all topics except for i, w represents all words in the article, w_i represents current word and w_{-i} represents all words except for w_i.

Formula (1) could be represented as follow after derivation:

$$P(z_i = j \mid z_{-i}, w) \propto \frac{n_{-i,j}^{(w_i)} + \beta}{n_{-i,j}^{(\bullet)} + W\beta} \frac{n^{(d_i)} + \alpha}{n_{-i,\bullet}^{(d_i)} + T\alpha} \quad (2)$$

where $n_{-i,j}^{(\bullet)}$ represents count of words belong to topic j except for current word. $n_{-i,j}^{(w_i)}$ represents count of word w_i belong to topic j in the article except for current one. $n^{(d_i)}$ represents total of words in article d_i, while $n_{-i,\bullet}^{(d_i)}$ represents count of words in document d_i not including the current one. α and β are hyperparameters that determine extent of smooth of this empirical distribution, and how heavily this distribution can be chosen to give the desired resolution in the resulting distribution. W stands for count of words while T stands for count of topics.

3.2.3 Training of topic model

We randomly selected sentences from 8000 documents in our corpus as training set and set number of topics $_x$as 10. Topic that contains most words in gene name dictionary and disease name dictionary was treated as a key topic. Then we manually assigned each word in gene name dictionary or disease name dictionary to key topic, and each word doesn't belong to the two dictionaries was assigned to the most probable topic of itself.

3.2.4 Prediction of key sentences

The sentences containing interactions among genes or diseases were marked as 'Key' and others were marked as 'None'. A MaxEnt classifier [1] was trained based on the topic distribution.

3.3 Extracting interactions from key sentences

In order to extract interactions from sentences, we used phrase structure parsing which generates parse tree of a sentence that can be analyzed for relationships among words. Stanford parser tool[2] (de Marneffe et al. 2006) is employed for sentence parsing. Figure 1 shows an example of phrase structure parse tree.

We extracted interactions by depth-first search in the parse tree. Each path between keyword nodes (e.g. gene or disease) and the root node were collected. A list of interaction verbs

---

[1] http://morphix-nlp.berlios.de/manual/node36.html

[2] http://nlp.stanford.edu/software/stanford-dependencies.shtml

were compiled from VerbNet[3], which consists of 1048 verbs. We captured interactions from the paths which contain an interaction verb.

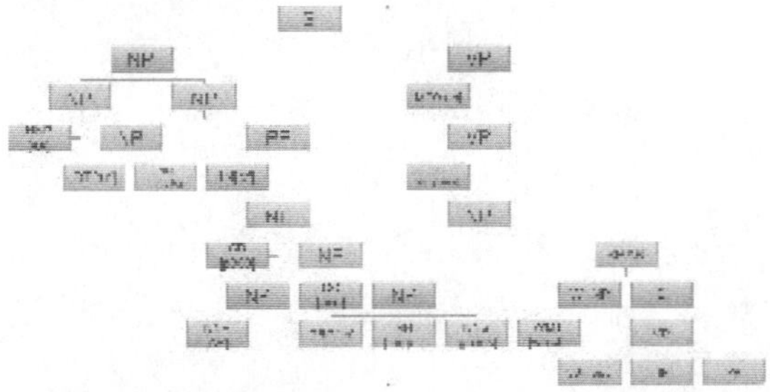

Figure **1**. Part of the phrase structure parse tree of the sentence “AA, an inhibitor of p300, can suppress AR and its target genes, which can induce cells cycle arrest and apoptosis of Lncap cells through AR signaling.”

For instance, two genes ‘AA’ and ‘AR’ could be extracted from sentence “AA, an inhibitor of p300, can suppress AR and its target genes, which can induce cells cycle arrest and apoptosis of Lncap cells through AR signaling”. The path from ‘AA’ to ‘AR’ in the syntactic tree is “NP(AA) ->NP ->NP ->S ->VP(can) ->VP(suppress) ->NP ->NP ->NP(AR)”, where ‘suppress (VP)’ is an interaction verb. Therefore, we consider there is a ‘suppression’ interaction between ‘AA’ and ‘AR’.

4 Interaction network analysis

The extracted interactions can be represented by an adjacency matrix, where $A_{i,j}=1$ if there is an edge between node i and j, and $A_{i,j}=0$ if there is no edge between node i and j. We establish disease-specific interaction network through searching for nodes within 3 distance unit from the target disease node. To gain the most related gene of the target disease, Centrality approach is used for calculating correlation of each gene based on its weight in this specific disease network.

4.1 Degree centrality

Degree centrality represents central tendency of each node in the network, the more direct connects it has, the more power it has in the network and so the more important it is. The degree centrality $C_D(v)$ of node v is calculated as follows:

$$C_D(v)=\sum_{j=1}^{n} A_{ij} \tag{3}$$

4.2 Betweenness centrality

Betweenness centrality reflects the ability of a node taking control of other nodes' communication and the capability of controlling resources in the network. The more nodes that shortest paths pass through, the more communications of other nodes depend on it, and the more betweenness centrality the node has. The betweenness centrality $C_B(v)$ of node v is calculated as follows:

$$C_B(v)=\sum_{s\neq v\neq t\in V}\frac{\sigma_{st}(v)}{\sigma_{st}} \tag{4}$$

where σ_{st} is the total number of shortest paths from node s to t and $\sigma_{st}(v)$ is the number of paths that pass through v.

4.3 Closeness centrality

Closeness centrality reflects the ability a node has of not being controlled by other nodes. The closeness centrality of a node measures how close it is to other nodes in the whole network. The smaller the total distance from a node to other nodes in the network, the less dependency the node has on nodes in the network, and thus the higher its centrality is. The closeness centrality $C_c(v)$ of node v is calculated as follows.

$$C_C(v)=\sum_{t\in V\backslash v} 2^{-d_G(v,t)} \tag{5}$$

where $d_G(v,t)$ represents distance from node v to node t.

4.4 Weighted centrality

Formula (6) is applied to assigne weights for each measure of centrality equally:

$$C_A(v)=\frac{C_D(v)}{3C_D}+\frac{C_B(v)}{3C_B}+\frac{C_C(v)}{3C_C} \tag{6}$$

where C_D represents the largest degree centrality of all nodes in the network, C_B represents the largest betweenness centrality of the whole network and C_C represents the largest closeness centrality among all nodes.

5 Results and Discussion

As a common disease with high incidence, breast cancer gains much attention among researchers and has a rather large literature accumulation.

[3] http://verbs.colorado.edu/~mpalmer/projects/verbnet.html

We used breast cancer as testing disease for system evaluation.

The corpus contains 3,209,385 sentences from 44,064 articles. All articles were extracted from PMC with keyword of "breast cancer" (search date: March 1 2013). The gene name dictionary consists of 19,195 gene names searched from OMIM database while the disease dictionary consists of 5644 disease names from Genetic Association database (GAD).

5.1 Evaluation on key sentence extraction

MaxEnt classifier is applied with topic features for key sentences extraction. We randomly selected sentences from 8000 documents in our corpus as training set. We set number of topics K as 10. The results of topics-words distribution predicted by Gibbs Sampling based topic model and topic correction are shown in Table 1.

Topic0	Topic1	Topic2	Topic3	Topic4
molecul	use	increase	cancer	cluster
receptor	analysis	rate	organis	compari
body	table	exhibit	gene	melanog
clone	differen	consider	MLL	identical
organis	significa	evolutio	HBB	place
mutator	set	degree	DLC1	share
band	map	due	GRXCR	rDNA
expressi	group	position	XRCC1	parental
replicate	score	distance	GST01	pattern
Topic5	**Topic6**	**Topic7**	**Topic8**	**Topic9**
indicate	observe	control	chromos	growth
test	Demons	express	carry	medium
line	dominan	suppress	male	assay
determi	fact	elegans	female	conditio
experim	reductio	germlin	cross	colony
represen	weak	deficien	homozy	culture
measure	strong	distinct	segregat	syntheti
derive	enhance	close	recover	survival
conversi	still	segment	hybrid	cell

Table 1: The results of topics-words distribution predicted by Gibbs Sampling based topic model and topic correction.

There are totally 1037,637 key sentences were extracted, and the extraction precision is 66.4%.

5.2 Interaction network analysis

5.2.1 Degree centrality

The breast cancer related gene-interaction network consists of 4636 distinct gene nodes and 19,972 interactions extracted among them. Figure 2 illustrates degree centrality of the interaction network of breast cancer. Different color and size indicate different degree centrality of each node. The node in red with the largest degree centrality 1069 in the figure represents breast cancer. This indicates that 1069 genes have direct interactions with breast cancer referred in all sentences.

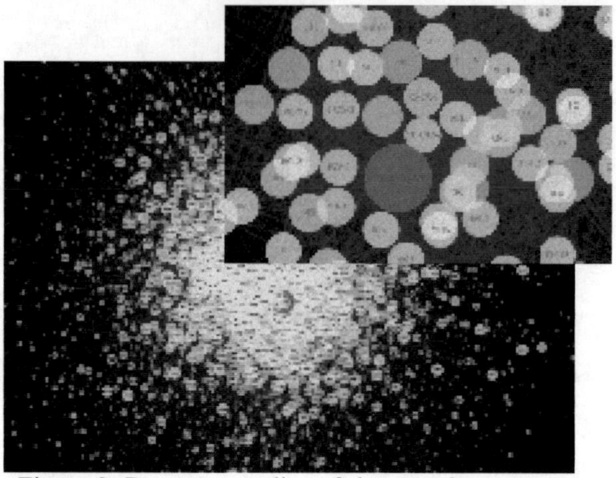

Figure 2. Degree centrality of the gene-breast cancer interaction network.

Figure 3 shows the relationship between each degree centrality and its count of nodes.

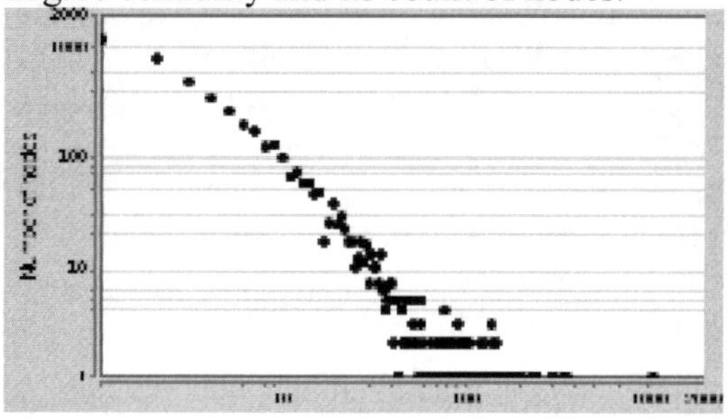

Figure 3. The relationship between each degree centrality and its count of nodes.

As shown in Figure 3, the node with maximum degree centrality 1069 is target disease while most of other nodes distribute from degree centrality of 1 to 10 which are considered as least related genes. Table 2 lists part of ranks of all 1069 genes in the order of degree centrality.

Gene	Degree Centrality
TNF	359
EGFR	342
CRC	301
IL-6	245
EGF	200
BRCA1	195
HR	193
GAPDH	190
AR	188
ATM	148
TP53	138
BRCA2	94

Table 2: Part of ranks of all 1069 genes in the order of degree centrality.

From Table 2, we can find that BRCA1 and BRCA2 are known familial breast cancer genes which have gained authority validation. Although their mutations are not common in sporadic breast cancer patients, they accounts for approximately 80% to 90% among all hereditary breast cancer.

TP53 is a kind of mutant gene with high penetrance which has also been verified association with breast cancer in genetics. Moreover, ATM and AR are low frequency genes belong to specific loci, about 5% to 10% of breast cancer relate to at least one or more changes in the susceptibility genes mentioned above.

The result of CRC in contrast is more like some kind of institution's name: Cooperative Research Centre for Discovery of Genes for Common Human Diseases or the abbreviation of another disease: Colorectal Cancer (CRC). There haven't been any evidence reveals direct correlation between CRC gene and breast cancer, we can only consider this as a misrecognition.

In addition to genes described above, other genes in the list have also been verified in authoritative sites or papers. These results preliminarily verified the accuracy of our system.

5.2.2 Betweenness centrality

Figure 4 illustrates betweenness centrality of the interaction network of breast cancer. Color and size of each point reflect betweenness of the node, which indicate the ability to control other nodes in the network. Nodes in green have the minimum betweenness centrality while the color of jade-green shows larger betweenness centrality. Yellow nodes indicate betweenness centrality larger than jade-green and orange represents the largest.

Figure 4. Betweenness centrality of the gene-breast cancer interaction network

Figure 5 shows relationship between each betweenness centrality and its count of neighbors.

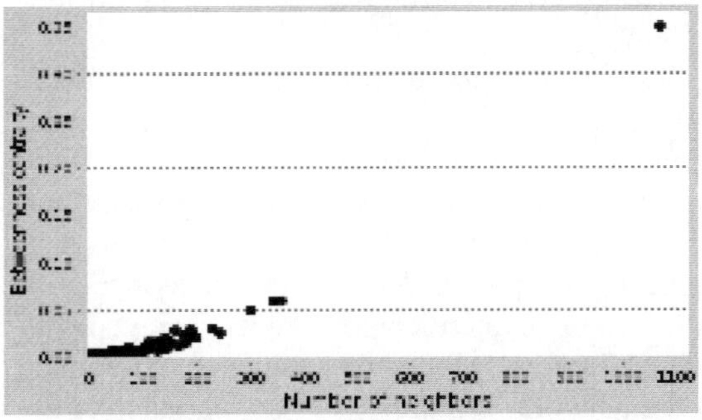

Figure 5. Relationship between each betweenness centrality and its count of neighbors.

As shown in Figure 5, the more adjacent nodes, the larger betweenness centrality. The node with most neighbors of 1068 has maximum betweenness centrality of 0.35 while most nodes in the network have the count of neighbors from 0 to 200 with their betweenness centrality between 0 and 0.04. Table 3 lists part of ranks of all 1069 genes in the order of betweenness centrality.

Gene	Betweenness Centrality
TNF	0.05981684
EGFR	0.05912439
CRC	0.04896846
AR	0.02892632
GAPDH	0.02877095
AD	0.02863766
IL-6	0.02545676
HR	0.02381936
BRCA1	0.02202402
TP53	0.01603455
ATM	0.01566084
BRCA2	0.00507333

Table 3: Part of ranks of all 1069 genes in the order of betweenness centrality.

As can be seen from Table 3, the rank of betweenness centrality is approximately matched with the rank of degree centrality. TNF, EGFR and CRC are still the highest ranked genes while IL-6, AR, HR , GAPDH and ATM simply exchanged their order. AR, androgen receptor, has a quick raise in the rank list. It plays a vital role in the development and maintenance of male reproductive function and the cause of prostate cancer, but the effect and function on breast cancer of AR have not been clear until 2010 (most of the literature published before 2010). This result shows that the genes excavated by our system not only include genes in the known interaction network, but also reflect research tendency at present or in a certain period of time. This also indicates the effectiveness of understanding scientific research tendency of our system.

As the definition of betweenness centrality, it reflects the ability to affect other nodes in the network. If a gene interacts with another gene through an intermediate gene such as suppression or promotion, then the role played by this intermediate gene is decisive in this association. The more intermediate roles played in associations, the greater the influence of the gene in the network. Similarly, among all genes in the neighborhood of a specific gene, the greater the betweenness centrality of a gene, the more influence it has on that specific gene.

5.2.3 Closeness centrality

Figure 6 illustrates closeness centrality of the interaction network of breast cancer.

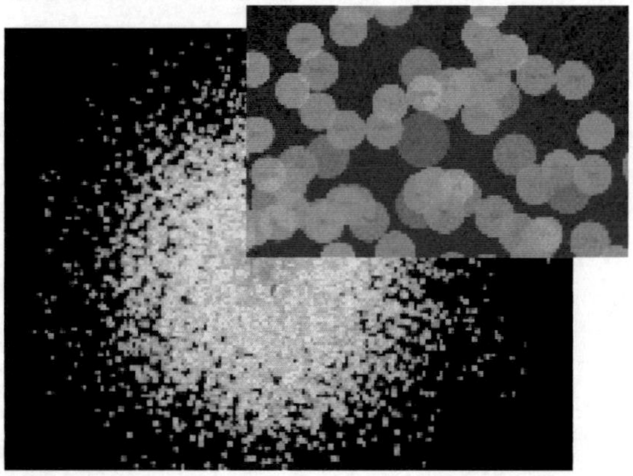

Figure 6. Closeness centrality of the gene-breast cancer interaction network.

As can be seen from Figure 6, red node at the center of the network represents breast cancer and neighboring orange nodes stand for direct related genes while peripheral nodes in green represents least related genes. Figure 7 shows relationship between each closeness centrality and its count of neighbors.

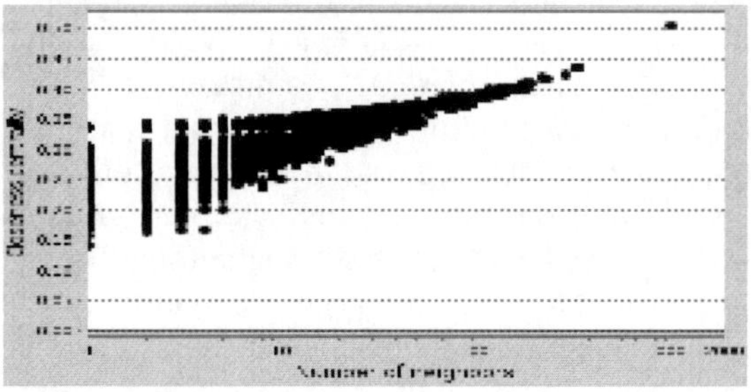

Figure 7. Relationship between each closeness centrality and its count of neighbors.

Figure 7 shows the tendency of closeness centrality in the network while number of neighbors increases. There is an approximate positive correlation between the count of neighbors and the closeness centrality of nodes but not so obvious compared with betweenness centrality or degree centrality. For instance, the closeness centrality ranges from 0.14 to 0.34 for nodes with only one neighbor. This tendency represents that closeness centrality reflect geographical centricity of each node more efficiently compared with degree centrality and betweenness centrality with less dependence on count of neighbors. For example, if a node has only one edge to the center of the network, this node is bound to own large closeness centrality even though this edge is the only edge it has. Meanwhile, another node has much more than one edge but far away from the center of the network, the closeness centrality of it can never be larger than the former one. Table 4 lists part of ranks of all 1069 genes in the order of closeness centrality.

Gene	Closeness Centrality
TNF	0.43612418
EGFR	0.43550963
CRC	0.4247366
PTEN	0.41920608
IL-6	0.41814738
AR	0.41092005
EGF	0.40954064
BRCA1	0.40914306
STAT3	0.4088544
MMP-9	0.40386793
HR	0.40330579
MMP-2	0.40031085

Table 4: Part of ranks of all 1069 genes in the order of closeness centrality.

Table 4 shows that list ordered by closeness centrality is generally similar to list ordered by degree centrality and betweenness centrality. TNF, EGFR and CRC are still highest ranking genes. However, genes like STAT3, MMP-9 and MMP-2 appear firstly in the list where STAT3 ranks 18 in degree centrality and 14 in betweenness centrality. The details of STAT3 has been clearly described in Hsieh FC et al. STAT3 full-called signal transducer and activator of transcription 3, which is often detected in breast cancer tissues and its cell lines. STAT3 has already been defined as an oncogene since its activated form in nude mice can produce malignant transformation of cultured cells and ultimately form tumors. MMP-9 and MMP-2 are gelatinase, proteolytic enzymes involved in process of tumor invasion which is considered as a potential tumor marker in breast cancer.

All these three genes can be identified as direct related genes with breast cancer. These associations which are not obvious in degree centrality and betweenness centrality indicating the effectiveness of closeness centrality in finding related gene to a specific disease.

5.3 Result Evaluation

We enumerate 31 top genes ranked with weighted centrality considered as related to breast cancer due to our system. Table 5 lists the gene or disease symbol, ID, and full name from OMIM database.

Gene Symbol	Gene ID	Gene Full Name
TNF	*191160	TUMOR NECROSIS FACTOR
EGFR	*131550	EPIDERMAL GROWTH FACTOR RECEPTOR
CRC		COLORECTAL CANCER
PTEN	+601728	PHOSPHATASE AND TENSIN HOMOLOG
IL-6	*147620	INTERLEUKIN 6
AR	*313700	ANDROGEN RECEPTOR
BRCA1	*113705	BREAST CANCER 1 GENE
EGF	*131530	EPIDERMAL GROWTH FACTOR
GAPDH	*138400	GLYCERALDEHYDE-3-PHOSPHATE DEHYDROGENASE
HR	*602302	HAIRLESS, MOUSE, HOMOLOG OF
AML	#601626	LEUKEMIA, ACUTE MYELOID
CD4	*186940	CD4 ANTIGEN
STAT3	*102582	SIGNAL TRANSDUCER AND ACTIVATOR OF TRANSCRIPTION 3;
AD	#104300	ALZHEIMER DISEASE
MMP-9	*120361	MATRIX METALLOPROTEINASE 9
MS	#126200	MULTIPLE SCLEROSIS, SUSCEPTIBILITY TO
RD	#111620	RADIN BLOOD GROUP ANTIGEN
MYC	*190080	V-MYC AVIAN MYELOCYTOMATOSIS VIRAL ONCOGENE HOMOLOG
S6	*185520	SURFACE ANTIGEN 6
TP53	*191170	TUMOR PROTEIN p53
ATM	*607585	ATAXIA-TELANGIECTASIA MUTATED GENE
IL-8	*146930	INTERLEUKIN 8
AP1		activator protein-1
MMP-2	*120360	MATRIX METALLOPROTEINASE 2
GC	+139200	GROUP-SPECIFIC COMPONENT
FBS	#227810	FANCONI-BICKEL SYNDROME
ES	#612219	EWING SARCOMA
RA	#180300	RHEUMATOID ARTHRITIS
CXCR4	*162643	CHEMOKINE, CXC MOTIF, RECEPTOR 4
IL-10	*124092	INTERLEUKIN 10
BRCA2	*600185	BRCA2 GENE

Table 5: The gene or disease symbol, ID, and full name from OMIM database.

The Genes and diseases in Table 5 inferred by degree, betweenness, closeness centralities and the relevance are listed in Table 6.

Gene	Degree	Betweenness	Closeness	Relevance
TNF	359	0.05985761	0.43401678	Yes
EGFR	342	0.05904224	0.4332496	Yes
CRC	301	0.04875035	0.4225186	No
PTEN	229	0.03029572	0.41695765	Yes
IL-6	245	0.02541463	0.41613797	Yes
AR	188	0.02883127	0.40890333	Yes
BRCA1	195	0.02190664	0.40704484	Yes
EGF	200	0.01992148	0.40747222	Yes
GAPDH	190	0.02868382	0.39946818	Yes
HR	193	0.02371613	0.40136172	Yes
AML	177	0.02417702	0.39779619	Disease
CD4	179	0.01865428	0.40467501	Yes
STAT3	182	0.01563346	0.40683148	Yes
AD	159	0.02853342	0.39769428	Yes
MMP-9	160	0.01347212	0.40188126	Yes
MS	148	0.01806096	0.39967388	Disease
RD	166	0.0113587	0.3970162	No
MYC	141	0.02132884	0.39052411	Yes
S6	136	0.01504618	0.39912581	Yes
TP53	138	0.01607533	0.39607076	Yes
ATM	148	0.01556309	0.39170662	Yes
IL-8	146	0.00944026	0.40108518	Yes
AP1	141	0.01531257	0.39286317	Yes
MMP-2	138	0.01241541	0.39837468	Yes
GC	131	0.01515181	0.39055686	No
FBS	126	0.0117904	0.39749061	No
ES	128	0.01325333	0.39283003	No
RA	133	0.01256221	0.3894464	Disease
CXCR4	138	0.01019905	0.39039316	Yes
IL-10	128	0.00680617	0.39045862	Yes
BRCA2	94	0.00504479	0.38194046	Yes

Table 6: Genes inferred by degree, betweenness, and closeness centralities and the relevance.

As results listed in Table 6, all 31 top ranked genes and diseases have been checked relevance with breast cancer through NCBI database. Terms marked as 'No' are none-relevant to breast cancer and words marked as 'disease' are related diseases to breast cancer. The accuracy rate is 83.9% for these top 31 genes and diseases and 74.2% for these top 31 genes.

6 Conclusion

Understanding the role of genetics in diseases is one of the major goals of the post-genome era. We have proposed an automatic gene-disease association extraction approach based on text mining and network analysis.

Gene-breast cancer interaction network analysis demonstrated that degree, betweenness, and closeness centralities can estimate disease related genes effectively. And closeness centrality is able to find disease related genes which are not obvious ranked by degree centrality and betweenness centrality. In addition, this result showed that the genes excavated by our system not only include genes in the known interaction network, but also reflect research tendency at present or in a certain period of time. This also indicates the effectiveness of understanding scientific research tendency of our system.

Acknowledgment

This research has been partially supported by the National High-Tech Research & Development Program of China 863 Program under Grant No. 2012AA011103, National Natural Science Foundation of China under Grant No. 61203312, National Program on Key Basic Research Project of China (973 Program) under Grant No. 2014CB347600, the Scientific Research Foundation for the Returned Overseas Chinese Scholars, State Education Ministry, and Key Science and Technology Program of Anhui Province under Grant No. 1206c0805039.

References

Adamic, L.A., Wilkinson, D., Huberman, B.A., and Adar, E. 2002. A literature based method for identifying gene-disease connections. In *Proceedings of the IEEE Computer Society Conference on Bioinformatics*, Stanford, CA, pp. 109–117.

Aerts, S., Lambrechts, D., Maity, S., Van Loo, P., Coessens, B., De Smet, F., Tranchevent, L.-C. C., De Moor, B., Marynen, P., Hassan, B., Carmeliet, P. & Moreau, Y. 2006. Gene prioritization through genomic data fusion. *Nature biotechnology* 24(5):537–544.

Al-Mubaid, H., and Singh, R.K. 2005. A new text mining approach for finding protein-to-disease associations. *Am J Biochem Biotechnol*, 1:145–152.

Bader, G., Betel, D., Hogue, C. 2003. Bind – the biomolecular interaction network database. *Nucleic Acids Research*, 31, pp. 248–250.

Benson, D.A., Karsch-Mizrachi, I., Lipman, D.J., Ostell, J., Ouellette, B.F.F., Rapp, B.A. and Wheeler, D.L. 2000. GenBank. *Nucleic Acids Research*, 28. pp. 15–18.

Blei, D. and McAuliffe, J. 2007. Supervised topic models. Neural Information Processing System 21.

Blei, D.M., Ng, A., Jordan, M.I. 2002. Latent Dirichlet Allocation. NIPS.

Chen, J.Y., Shen, C., Sivachenko, A.Y. 2006. Mining Alzheimer disease relevant proteins from integrated protein interactome data. *Pac. Symp. Biocomput.*, 11, 367–378.

Chen, J., Bardes, E. E., Aronow, B. J. & Jegga, A. G. 2009. Toppgene suite for gene list enrichment analysis and candidate gene prioritization, *Nucleic Acids Research*, 37(Web Server issue): gkp427+.

Christopher D. Manning and Hinrich Schjtze. 1999. Foundations of statistical natural language processing. Cambridge, MA: MIT Press.

Chun, H., Tsuruoka, Y., Kim, J. Shiba, R., Nagata, N., Hishiki, T., and Tsujii, J. 2006. Extraction of gene-disease relations from MEDLINE using domain dictionaries and machine learning. In *Proceedings of the Pacific Symposium on Biocomputing*, pp. 4–15.

Erkan, G., Radev, D., Ozgur, A. 2007. Semi-supervised classification for extracting protein interaction sentences using dependency parsing. In *Proceedings of the Joint Conference on Empirical Methods in Natural Language Processing and Computational Natural Language Learning*, Prague, Czech Republic, pp. 228–237.

Freudenberg, J., and Propping, P. 2002. A similarity-based method for genomewide prediction of disease-relevant human genes. *Bioinformatics*, 18 (Suppl. 2), pp. S110–S115.

Gillick, D., Sentence Boundary Detection and the Problem with the U.S. NAACL 2009. pp. 241–244,

Glenisson, P., Coessens, B., Vooren, S. V., Mathys, J., Moreau, Y., and De Moor, B. 2004. TXTGate: profiling gene groups with text-based information. *Genome Biol.*, 5, R43.

Griffiths, T., 2002. Gibbs sampling in the generative model of Latent Dirichlet Allocation. http://citeseerx.ist.psu.edu/viewdoc/summary?doi=10.1.1.138.3760.

Huang, D.W., Sherman, B.T., and Lempicki, R.A. 2009. Systematic and integrative analysis of large gene lists using david bioinformatics resources. *Nat. Protoc.*, 4: 44–57.

Hutz, J., Kraja, A., McLeod, H. & Province, M. 2008. Candid: a flexible method for prioritizing candidate genes for complex human traits., *Genetic Epidemiology* 32(8): 779–790.

Kerrien, S., Aranda, B., Breuza L., Bridge, A., Broackes-Carter, F., and Chen, C. 2002. The IntAct molecular interaction database in 2012. *Nucleic Acids Research*, 40, pp. 841–846.

Klein, D. and Christopher D. M. 2003. Accurate Unlexicalized Parsing. In *Proceedings of the 41st Meeting of the Association for Computational Linguistics*, pp. 423–430.

Krallinger, M., Leitner, F., Valencia, A. 2010. Analysis of biological processes and diseases using text mining approaches. *Methods Mol Biol,* 593: 341–82.

Ma, X., Lee, H., Wang, L. & Sun, F. 2007. Cgi: a new approach for prioritizing genes by combining gene expression and protein-protein interaction data, *Bioinformatics* 23(2): 215–221.

Martin, D., Brun. C., Remy, E., Mouren, P., Thieffry, D., and Jacq, B. 2004. GOToolbox: functional analysis of gene datasets based on gene ontology. *Genome Biol.*, 5, R101.

McKusick,V. 2007. Mendelian inheritance in man and its online version, OMIM. *Am. J. Hum. Genet.*, 80, pp. 588–604.

Morrison, J. L., Breitling, R., Higham, D. J., and Gilbert, D. R. 2005. Generank: using search engine technology for the analysis of microarray experiments., BMC Bioinformatics 6: 233. URL: http://www.biomedsearch.com/nih/GeneRank-using-search-engine-technology/16176585.html

OMIM. 2007. Online Mendelian inheritance in man, OMIM (TM).McKusick-Nathans Institute of Genetic Medicine, Johns Hopkins University (Baltimore, MD) and National Center for Biotechnology Information, National Library of Medicine (Bethesda, MD).

Özgür, A., Vu, T., Erkan, G., and Radev D. R. 2008. Identifying gene-disease associations using centrality on a literature mined gene-interaction network. *Bioinformatics*, 24. pp. 277–285.

Schwikowski, B., Uetz, P., and Fields, S. 2000. A network of protein-protein interactions in yeast. *Nat.Biotechnol.*, 18, pp. 1257–1261.

Subramanian, A., Tamayo, P., Mootha, V.K., Mukherjee, S., Ebert, B.L., Gillette, M.A., Paulovich, A., Pomeroy, S.L., Golub, T.R., Lander, E.S., and Mesirov, J.P. 2005. Gene set enrichment analysis: a knowledge-based approach for interpreting genome-wide expression profiles. *Proc. Natl Acad.* Sci. USA, 102, pp. 15545–15550.

Hwang, T., Zhang, W., Xie, M., Liu, J., and Kuang, R. 2011. Inferring disease and gene set associations with rank coherence in networks. *Bioinformatics*, 27(19): 2692–2699.

Temkin, J. and Gilder, M. 2003. Extraction of protein interaction information from unstructured text using a context-free grammar. *Bioinformatics*, 19:2046–2053.

Wuchty, S., Oltvai, Z.N., Barabási, A.L. 2003. Evolutionary conservation of motif constituents in the yeast protein interaction network. *Nat. Genet.*, 35:176–179.

Yakushiji, A., Miyao, Y., Tateisi, Y., and Tsujii J. 2005. Biomedical information extraction with predicate argument structure patterns. In *Proceedings of the Eleventh Annual Meeting of the Association for Natural Language Processing,* pp. 93–96.

Zanzoni, A., Montecchi-Palazzi, L., Quondam, M., Ausiello, G., Helmer-Citterich, M., Cesareni, G. 2002. Mint: A molecular interaction database. FEBS Letters, 513: 135–140.

Negation scope and spelling variation for text-mining of Danish electronic patient records

Cecilia Engel Thomas[1], Peter Bjødstrup Jensen[2,3], Thomas Werge[4], and Søren Brunak[1,3]

[1]Center for Biological Sequence Analysis, Department of Systems Biology, Technical University of Denmark, Kemitorvet, Building 208, DK-2820 Lyngby, Denmark.
[2]OPEN, University of Southern Denmark, Campusvej 55, DK-5230 Odense, Denmark.
[3]NNF Center for Protein Research, Department of Disease Systems Biology, Faculty of Health and Medical Sciences, University of Copenhagen, DK-2200 Copenhagen, Denmark. [4]The Research Institute of Biological Psychiatry, Mental Health Centre Sct. Hans, Copenhagen University Hospital, DK-4000 Roskilde, Denmark.

Abstract

Electronic patient records are a potentially rich data source for knowledge extraction in biomedical research. Here we present a method based on the ICD10 system for text-mining of Danish health records. We have evaluated how adding functionalities to a baseline text-mining tool affected the overall performance.

The purpose of the tool was to create enriched phenotypic profiles for each patient in a corpus consisting of records from 5,543 patients at a Danish psychiatric hospital, by assigning each patient additional ICD10 codes based on free-text parts of these records. The tool was benchmarked by manually curating a test set consisting of all records from 50 patients. The tool evaluated was designed to handle spelling and ending variations, shuffling of tokens within a term, and introduction of gaps in terms. In particular we investigated the importance of negation identification and negation scope.

The most important functionality of the tool was handling of spelling variation, which greatly increased the number of phenotypes that could be identified in the records, without noticeably decreasing the precision. Further, our results show that different negations have different optimal scopes, some spanning only a few words, while others span up to whole sentences.

1. Introduction

Electronic patient records (EPRs) file patient treatment data over time and contain structured data, such as medication information and laboratory test results, as well as unstructured data contained in free text. Previously unstructured data has been used for a range of purposes such as diagnosis detection (e.g. Meyste, 2006; Suzuki, 2008; Liao, 2010), decision support (Tremblay, 2009), and temporal investigation of adverse drug reactions (Eriksson, to appear 2014). Structured EPR data will primarily contain diagnoses relevant to the current hospitalization, whereas free text will contain additional information about adverse drug reactions and the general health status of the patient. By utilizing unstructured EPR data, it is possible to obtain a much richer phenotypic profile of each patient, which can be applied to the investigation of disease-disease correlations, patient stratification, and underlying molecular level disease etiology (Jensen, 2012).

Several tools for text mining of free text in English medical records have been developed previously. We present a non-English contribution to the field. We have developed a simple parser based on the ICD10 classification system for a Scandinavian language; Danish, which performs well and is relatively fast to implement. The parser handles a number of variations such as spelling and ending when matching between the corpus and the dictionary. We have evaluated the importance of taking these variations into account in a Danish context.

An additional focus of this work was to evaluate how negations should be handled in a Danish context. It has previously been shown that it is important to consider negations when medical text mining and several methods such as NegScope (Agarwal, 2010), NegFinder (Mutalik, 2001) and NegEx (Chapman, 2001) have been developed. These methods have shown good performance, but they have all been specifically developed for application to English text, and can thus not be directly transferred to our purpose. Instead we have here implemented a simple method for handling negations, and subsequently evaluated the scope of negations.

2. Materials and methods

The text-mining tool presented here uses a dictionary based on the Danish version of the ICD10 system to search for mentioning of disease terminology terms in the corpus consisting of EPRs. Five add-on functionalities for the text-mining tool were evaluated. These were; handling of A) spelling, B) ending variations, C) allowing a gap in terms when matching, D) allowing shuffling of tokens in term when matching, and E) handling of negations.

The EPRs used here were 5,543 records from the Sct. Hans Psychiatric Hospital (Roque, 2011). The free text in these records consists of many different note types, written by a range of different types of medical and non-medical personnel including doctors, psychiatrists, nurses and social workers.

A test set of all records from a randomly selected set of 50 patients (roughly 1% of cohort) was manually curated. 5,765 disease related terms (hits) were found in the test set. On average each patient was associated with a total of 115.3 hits, which covered an average of 16.96 different ICD10 codes. Each hit was traced back to its origin in the corpus, and based on the context (sentence or entire note) it was evaluated whether the hit was correctly associated with the patient in the text.

2.1 Generation of spelling and ending variants

The ICD10 terms in the dictionary are supplemented with synonyms comprised of spelling and ending variants to allow a degree of fuzzy mapping between the corpus and the dictionary. Spelling (A) and ending (B) variants are generated by comparing all unique tokens of the corpus that exceed three letters with all unique tokens of the dictionary. Spelling variants (A) are generated by allowing a Damarau Levehnstein[1] edit distance of one between corpus and dictionary tokens. Ending variations (B) are generated by testing if a token becomes identical to a dictionary term if they are both stemmed for typical Danish endings.

2.2 Text-mining

A potential hit is a token or a set of tokens in a sentence, which match a full term in the dictionary. When matching one gap, comprised of an interposed word, is allowed (C) in the token string that is not found in the dictionary term. When matching a string of tokens to a dictionary term, shuffling of words is allowed (D), such that the order of the words is not important.

If a potential hit is found, the preceding part of the sentence is checked for negations (E). If a negation is found the potential hit is discarded. The end result is a list of hits with their matching ICD10 codes.

The negations evaluated here are both true negations like "ingen" and "ikke" ("none" and "no"), and alternative subjects such as family members. These alternative subjects are included as a form of negations, as a clinical term mentioned in the same sentence as an alternative subject, will often refer to that subject rather than the patient covered by the record.

2.3 Evaluation of features

All different combinations of functionalities A-D were tested and compared to the baseline text-mining tool with no add-on functionalities. The total number of hits and unique hits that a run of the tool results in were evaluated. Total hits include all hits, whereas unique hits consider simply how many unique 3-digit ICD10 terms are represented.

As described above each hit generated from the test set was evaluated to determine if it was correctly associated with the patient or not. Two different types of precisions were calculated: I) incidence precision, which is the number of correct hits divided by the total number of hits; II) association precision, where a hit is counted as correct as long as the corresponding ICD10 code is correctly associated with the patient at least once. Here it is assumed that as long as an ICD10 code is correctly associated with the patient once, it does not matter if the same ICD10 code is also incorrectly associated with the patient elsewhere.

2.4 Evaluation of negations and their scope

A random sample of 500 potential hits that were disqualified by the negation step was manually curated, and it was evaluated whether it was correct to negate the potential hits or not. The total number of negated hits, incidence precision and the distance, in terms of number of tokens, between the negation and the term it negates, i.e. the scope of the negations were calculated for all the negations. The same measures were calculated for each individual negation word occurring in the test set (data not shown).

[1] The Daramau Levehnstein edit distance is the number of edits needed to turn one token into another token. An edit can be a substitution, deletion or insertion of a letter, or the reversal of a pair of letters.

In order to investigate the influence of the distance between the hit and the negation further, the incidence precision for each distance was also calculated.

3. Results

The incidence precision of the tool with all features enabled was 0.867 and the association precision was slightly higher at 0.888. Enabling or disabling of fuzzy mapping features does not seem to affect the precision of the method. In contrast to this, both the total number of hits and the number of unique hits increase as more features are enabled. This is especially true for enabling feature A (spelling) and B (ending). Results for all runs can be seen in Figure 1 and Table 1

Figure 2 shows the results from evaluation of the negations for all 500 negated sentences. The correlation between the precision of a negation and its distance from the hits can be seen in Figure 2. As can be seen not all distances are represented in the test set. It seems that incidence precision is at least partly inversely related to the distance between the candidate hit and the negation.

Two negations are by far the most used in the records. These are 'ikke' and 'ingen', which are both true negations. Whereas 'ingen' has a very high incidence precision at 0.946 'ikke' has a precision of only 0.573. These two negations also have very different negation scopes as can be seen on the plot in Figure 2 illustrating that different negation words can have very different scopes.

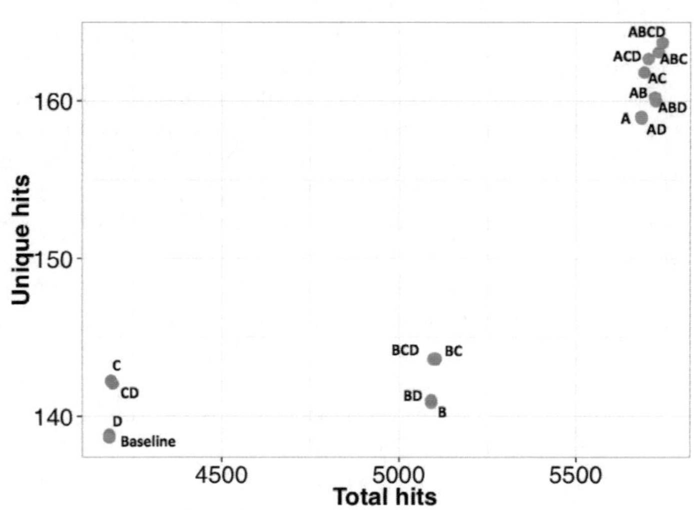

Figure 1: Number of hits generated for each run. A: spelling, B: ending, C: gap, D: shuffling.

Features	Incidence precision	Association precision
Baseline	0.872	0.889
D	0.872	0.889
C	0.872	0.89
CD	0.872	0.89
B	0.874	0.891
BD	0.874	0.891
BC	0.874	0.892
BCD	0.874	0.893
A	0.867	0.889
AD	0.867	0.886
AC	0.868	0.891
ACD	0.867	0.888
AB	0.867	0.889
ABD	0.867	0.887
ABC	0.868	0.891
ABCD	0.867	0.888

Table 1: Precision for all runs.

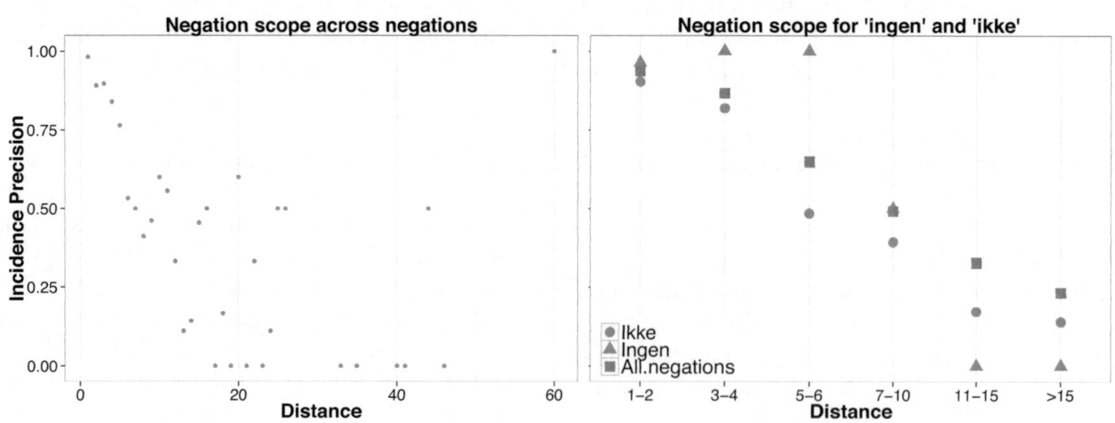

Figure 2: Evaluation of negation scopes for all negations (left) and 'ingen' and 'ikke' (right).

Negation	Total occurrences	Incidence precision	Average distance
All negations	500	0.722	4.9
True neg.	449	0.724	4.7
Subject neg.	51	0.706	6.4

Table 2: Evaluation parameters for negations.

Negation cutoff	Total hits	Unique hits	Incidence precision
None	5741	164	0.867
4	5964	171	0.854
10	5836	166	0.864

Table 3: Performance with hard negation cutoffs.

4. Discussion

4.1 Fuzzy mapping features

Quantitatively the precision of the tool presented here is on par with other similar tools such as MedLEE; 0.89 (Friedman 2004) and the tool presented in Meystre 2006; 0.76, despite that a relatively simple approach presented here.

Allowing ending variants (B) gives a significant increase in total hits, but only a minor increase in unique hits. This was investigated further, and it was revealed that the term 'ryger' ("smoking" or "smoker") was responsible for this peculiarity, as the term 'ryge' matches 'ryger' when spelling variation is allowed. More than 4/5 of the total hits generated when enabling ending variation were due to this one synonym generated. The same problem is apparent when allowing spelling variants (A) as this also allows 'ryger' as a synonym.

It is debatable whether it is even worth including gap variations (D), since only very few hits are generated. However, there seems to be a synergistic effect between allowing gaps and shuffling and one must keep in mind that gap and shuffling variations only come into effect when a hit has more than one token, and only around 12% of all hits identified, have more than one token. Therefore gap and shuffling variations would make a bigger difference in a corpus where hits with more words are more frequent.

4.2 Negation evaluation

The data indicates that higher distance leads to lower precision. In order to improve the use of negations we tested two hard precision cutoffs (4 and 10) to limit the scope of negations. Using these hard cutoffs increased the precision of the negations from 0.722 to 0.921 and 0.820, respectively. This is comparable to the precisions reported for other tools such as NegEx; 0.845 (Chapman 2001) and NegFinder; 0.977/0.918 (Mutalik 2001), though one must keep in mind that these are tested on different corpora. Setting negation cutoffs also resulted in an increase in number of hits identified, but did lead to slightly lower precisions for the hits generated compared to no cutoff (see Table 3).

4.3 Limitations

The tool presented here was developed for EPRs from a psychiatric hospital, which does not guarantee its direct applicability to EPRs from other indication areas, as these psychiatric EPRs contain a high proportion of notes entered by nurses and other personnel that are not medical doctors. One possible issue related to this is that the EPRs used here do not show widespread use of abbreviations and acronyms for disease terms, thus a method for handling abbreviations was not implemented. However, this might be necessary for EPRs from other clinical domains.

Additionally the tool is limited to handle the 10 real and 24 subject negations present in the manually constructed negation list and negations are only allowed to negate terms in the succeeding part of the sentence, which will not be true for all negation usages.

In the approach described here it is assumed that a disease term found in a patients journal, is related to the given patient unless negated. This assumption is accepted here to preserve the simplicity of the approach, but is actually handled to so some extent by including subject negations.

5. Conclusion

We have shown here that it is possible to make a text-mining tool for a non-English language that has good performance in a quick and simple way. The full tool described here has rather good precision and many patient-disease relations were identified that could be used to enrich the phenotypes of the patients. Large variations in the precision of the different negations were found, but restricting the scopes of negations, contributes to increasing the precision of the negations. Furthermore, this also resulted in an increase in the number of hits generated without severely affecting the precision of the hits.

Acknowledgements

We thank Henriette Schmock, Sct. Hans Hospital, for help interpreting details in the corpus and the Novo Nordisk Foundation for support.

References

Agarwal, Shashank and Yu, Hong (2010) Biomedical negation scope detection with conditional random fields, J Am Med Inform Assoc., 17:696-701.

Chapman, Wendy W., Bridewell, Will, Hanbury, Paul, Cooper, Gregory F., and Buchanan, Bruce G. (2001) A Simple Algorithm for Identifying Negated Findings and Diseases in Discharge Summaries, Journal of Biomedical Informatics 34, 301–310.

Eriksson, Robert, Werge, Thomas, Jensen, Lars J., and Brunak, Søren (to appear 2014) Dose-specific adverse drug reaction identification in electronic patient records: temporal data mining in an inpatient psychiatric population.

Friedman, Carol, Shagina, Lyudmila, Lussier, Yves, and Hripcsak, George (2004) Automated encoding of clinical documents based on natural language processing, J Am Med Inform Assoc., 11(5):392-402.

Jensen, Peter B., Jensen, Lars J., and Brunak, Søren (2012) Mining electronic health records: towards better research applications and clinical care, Nature Rev. Genetics 13(6):395-405.

Liao, Katherine P., Cai, Tianxi, Gainer, Vivian, Goryachev, Sergey, Zeng-Treitler, Qing, Raychaudhuri, Soumya, Szolovits, Peter, Churchill, Susanne, Murphy, Shawn, Kohane, Isaac, Karlson, Elizabeth W., and Plenge, Robert M. (2010) Electronic medical records for discovery research in rheumatoid arthritis, Arthritis Care Res (Hoboken) 62;1120-1127.

Meystre, Stephane and Haug, Peter J. (2006) Natural language processing to extract medical problems from electronic clinical documents: performance evaluation, J Biomed Inform 39;589-599.

Mutalik, Pradeep G., Deshpande, Aniruddha, and Nadkarni, Prakash M. (2001) Use of General-purpose Negation Detection to Augment Concept Indexing of Medical Documents: A Quantitative Study Using the UMLS, J Am Med Inform Assoc. 8:598–609.

Park, Juyong, Lee, Deok-Sun, Christakis, Nicholas A., and Barabási, Albert-László (2009) The impact of cellular networks on disease comorbidity, Molecular Systems Biology 5:262.

Prather, J.C., Lobach, D.F., Goodwin, L.K., Hales, J.W., Hage, M.L., and Hammond, W.E. (1997) Medical data mining: knowledge discovery in a clinical warehouse, Proc AMIA Annu Fall Symp; 101-105.

Roque, Francisco S. Jensen, Peter B., Schmock, Henriette, Dalgaard, Marlene, Andreatta, Massimo, Hansen, Thomas, Søeby, Karen, Bredkjær, Søren, Juul, Anders, Werge, Thomas, Jensen, Lars J., and Brunak, Søren (2011) Using electronic patient records to discover disease correlations and stratify patient cohorts, PLOS computational biology.

Suzuki, T., Yakoi, H., Fujita, S., and Takabayashi, K. (2008) Automatic DPC code selection from electronic medical records: text mining trial of discharge summary, Methods Inf Med 47;541-548.

Tremblay, Monica C., Berndt, Donald J., Luther, Stephen L., Foulis, Philip R., and French, Dustin D. (2009) Identifying fall-related injuries: Text mining the electronic medical record, Inf Technol Manag 10;253-26.

Building a semantically annotated corpus for congestive heart and renal failure from clinical records and the literature

Noha Alnazzawi, Paul Thompson and Sophia Ananiadou
School of Computer Science, University of Manchester, UK
alnazzan@cs.man.ac.uk, {paul.thompson, sophia.ananiadou@manchester.ac.uk}

Abstract

Narrative information in Electronic Health Records (EHRs) and literature articles contains a wealth of clinical information about treatment, diagnosis, medication and family history. This often includes detailed phenotype information for specific diseases, which in turn can help to identify risk factors and thus determine the susceptibility of different patients. Such information can help to improve healthcare applications, including Clinical Decision Support Systems (CDS). Clinical text mining (TM) tools can provide efficient automated means to extract and integrate vital information hidden within the vast volumes of available text. Development or adaptation of TM tools is reliant on the availability of annotated training corpora, although few such corpora exist for the clinical domain. In response, we have created a new annotated corpus (PhenoCHF), focussing on the identification of phenotype information for a specific clinical sub-domain, i.e., congestive heart failure (CHF). The corpus is unique in this domain, in its integration of information from both EHRs (300 discharge summaries) and literature articles (5 full text papers). The annotation scheme, whose design was guided by a domain expert, includes both entities and relations pertinent to CHF. Two further domain experts performed the annotation, resulting in high quality annotation, with agreement rates up to 0.92 F-Score.

1 Introduction

An ever-increasing number of scientific articles is published every year. For example, in 2012, more than 500,000 articles were published in MEDLINE (U.S. National Library of Medicine , 2013). A researcher would thus need to review at least 20 articles per day in order to keep up to date with latest knowledge and evidence in the literature (Perez-Rey et al., 2012).

EHRs constitute a further rich source of information about patients' health, representing different aspects of care (Jensen et al., 2012). However, clinicians at the point of care have very limited time to review the potentially large amount of data contained within EHRs. This presents significant barriers to clinical practitioners and computational applications (Patrick et al., 2006).

TM tools can be used to extract phenotype information from EHRs and the literature and help researchers to identify the characteristics of CHF and to better understand the role of the deterioration in kidney function in the cycle of progression of CHF.

2 Related work

There are many well-known publicly available corpora of scientific biomedical literature, which are annotated for biological entities and/or their interactions (often referred to as *events*) (Roberts et al., 2009; Xia & Yetisgen-Yildiz, 2012). Examples include GENIA (Kim et al., 2008), BioInfer (Pyysalo et al., 2007) GREC (Thompson et al., 2009), PennBioIE (Kulick et al., 2004), GENETAG (Tanabe et al., 2005) and LLL'05 (Hakenberg et al., 2005). However, none of these corpora is annotated with the types of entities and relationships that are relevant to the study of phenotype information.

On the other hand, corpora of clinical text drawn from EHRs are rare, due to privacy and confidentiality concerns, but also because of the time-consuming, expensive and tedious nature of producing high quality annotations, which are reliant on the expertise of domain experts (Uzuner et al., 2011). A small number of corpora, however, have been made available, mainly in the context of shared task challenges, which aim to encourage the development of information extraction (IE) systems. These corpora vary in terms of the text type and annotation granularity. For example, the corpus presented in (Pestian et al., 2007) concerns only structured data from radiology reports, while the corpus presented in (Meystre & Haug, 2006) contains unstructured parts of EHRs, but annotated with medical problem only at the document level.

Other corpora are more similar to ours, in that that they include text-bound annotations corresponding to entities or relations. CLEF (Clinical E-Science Framework) (Roberts et al., 2008) was one of the first such corpora to include detailed semantic annotation. It consists of a number of different types of clinical records, including clinic letters, radiology and histopathology reports, which are annotated with a variety of clinical entities, relations between them and co-reference. However, the corpus has not been made publicly available. The more recent 2013 CLEF-eHEALTH challenge (Suominen et al., 2013) corpus consists of EHRs annotated with named entities referring to disorders and acronyms/abbreviations, mapped to UMLS concept identifiers.

The Informatics for Integrating Biology at the Bedside (i2b2) NLP series of challenges have released a corpus of de-identified clinical records annotated to support a number of IE challenges with multiple levels of annotation, i.e., entities and relations (Uzuner et al., 2008; Uzuner, 2009). The 2010 challenge included the release of a corpus of discharge summaries and patient reports in which named entities and relations concerning medical problems, tests and treatments were annotated (Uzuner et al., 2011). A corpus of EHRs from Mayo Clinic has been annotated with both linguistic information (part-of-speech tags and shallow parsing results) and named entities corresponding to disorders (Ogren et al., 2008; Savova et al., 2010).

3 Description of the corpus

The discharge summaries in our PhenoCHF corpus constitute a subset of the data released for the second i2b2 shared task, known as "recognising obesity" (Uzuner, 2009). PhenoCHF corpus was created by filtering the original i2b2 corpus, such that only those summaries (a total of 300) for patients with CHF and kidney failure were retained.

The second part of PhenoCHF consists of the 5 most recent full text articles (at the time of query submission) concerning the characteristics of CHF and renal failure, retrieved from the PubMed Central Open Access database.

4 Methods and results

The design of the annotation schema was guided by an analysis of the relevant discharge summaries, in conjunction with a review of comparable domain specific schemata and guidelines, i.e., those from the CLEF and i2b2 shared tasks. The schema is based on a set of requirements developed by a cardiologist. Taking into account our chosen focus of annotating phenotype information relating to the CHF disease, the cardiologist was asked firstly to determine a set of relevant entity types that relate to CHF phenotype information and the role of the decline in kidney function in the cycle of CHF (exemplified in Table 1), secondly to locate words that modify the entity (such as polarity clues) and thirdly to identify the types of relationships that exist between these entity types in the description of phenotype information (Table 2) .

Secondly, medical terms in the records are mapped semi-automatically onto clinical concepts in UMLS, with the aid of MetaMap (Aronson, 2001).

The same annotation schema and guidelines were used for both the discharge summaries and the scientific full articles. In the latter, certain annotations were omitted, i.e., organ entities, polarity clues and relations. This decision was taken due to the differing ways in which phenotype information is expressed in discharge summaries and scientific articles. In discharge summaries, phenotype information is explicitly described in the patient's medical history, diagnoses and test results. On the other hand, scientific articles summarise results and research findings. This means that certain types of information that occur frequently in discharge summaries are extremely rare in scientific articles, such that their occurrences are too sparse to be useful in training TM systems, and hence they were not annotated.

The annotation was carried out by two medical doctors, using the Brat Rapid Annotation Tool (brat) (Stenetorp et al., 2012), a highly-configurable and flexible web-based tool for textual annotation.

Annotations in the corpus should reflect the instructions provided in the guidelines as closely as possible, in order to ensure that the annotations are of ahigh quality. A standard means of providing evidence regarding the reliability of annotations in a corpus is to calculate a statistic known as the inter-annotator agreement (IAA). IAA provides assurance that different annotators can produce the same annotations when working independently and separately. There are several different methods of calculating IAA, which can be influenced by the exact nature of the annotation task. We use the measures of precision, recall and F-measure to indicate the level of inter-annotator reliability (Hripcsak & Rothschild, 2005). In order to carry out such calculations, one set of annotations is considered as a gold standard and the total number of correct entities is the total number of entities annotated by this annotator.

Precision is the percentage of correct positive predictions annotated by the second annotator, compared to the first annotator's assumed gold standard. It is calculated as follows:

$$P = TP / TP + FP$$

Recall is the percentage of positive cases recognised by the second annotator. It is calculated as follows:

$$R = TP / TP + FN$$

F-score is the harmonic mean between precision and recall.

$$F\text{-}score = 2 * (Precision * Recall) / Precision + Recall$$

We have calculated separate IAA scores for the discharge summaries and the scientific articles. Table 3 summarises agreement rates for term annotation in the discharge summaries, showing results for both individual entity types and macro-averaged scores over all entity types. Relaxed matching criteria were employed, such that annotations added by the two annotators were considered as a match if their spans overlapped. In comparison to related efforts, the IAA rates shown in Table 3 are high. However, it should be noted that the number of targeted classes and relations in our corpus is small and focused, compared to other related corpora.

Agreement statistics for scientific articles are shown in Table 4. Agreement is somewhat lower than for discharge summaries, which this could be due to the fact that the annotators (doctors) are more used to dealing with discharge summaries in their day-to-day work, and so are more accustomed to locating information in this type of text. Scientific articles are much longer and generally include more complex language, ideas and analyses, which may require more than one reading to fully comprehend the information within them. Table 5 shows the agreement rates for relation annotation in the discharge summaries. The agreement rates for relationships are relatively high. This can partly be explained by the deep domain knowledge possessed by the annotators and partly by the fact that the relationships to be identified were relatively simple, linking only two pre-annotated entities.

Entity Type	Description	Example
Cause	any medical problem that contributes to the occurrence of CHF	
Risk factors	A condition that increases the chance of a patient having the CHF disease	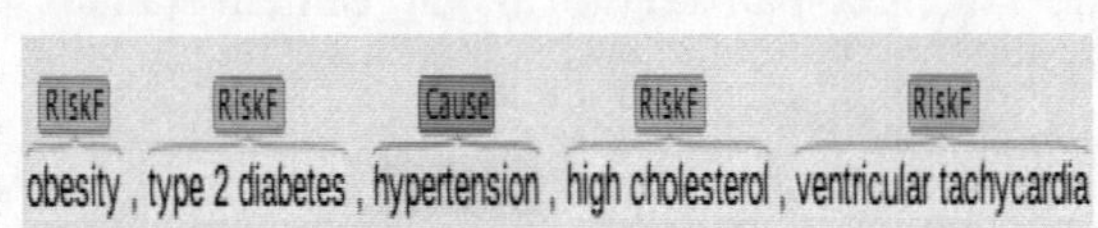
Sign & symptom	any observable manifestation of a disease which is experienced by a patient and reported to the physician	
Non-traditional risk factor	Conditions associated with abnormalities in kidney functions that put the patient at higher risk of developing "signs & symptoms" and causes of CHF	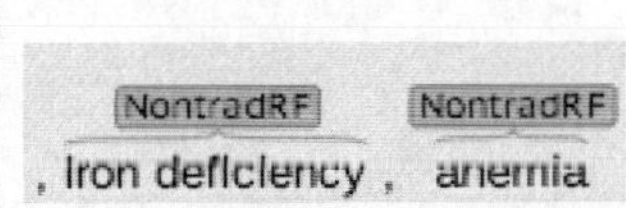
Organ	Any body part	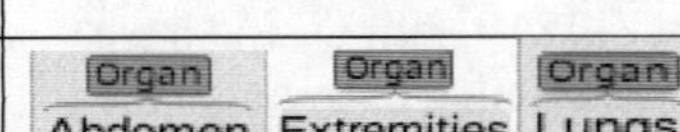

Table 1. Annotated phenotype entity classes

Relation Type	Description	Example
Causality	This relationship links two concepts in cases in which one concept causes the other to occur.	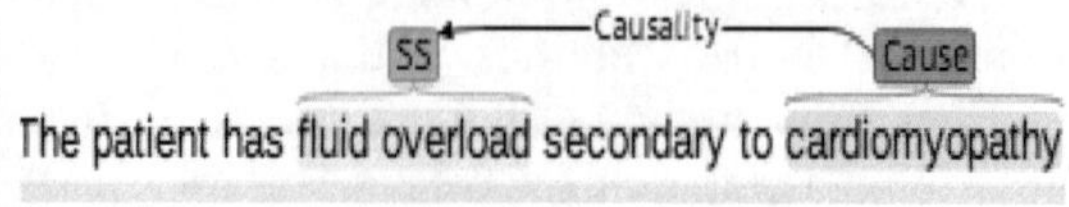
Finding	This relationship links the organ to the manifestation or abnormal variation that is observed during the diagnosis process.	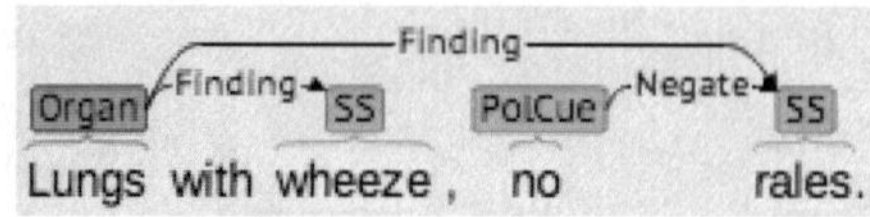
Negate	This is one-way relation to relate a negation attribute (polarity clue) to the condition it negates.	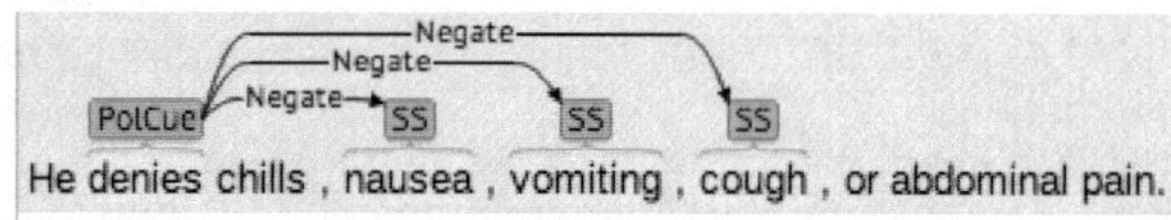

Table 2. Description of Annotated Relations

	Causality	Risk factor	Sign & Symptom	Non-traditional risk factor	Polarity clue	Organ	Macro-average
F-score	0.95	0.94	0.97	0.83	0.94	0.92	0.92

Table 3. Term annotation agreement statistics for discharge summaries

	Cause	Risk factor	Sign & Symptoms	Non-traditional risk factor	Macro-average
F-score	0.82	0.84	0.82	.77	0.81

Table 4. Overall agreement statistics for terms annotation in scientific articles

	Causality	Finding	Negate	Macro-average
F-score	0.86	0.94	0.95	0.91

Table 5. Relation annotation and agreement statistics for discharge summaries

5 Conclusion

This paper has described the creation of a new annotated corpus to facilitate the customisation of TM tools for the clinical domain. The corpus[1] consists of 300 discharge summaries and 5 full-text articles from the literature, annotated for CHF phenotype information, including causes, risk factors, sign & symptoms and non-traditional risk factors. Discharge summaries have also been annotated with relationships holding between pairs of annotated entities. A total 7236 of entities and 1181 relationships have been annotated. Extracting phenotype information can have a major impact on our deeper understanding of disease ethology, treatment and prevention (Xu et al., 2013). Currently we are working on confirming the utility of the annotated corpus in training and customising TM tools, i.e., adapting different sequence tagging algorithms (such as Conditional Random Fields (CRF) and Hidden Markov Model (HMM)) to extract comprehensive clinical information from both discharge summaries and scientific articles.

[1] Guidelines and stand-off annotation are publicly available at https://code.google.com/p/phenochf-corpus/source/browse/trunk

References

MEDLINE citation counts by year of publication.

Aronson, A.R. (2001). *Effective mapping of biomedical text to the UMLS Metathesaurus: the MetaMap program*. Proceedings of the AMIA Symposium, American Medical Informatics Association.

Hakenberg, J., Plake, C., Leser, U., Kirsch, H. and Rebholz-Schuhmann, D. (2005). *LLL'05 challenge: Genic interaction extraction-identification of language patterns based on alignment and finite state automata*. Proceedings of the 4th Learning Language in Logic workshop (LLL05).

Hripcsak, G. and Rothschild, A.S. (2005). Agreement, the f-measure, and reliability in information retrieval. *Journal of the American Medical Informatics Association*, 12(3): 296-298.

Jensen, P.B., Jensen, L.J. and Brunak, S. (2012). Mining electronic health records: towards better research applications and clinical care. *Nature Reviews Genetics*, 13(6): 395-405.

Kim, J.-D., Ohta, T. and Tsujii, J. (2008). Corpus annotation for mining biomedical events from literature. *BMC Bioinformatics*, 9(10).

Kulick, S., Bies, A., Liberman, M., Mandel, M., McDonald, R., Palmer, M., Schein, A., Ungar, L., Winters, S. and White, P. (2004). *Integrated annotation for biomedical information extraction*. Proc. of the Human Language Technology Conference and the Annual Meeting of the North American Chapter of the Association for Computational Linguistics (HLT/NAACL).

Meystre, S. and Haug, P.J. (2006). Natural language processing to extract medical problems from electronic clinical documents: performance evaluation. *Journal of Biomedical Informatics*, 39(6): 589-599.

Ogren, P.V., Savova, G.K. and Chute, C.G. (2008). *Constructing Evaluation Corpora for Automated Clinical Named Entity Recognition*. LREC.

Patrick, J., Wang, Y. and Budd, P. (2006). *Automatic Mapping Clinical Notes to Medical Terminologies*. Australasian Language Technology Workshop.

Perez-Rey, D., Jimenez-Castellanos, A., Garcia-Remesal, M., Crespo, J. and Maojo, V. (2012). CDAPubMed: a browser extension to retrieve EHR-based biomedical literature. *BMC Medical Informatics and Decision Making*, 12(1): 29.

Pestian, J.P., Brew, C., Matykiewicz, P., Hovermale, D., Johnson, N., Cohen, K.B. and Duch, W. (2007). *A shared task involving multi-label classification of clinical free text*. Proceedings of the Workshop on BioNLP 2007: Biological, Translational, and Clinical Language Processing, Association for Computational Linguistics.

Pyysalo, S., Ginter, F., Heimonen, J., Björne, J., Boberg, J., Järvinen, J. and Salakoski, T. (2007). BioInfer: a corpus for information extraction in the biomedical domain. *BMC Bioinformatics*, 8(1): 50.

Roberts, A., Gaizauskas, R., Hepple, M., Demetriou, G., Guo, Y., Setzer, A. and Roberts, I. (2008). *Semantic annotation of clinical text: The CLEF corpus*. Proceedings of the LREC 2008 workshop on building and evaluating resources for biomedical text mining.

Roberts, A., Gaizauskas, R., Hepple, M., Demetriou, G., Guo, Y., Roberts, I. and Setzer, A. (2009). Building a semantically annotated corpus of clinical texts. *Journal of Biomedical Informatics*, 42(5): 950-966.

Savova, G.K., Masanz, J.J., Ogren, P.V., Zheng, J., Sohn, S., Kipper-Schuler, K.C. and Chute, C.G. (2010). Mayo clinical Text Analysis and Knowledge Extraction System (cTAKES): architecture, component evaluation and applications. *Journal of the American Medical Informatics Association*, 17(5): 507-513.

Stenetorp, P., Pyysalo, S., Topić, G., Ohta, T., Ananiadou, S. and Tsujii, J.i. (2012). *BRAT: a web-based tool for NLP-assisted text annotation*. Proceedings of the Demonstrations at the 13th Conference of the European Chapter of the Association for Computational Linguistics, Association for Computational Linguistics.

Suominen, H., Salanterä, S., Velupillai, S., Chapman, W.W., Savova, G., Elhadad, N., Pradhan, S., South, B.R., Mowery, D.L. and Jones, G.J. (2013). Overview of the ShARe/CLEF eHealth Evaluation Lab 2013. *Information Access Evaluation. Multilinguality, Multimodality, and Visualization*, Springer: 212-231.

Tanabe, L., Xie, N., Thom, L.H., Matten, W. and Wilbur, W.J. (2005). GENETAG: a tagged corpus for gene/protein named entity recognition. *BMC Bioinformatics*, 6(Suppl 1): S3.

Thompson, P., Iqbal, S., McNaught, J. and Ananiadou, S. (2009). Construction of an annotated corpus to support biomedical information extraction. *BMC Bioinformatics*, 10(1): 349.

Uzuner, Ö., Goldstein, I., Luo, Y. and Kohane, I. (2008). Identifying patient smoking status from medical discharge records. *Journal of the American Medical Informatics Association*, 15(1): 14-24.

Uzuner, Ö. (2009). Recognizing obesity and comorbidities in sparse data. *Journal of the American Medical Informatics Association*, 16(4): 561-570.

Uzuner, Ö., South, B.R., Shen, S. and DuVall, S.L. (2011). 2010 i2b2/VA challenge on concepts, assertions, and relations in clinical text. *Journal of the American Medical Informatics Association*, 18(5): 552-556.

Xia, F. and Yetisgen-Yildiz, M. (2012). *Clinical corpus annotation: challenges and strategies.* Proceedings of the Third Workshop on Building and Evaluating Resources for Biomedical Text Mining (BioTxtM'2012) in conjunction with the International Conference on Language Resources and Evaluation (LREC), Istanbul, Turkey.

Xu, R., Li, L. and Wang, Q. (2013). Towards building a disease-phenotype knowledge base: extracting disease-manifestation relationship from literature. *Bioinformatics*, 29(17): 2186-2194.

Precise Medication Extraction using Agile Text Mining

Chaitanya Shivade[*], **James Cormack**[†], **David Milward**[†]
[*]The Ohio State University, Columbus, Ohio, USA
[†]Linguamatics Ltd, Cambridge, UK
shivade@cse.ohio-state.edu,
{james.cormack,david.milward}@linguamatics.com

Abstract

Agile text mining is widely used for commercial text mining in the pharmaceutical industry. It can be applied without building an annotated training corpus, so is well-suited to novel or one-off extraction tasks. In this work we wanted to see how efficiently it could be adapted for healthcare extraction tasks such as medication extraction. The aim was to identify medication names, associated dosage, route of administration, frequency, duration and reason, as specified in the 2009 i2b2 medication challenge.

Queries were constructed based on 696 discharge summaries available as training data. Performance was measured on a test dataset of 251 unseen documents. F1-scores were calculated by comparing system annotations against ground truth provided for the test data.

Despite the short amount of time spent in adapting the system to this task, it achieved high precision and reasonable recall (precision of 0.92, recall of 0.715). It would have ranked fourth in comparison to the original challenge participants on the basis of its F-score of 0.805 for phrase level horizontal evaluation. This shows that agile text mining is an effective approach towards information extraction that can yield highly accurate results.

1 Introduction

Medication information occupies a sizeable portion of clinical notes, especially discharge summaries. This includes medications on admission, during hospital course, and at discharge. This information is useful for clinical tasks such as inferring adverse drug reactions, clinical trial recruitment, etc. The i2b2 Natural Language Processing (NLP) challenges encourage the development of systems for clinical applications, using a shared task, publicly available clinical data, and comparison of performance with the other participating systems, subject to rigid evaluation metrics. The 2009 challenge (Uzuner, Solti, & Cadag, 2010) aimed to extract mentions of medication names, associated dosage, route of administration, frequency, duration and the reason for medication.

The project used the Linguamatics Interactive Information Extraction (I2E) platform. This combines NLP, terminologies and search technology to provide a unique "agile" text mining approach (Milward et al., 2005) that can yield highly precise results in a small amount of time. The approach involves semantic annotation and indexing of data followed by interactive design of queries that capture typical syntactic and semantic features of the desired information. While the system uses machine learning approaches within its core linguistic processing, the final set of queries are essentially syntactic/semantic rules identifying specific information in the text.

2 Section Identification

Although discharge summaries are considered to be unstructured data, there are typical characteristics associated with them. There is a specific flow of information within every discharge summary, starting with details of patient's admission, followed by the hospital course and ending with discharge instructions. Other common sections include chief complaint, physical examination, etc. There were more than twenty headings to express discharge medications in the training data ("Medications on discharge," "Discharge meds," etc.). The training data was processed to identify section headings and multiple forms of the same heading were normalized to a single heading. The plain text was converted into XML with tags representing section names.

3 Offset Information

To allow evaluation of results in the i2b2 format, the text was preprocessed to include line numbers and word numbers as further XML annotations.

4 Natural Language Processing

Indexing documents with I2E uses a standard NLP pipeline involving tokenization of the text, part-of-speech tagging, and linguistic chunking. The output of the pipeline provides useful linguistic information, particularly about the location of noun phrases and verb phrases, for use in entity extraction and querying.

5 Terminologies

The I2E platform uses hierarchical terminologies to extract entities from the text. These can include freely available terminologies such as MeSH, and the NCI thesaurus, as well as proprietary terminologies such as MedDRA. A series of regular expressions allow for the indexing of numeric terms (integers, fractions, decimal numbers) and measurement units (length, time, weight, etc.). In addition, custom terminologies can be created for specific tasks by combining or merging existing terminologies, or by using the system itself to help discover terminology from the data.

6 Querying

The I2E framework provides an interactive querying experience that is similar to a web search. While users can enter text queries just as one might in an internet search engine, the query interface also allows specification of linguistic and non-linguistic units as 'containers' for other units. For example, it is possible to search for a noun phrase within a sentence and to specify words, regular expressions and concepts from terminologies. Non-linguistic units can be customized to regulate the ordering of items within the container, the number of items that may occur between two items and whether they are constrained by linguistic boundaries, such as the sentence. The output of the query can also be customized so as to provide structured representation of the query results.

As an example, one of the typical ways a medication is prescribed follows the construct: "Aspirin 625 mg p.o. b.i.d." This means Aspirin with a dosage of 625 milligrams is to be consumed orally (p.o.), twice a day (b.i.d.). A query to capture this construct can be constructed as a non-linguistic phrase, starting with (a) a pharmacological substance (a concept from the appropriate branch of the NCI-thesaurus), followed by (b) a numerical term, (c) a unit for measuring weight, (d) a dosage abbreviation and finally, (e) an abbreviation for the frequency of medication.

A query containing items only for (a), (b) and (c) will give results for all phrases containing a pharmacological substance followed by its dosage (Aspirin 625 mg, Tylenol 350 mg, etc.). The graphical query interface is sufficiently flexible to allow many different orderings of these constructs and to negate false positive results.

User defined terminologies can be systematically constructed to allow consistent matching of lists of terms and to generate concise queries. For example, candidates for abbreviations corresponding to the route of administration were found by constructing a query with items for (a), (b), (c) and (e) and an empty word container for (d). This gave all phrases containing (a), (b), (c), and any word in the discharge summary that was followed by (e). The results of this query were candidates for route of administration. The efficiency of querying in I2E provides an opportunity to interactively refine parts of the final query and discover terms in the training data that might be missed by regular expressions and thesauri.

Queries can also be limited to specific sections of the document. The pre-processing step described above identified sections in discharge summaries of the i2b2 medications challenge corpus. The queries can thus be limited to only a few specific sections such as "Medications on Admission" and "Medications on Discharge" by embedding the query in a section container. The challenge specified not to include medications mentioned as allergies for a patient. Results obtained in the allergies section of discharge summaries were therefore ignored using this approach.

7 Post-processing

I2E's default output is an HTML table with columns corresponding to different containers used in the query. Output can also be limited to predefined columns of interest. Multiple queries are often required to capture different pieces of information spread across the corpus. In the i2b2 challenge, there are multiple fields associated with every mention of medication. A single structured record corresponding to every mention of medication is expected as an output. Spasic et al. (2010) view the challenge as a template filling task where the participating system is expected to fill slots in a template. Thus, the output can be configured to be 6 columns representing each of the templates. Following their terminology, different semantic queries filled different slots of the same template. These slots were aggregated into a single template using post-processing.

Multiple issues had to be taken care of in this step. Different queries captured parts of the text corresponding to the same slot. For example, a query aimed at capturing a particular linguistic construct may extract frequency as "daily after dinner," while another query may capture its substring "daily." In this case, the former extraction, which is the longer string, received priority as per the challenge specifications. Another important problem encountered was that of multiple matches for the same field. For example, Insulin and Aspart were identified as separate pharmacological substances during the indexing process. However, "Insulin aspart" is considered as a single medication name as per the challenge specifications. Two separate templates are thus created. The results of the post processing collapse them into one. Certain terms from the terminologies did not match the definition of a medication, since terminology branches are often generic. For example, the Chemicals and Drugs branch of MeSH constitutes terms such as coffee. Therefore, a list of false positives for medication names corresponding to these matches was generated from the training data.

8 Experiments

The i2b2 website offers downloading of the NLP dataset for the 2009 challenge after signing a Data Usage Agreement. The training data consists of 696 discharge summaries. A subset of ten documents with gold standard annotations has been made available by the organizers. The test dataset consists of 251 documents which were annotated by the participants under a community annotation experiment conducted by the organizers (Uzuner, Solti, Xia, et al. 2010). These 251 documents and their corresponding gold standard annotations are also available. The performance was calculated using phrase level and token level metrics for horizontal and vertical evaluations as defined in (Uzuner, Solti, & Cadag, 2010). The phrase level horizontal evaluation measures the performance of a system across all six fields. This was used as a primary metric to rank the results in the challenge.

Terminology	P	R	F1
NCI	0.953	0.657	0.777
MeSH	0.923	0.563	0.699
NCI + MeSH	0.932	0.688	0.792
NCI + FDA	0.947	0.678	0.790
MeSH + FDA	0.921	0.571	0.705
NCI + MeSH + FDA	0.931	0.698	0.798
NCI + MeSH + FDA + RxNorm	0.92	0.715	0.805

Table 1: Comparison of Different Terminologies.

In order to assess the utility of different terminologies, the same set of queries were modified by replacing the concept from one with the corresponding concept in another. For example: Pharmacological substance from NCI was replaced with Chemicals and Drugs from MeSH. This offered an objective way to compare the coverage of MeSH and NCI with respect to medication names. Coverage of multiple terminologies can be leveraged by aggregating the results of queries resulting from different terminologies. NCI thesaurus, MeSH, a list of FDA drug labels, and RxNorm were used. In addition a custom terminology was prepared by capturing medication names in the training data that were missed by the terminologies. The best F-score was obtained when query results for all sources were aggregated. Addition of sources resulted in a drop in precision but increased recall. Table 1 summarizes these results, where columns P and R denote precision and recall respectively.

9 Results

Twenty teams representing 23 organizations and nine countries participated in the medication challenge. The other systems used a variety of rule-based, machine-learning and hybrid systems, with the most popular being rule-based systems (Uzuner et al., 2010). The best ranked system, detailed in Patrick & Li (2009), was an example of a hybrid system, using both rule-based and statistical classifiers.

No.	Group	P	R	F1
1	USyd	0.896	0.82	0.857
2	Vanderbilt	0.840	0.803	0.821
3	Manchester	0.864	0.766	0.812
*	I2E	0.920	0.715	0.805
4	NLM	0.784	0.823	0.803
5	BME - Humboldt	0.841	0.758	0.797
6	OpenU	0.850	0.748	0.796
7	UParis	0.799	0.761	780
8	LIMSI	0.827	0.725	0.773
9	UofUtah	0.832	0.715	0.769
10	U Wisconsin Madison	0.904	0.661	0.764

Table 2: Phrase level horizontal evaluation

Phrase level horizontal evaluation was used as a metric to rank the performance of participants in the challenge. Table 2 compares the performance of I2E with the top ten participants in the challenge using this metric. It achieves highly precise results as compared to other participants of the challenge. The vertical evaluation which measures the performance along individual fields showed that the system performed poorly on duration and reason, in common with other systems. As reported by the organizers of the challenge (Uzuner et al., 2010), capturing duration and reason is a hard task. They report that this is primarily due to the variation in length and content of these fields in the training and testing data.

10 Conclusion

Extracting information through interactive design of queries can achieve highly precise results in a short amount of time. Much of the time in this project was spent on pre-processing documents to allow the results to conform to the i2b2 format. The time taken on query development was of the order of a few weeks, including a couple of days training in the system at the start of the project. This process requires far less specialist knowledge of Artificial Intelligence than other solutions to this challenge and the easy to use interface means refinement is straightforward. Clearly, recall still needs to be improved: our best system would have been ranked 4th out of 21 systems in the phrase level horizontal evaluation. Examination of the training material suggests this is due to gaps in the drug coverage provided by the terminologies rather than gaps in the query patterns. We will therefore concentrate on extending drug coverage in our future work.

Acknowledgments

The authors would like to thank Tracy Gregory, Himanshu Agarwal and Matthijs Vakar for their help in this project.

References

Milward, D. et al., 2005. Ontology-based interactive information extraction from scientific abstracts.

Comparative and functional genomics, 6(1-2), pp.67–71.

Spasic, I. et al., 2010. Medication information extraction with linguistic pattern matching and semantic rules. *Journal of the American Medical Informatics Association : JAMIA*, 17(5), pp.532–5.

Uzuner, O., Solti, I., Xia, F., et al., 2010. Community annotation experiment for ground truth generation for the i2b2 medication challenge. *Journal of the American Medical Informatics Association : JAMIA*, 17(5), pp.519–23.

Uzuner, O. Solti, I. & Cadag, E., 2010. Extracting medication information from clinical text. *Journal of the American Medical Informatics Association : JAMIA*, 17(5), pp.514–8

Patrick J & Li M. A Cascade Approach to Extracting Medication Events. Proceedings of the Third i2b2 Workshop on Challenges in Natural Language Processing for Clinical Data, 2009.

Applying UMLS for Distantly Supervised Relation Detection

Roland Roller and **Mark Stevenson**
University of Sheffield
Regent Court, 211 Portobello
S1 4DP Sheffield, UK
{R.Roller,M.Stevenson}@dcs.shef.ac.uk

Abstract

This paper describes first results using the Unified Medical Language System (UMLS) for distantly supervised relation extraction. UMLS is a large knowledge base which contains information about millions of medical concepts and relations between them. Our approach is evaluated using existing relation extraction data sets that contain relations that are similar to some of those in UMLS.

1 Introduction

Distant supervision has proved to be a popular approach to relation extraction (Craven and Kumlien, 1999; Mintz et al., 2009; Hoffmann et al., 2010; Nguyen and Moschitti, 2011). It has the advantage that it does not require manually annotated training data. Distant supervision avoids this by using information from a knowledge base to automatically identify instances of a relation from text and use them in order to generate training data for a relation extraction system.

Distant supervision has already been applied to the biomedical domain (Craven and Kumlien, 1999; Thomas et al., 2011). Craven and Kumlien (1999) were the first to apply distant supervision and used the Yeast Protein Database (YPD) to detect sentences containing subcellar-localization relations. Thomas et al. (2011) trained a classifier for protein-protein interactions (PPI) using the knowledge base IntAct and evaluated their approach on different PPI corpora.

There have also been recent applications of distant supervision outside the biomedical domain. The use of Freebase to train a classifier, e.g. (Mintz et al., 2009; Riedel et al., 2010), has proved popular. Other, such as Hoffmann et al. (2010), use Wikipedia info-boxes as the knowledge base.

Applications of distant supervision face several challenges. The main problem is ensuring the quality of the automatically identified training instances identified by the self-annotation. The use of instances that have been incorrectly labelled as positive can lower performance (Takamatsu et al., 2012). Another problem arises when positive examples are included in the set of negative training instances, which can occur when information is missing from the knowledge base (Min et al., 2013; Ritter et al., 2013; Xu et al., 2013).

Evaluation of relation extraction systems that use distant supervision represents a further challenge. In the ideal case an annotated evaluation set is available. Others, such as Ritter et al. (2013) and Hoffmann et al. (2011), use Freebase as knowledge base and evaluate their classifier on an annotated New York Times corpus. However, if no evaluation set is available leave-out can be used where the data identified using distant supervision used for both training and testing (Hoffmann et al., 2010).

This paper makes use of the Unified Medical Language System (UMLS) as a knowledge source for distant supervision. It is widely used for biomedical language processing and readily available. The advantage of UMLS is that it contains information about a wide range of different types of relations and therefore has the potential to generate a large number of relation classifiers. To our knowledge, it has not been used as a knowledge source to train relation extraction systems.

Evaluating such as wide range of relation classifiers is not straightforward due to the lack of gold-standard data. As an alternative approach we make use of existing annotated data sets and identify ones which contain relations that are similar to those included in UMLS.

The next section provides a short description of UMLS. We then describe how we acquire existing data sets to evaluate certain relations. In section 4 we present our first results using UMLS for distant supervision.

2 Unified Medical Language System

The *Unified Medical Language System*[1] is a set of files and software which combines different biomedical vocabularies, knowledge bases and standards. The Metathesaurus is a database within UMLS which contains several million biomedical and health related names and concepts and relationships among them. All different names of a concept are unified by the Concept Unique Identifiers (CUI). MRREL is a subset of the Metathesaurus and involves different relationships between different medical concepts defined by a pair of CUIs. Many of them are child-parent relationships, express a synonymy or are vaguely defined as broader or narrower relation. Other relations are more specific, such as *has_location* or *drug_contraindicated_for*. This work focuses on more specific types of relations.

3 Acquiring Evaluation Data Sets

We examined a number of relation extraction data sets in order to identify ones that could be used to evaluate our system. The aim is to find a data set that is annotated with relations that are similar to some of those found in the UMLS. If an appropriate relation can be identified then a relation extraction system can be trained using information from the UMLS and evaluated using the data set.

To determine whether a data set is suitable we used MetaMap (Aronson and Lang, 2010) to identify the CUIs for each related item. We then compared each pair against the MRREL table to determine whether it is included as a relation. To increase coverage we also included parent and child nodes in the mapping process.

Table 1 shows the mappings obtained for two of the data sets: the DDI 2011 data set (Segura-Bedmar et al., 2011) and the data set described by Rosario and Hearst (2004).

The DDI data set contains information about drug-drug interactions and includes a single relation (DDI). The relations it contained were mapped onto 701 CUI pairs. 266 (37.9%) of these mappings could be matched to the MRREL relation *has_contraindicated_drug*. Many of the CUI pairs could also be mapped to the *isa* relationship in MRREL, but this is a very general relationship and the matches are caused by the large number of these in UMLS rather than it being a reasonable match for the DDI relation.

The data set described by Rosario and Hearst (2004) focuses on different relationships between treatments and diseases. The two most common relations TREAT_FOR_DIS (TREAT), denoting the treatment for a particular disease, and PREVENT (PREV), which indicates that a treatment can be used to prevent a disease. The MRREL *isa* relationship also matches many of these relations, again due to its prevalence in MRREL. Other MRREL relations (*may_be_prevented_by* and *may_be_treated_by*) match fewer CUI pairs but seem to be better matches for the TREAT and PREV relations.

Relation	MRREL
DDI (701)	has_contraindicated_drug (266), isa (185), may_treat (57), has_contraindication (51)
PREV (41)	isa (11), may_be_prevented_by (5)
TREAT (741)	isa (172), may_be_treated_by (118)

Table 1: Relation mapping to MRREL

It is important to note that it is not always possible to find a CUI mapping for each entity and the mapping process means that the mapping cannot be guaranteed to be correct in all cases. High coverage does not necessarily mean that a corpus is very similar to a certain MRREL relation, just that many of the CUI pairs which have been mapped to the related entities in the corpus occur often together in a certain MRREL relation. However, in the absence of any other suitable evaluation data we assume that high coverage is an indicator that the relations are strongly similar and use these two data sets for evaluation.

4 Distant Supervision using UMLS

In this section we carry out two different distant supervised experiments using UMLS. The first experiment will be evaluated on a subset of the DDI 2011 training data set using the MRREL relation *has_contraindicated_drug* and *has_contraindication*. The second experiment uses the MRREL relations *may_be_treated_by* and *may_be_prevented_by* and are evaluated on the Rosario & Hearst data set.

We use 7,500,000 Medline abstracts annotated with CUIs using MetaMap (choosing the best mapping as annotation) as a corpus for distant supervision. Our information extraction platform based on a system developed for the BioNLP

[1] https://www.nlm.nih.gov/research/umls/

Shared Task 2013 (Roller and Stevenson, 2013). In contrast to our previous work, our classification process relies on the Shallow Linguistic Kernel (Giuliano et al., 2006) in combination with LibSVM (Chang and Lin, 2011) taking the kernel as input.

4.1 Experiment 1: DDI 2011

The DDI 2011 data set was split into training and test sets for the experiments. Table 2 presents results that place the distant supervision performance in context. The *naive* classification approach predicts all candidate pairs as positive. The *supervised* approach is trained on the training set, using the same kernel method as our distant supervised experiments and evaluated on the test set. This represents the performance that can be obtained using manually labelled training data and can be considered as an upper bound for distant supervision.

Method	Prec. / Recall / F1
naive	0.098 / **1.000** / 0.178
supervised	**0.428** / 0.702 / **0.532**

Table 2: DDI 2011 baseline results

The distant supervision approach requires pairs of positive and negative CUI to be identified. These pairs are used to identify positive and negative examples of the target relation from a corpus. Pairs which occur in our target MRREL relation are used as positive CUI pairs. Negative pairs are generated by selecting pairs of CUIs that are occur in any other MRREL relation.

Sentences containing these CUI pairs are identified in the subset of the MetaMapped Medline. In the basic setup (*basic*), sentences containing a positive pair will be considered as a positive training example. There are many cases where just the occurrence of a positive MRREL pair does not express the target relation. In an effort to remove this noisy data we apply some simple heuristics. The first discards all training instances with more than five words (*5w*) between the two entities, an approach similar to one applied by Takamatsu et al. (2012). The second discards positive sentences containing a comma between the related entities (*com*). We found that commas often indicate a sentence containing a list of items (e.g. genes or diseases) and that these sentences do not form good training examples due to the multiple relations that are possible when there are several items. Finally we also apply a combination of both techniques (*5w+com*).

1000 positive examples were generated using each approach and used for training. Although it would be possible to generate more examples for some approaches, for example *basic*, applying the combination of techniques (*5w+com*) significantly reduces the number of instances available.

Method	has_contraindication (*P./R./F1*)	has_contraindicated_drug (*P./R./F1*)
basic	0.146 / 0.371 / 0.210	0.158 / **0.598** / 0.250
5w	0.109 / **0.641** / 0.187	0.207 / 0.487 / 0.290
com	**0.212** / 0.560 / **0.308**	0.177 / 0.498 / 0.261
5w+com	0.207 / 0.487 / 0.291	**0.214** / 0.471 / **0.294**

Table 3: Evaluation with DDI 2011

Table 3 presents results of the experiments. The results show that all applied techniques for both MRREL relations outperform the naive approach. The best results in terms of F1 score for the *has_contraindication* MRREL relation are obtained using the *com* selection technique. Applying just *5w* leads to worse results than using the *basic* approach. The situation for *has_contraindicated_drug* is different. The classifier provides for all techniques a better F1 score than the *basic* approach. The best results are achieved by using *5w+com*. It is interesting to see, that both MRREL relations provide similar average classification results, even if both relations are different from the target relation and cover completely different CUI pairs. It is also interesting that the MRREL relation *has_contraindication* has a lower coverage to the DDI relation than *has_contraindicated_drug*, but provides slightly better results overall. A problem with the distant supervised classification of these two MRREL relations is their low occurrence in our Medline subset. Using more training data will often lead to better results. In our case, if we apply the combined selection technique, there are fewer positive training instances than are available to the supervised approach, making it difficult to outperform the supervised approach.

4.2 Experiment 2: Rosario & Hearst

The second experiment addresses the problem of detecting the MRREL relations *may_be_prevented_by* and *may_be_treated_by*. Parts of the Rosario & Hearst data set are used to evaluate this relation. This data set differs in structure from the DDI data set. Instead of annotating the entities in the sentence according to its relation, the annotations in the data set indicate whether a certain relation occurs in the sentence. This data set does not contain any negative examples. If a sentence contains two entities, it will always describe a certain relation. A supervised classifier is created by dividing the data set into training and test sets. The test set contains 253 different sentences (221 describe a *TREAT* relation, 15 a *PREV* relation and 17 involve other relationships). Positive and negative CUI pairs are selected in a different way to the previous experiment. The two most frequent relations in the data set are *TREAT* and *PREV*. A classifier for a particular relation is trained using sentences annotated with the corresponding MRREL relation as positive instances. Negative instances are identified using the other relation. For example, the classifier for the *TREAT* relation is trained using positive examples identified using *may_be_treated_by* with negative examples generated using *may_be_treated_by*.

Table 4 shows the baseline results on the data set using a naive and a supervised approach on the two original relations *TREAT* and *PREV*. Performance of the naive approach for *TREAT* is very high since the majority of sentences in the data set are annotated with that relation.

Data Set	Method	Prec. / Recall / F1
TREAT	naive	0.874 / **1.000** / 0.933
	supervised	**0.944** / 0.923 / **0.934**
PREV	naive	0.059 / **1.000** / 0.112
	supervised	**0.909** / 0.667 / **0.769**

Table 4: Rosario & Hearst baseline results

Table 5 shows the results for the various distant supervision approaches. Again, 1000 positive training examples were used to train the classifier. Since the F-Score of the naive and the supervised approaches of *TREAT* are very high, it is difficult to compete with the *may_be_treated_by* distant supervised classifier. However, considering that just 15.9% of the *TREAT* instance pairs of the training set match the MRREL *may_be_treated_by* relation, the results are promising. Furthermore, the precision of all *may_be_treated_by* distant supervised experiments outperform the naive approach. The best results are achieved using *com* as selection technique.

The experiments using the *PREV* relation for evaluation are more interesting. Due to its low occurrence in the test set it is more difficult to detect this relation. The distant supervised classifier trained with the *may_be_prevented_by* relation easily outperforms the naive approach. The best overall F1 scoer results are achieved using the *5w* technique. As expected the distant supervised results are outperformed by the supervised approach. However, the recall for all distantly supervised approaches are at least as high as those obtained using the supervised approach.

Method	*may_be_treated_by* evaluated on TREAT *(P./R./F1)*	*may_be_prevented_by* evaluated on PREV *(P./R./F1)*
basic	0.926 / 0.733 / 0.818	0.286 / 0.667 / 0.400
5w	0.925 / 0.783 / 0.848	**0.407** / 0.733 / **0.524**
com	**0.928 / 0.819 / 0.870**	0.222 / 0.800 / 0.348
5w+com	0.924 / 0.769 / 0.840	0.361 / **0.867** / 0.510

Table 5: Evaluation with Rosario & Hearst data set

5 Conclusion and Discussion

In this paper we presented first results using UMLS to train a distant supervised relational classifier. Evaluation was carried out using existing evaluation data sets since no resources directly annotated with UMLS relations were available. We showed that using a distantly supervised classifier trained on MRREL relations similar to those found in the evaluation data set provides promising results.

Overall, our system works with some components which should be improved to achieve better results. First, we rely on a cheap and fast annotation using MetaMap, which might produce annotation errors. In addition, the use of noisy distant supervised training data decreases the classification quality. An improvement of the selection process and an improvement of the classification method, such as Chowdhury and Lavelli (2013), could lead to better classification results. In future we would also like to make further use of existing data sets with similar relations to those of interest to evaluate distant supervision approaches.

Acknowledgements

The authors are grateful to the Engineering and Physical Sciences Research Council for supporting the work described in this paper (EP/J008427/1).

References

A. Aronson and F. Lang. 2010. An overview of MetaMap: historical perspective and recent advances. *Journal of the American Medical Association*, 17(3):229–236.

Chih-Chung Chang and Chih-Jen Lin. 2011. LIBSVM: A library for support vector machines. *ACM Transactions on Intelligent Systems and Technology*, 2:27:1–27:27.

Md. Faisal Mahbub Chowdhury and Alberto Lavelli. 2013. Fbk-irst : A multi-phase kernel based approach for drug-drug interaction detection and classification that exploits linguistic information. In *Second Joint Conference on Lexical and Computational Semantics (*SEM), Volume 2: Proceedings of the Seventh International Workshop on Semantic Evaluation (SemEval 2013)*, pages 351–355, Atlanta, Georgia, USA, June. Association for Computational Linguistics.

Mark Craven and Johan Kumlien. 1999. Constructing biological knowledge bases by extracting information from text sources. In *In Proceedings of the Seventh International Conference on Intelligent Systems for Molecular Biology (ISMB)*, pages 77–86. AAAI Press.

Claudio Giuliano, Alberto Lavelli, and Lorenza Romano. 2006. Exploiting shallow linguistic information for relation extraction from biomedical literature. In *In Proc. EACL 2006*.

Raphael Hoffmann, Congle Zhang, and Daniel S. Weld. 2010. Learning 5000 relational extractors. In *Proceedings of the 48th Annual Meeting of the Association for Computational Linguistics*, ACL '10, pages 286–295, Stroudsburg, PA, USA. Association for Computational Linguistics.

Raphael Hoffmann, Congle Zhang, Xiao Ling, Luke Zettlemoyer, and Daniel S. Weld. 2011. Knowledge-based weak supervision for information extraction of overlapping relations. In *Proceedings of the 49th Annual Meeting of the Association for Computational Linguistics*, ACL '11, pages 541–550.

Bonan Min, Ralph Grishman, Li Wan, Chang Wang, and David Gondek. 2013. Distant supervision for relation extraction with an incomplete knowledge base. In *Proceedings of the 2013 Conference of the North American Chapter of the Association for Computational Linguistics: Human Language Technologies*, pages 777–782, Atlanta, Georgia, June. Association for Computational Linguistics.

Mike Mintz, Steven Bills, Rion Snow, and Dan Jurafsky. 2009. Distant supervision for relation extraction without labeled data. In *Proceedings of the Joint Conference of the 47th Annual Meeting of the ACL and the 4th International Joint Conference on Natural Language Processing of the AFNLP: Volume 2 - Volume 2*, ACL '09, pages 1003–1011, Stroudsburg, PA, USA. Association for Computational Linguistics.

Truc-Vien T. Nguyen and Alessandro Moschitti. 2011. End-to-end relation extraction using distant supervision from external semantic repositories. In *Proceedings of the 49th Annual Meeting of the Association for Computational Linguistics: Human Language Technologies: short papers - Volume 2*, HLT '11, pages 277–282, Stroudsburg, PA, USA. Association for Computational Linguistics.

Sebastian Riedel, Limin Yao, and Andrew McCallum. 2010. Modeling relations and their mentions without labeled text. In *Proceedings of the European Conference on Machine Learning and Knowledge Discovery in Databases (ECML PKDD '10)*.

Alan Ritter, Luke Zettlemoyer, Mausam, and Oren Etzioni. 2013. Modeling missing data in distant supervision for information extraction. In *Association for Computational Linguistics Vol. 1 (TACL)*.

Roland Roller and Mark Stevenson. 2013. Identification of genia events using multiple classifiers. In *Proceedings of BioNLP Shared Task 2013 Workshop*, Sofia, Bulgaria, August. Association for Computational Linguistics.

Barbara Rosario and Marti A. Hearst. 2004. Classifying semantic relations in bioscience texts. In *Proceedings of the 42nd Annual Meeting on Association for Computational Linguistics*, ACL '04, Stroudsburg, PA, USA. Association for Computational Linguistics.

Isabel Segura-Bedmar, Paloma Martnez, and Daniel Snchez-Cisneros. 2011. The 1st ddi extraction-2011 challenge task: Extraction of drug-drug interactions from biomedical texts. In *Proceedings of DDI Extraction-2011 challenge task.*, pages 1–9.

Shingo Takamatsu, Issei Sato, and Hiroshi Nakagawa. 2012. Reducing wrong labels in distant supervision for relation extraction. In *Proceedings of the 50th Annual Meeting of the Association for Computational Linguistics: Long Papers - Volume 1*, ACL '12, pages 721–729, Stroudsburg, PA, USA. Association for Computational Linguistics.

Philippe Thomas, Illés Solt, Roman Klinger, and Ulf Leser. 2011. Learning protein protein interaction extraction using distant supervision. In *Proceedings of Robust Unsupervised and Semi-Supervised Methods in Natural Language Processing*, pages 34–41.

Wei Xu, Raphael Hoffmann, Le Zhao, and Ralph Grishman. 2013. Filling knowledge base gaps for distant supervision of relation extraction. In *Proceedings of the 51st Annual Meeting of the Association for Computational Linguistics (Volume 2: Short Papers)*, pages 665–670, Sofia, Bulgaria, August. Association for Computational Linguistics.

Adverse Drug Event prediction combining shallow analysis and machine learning

Sara Santiso
Alicia Pérez
Koldo Gojenola
IXA Taldea (UPV-EHU)

Arantza Casillas
Maite Oronoz
IXA Taldea (UPV-EHU)
http://ixa.si.ehu.es

Abstract

The aim of this work is to infer a model able to extract cause-effect relations between drugs and diseases. A two-level system is proposed. The first level carries out a shallow analysis of Electronic Health Records (EHRs) in order to identify medical concepts such as drug brand-names, substances, diseases, etc. Next, all the combination pairs formed by a concept from the group of drugs (drug and substances) and the group of diseases (diseases and symptoms) are characterised through a set of 57 features. A supervised classifier inferred on those features is in charge of deciding whether that pair represents a cause-effect type of event.

One of the challenges of this work is the fact that the system explores the entire document. The contributions of this paper stand on the use of real EHRs to discover adverse drug reaction events even in different sentences. Besides, the work focuses on Spanish language.

1 Introduction

This work deals with semantic data mining within the clinical domain. The aim is to automatically highlight the Adverse Drug Reactions (ADRs) in EHRs in order to alleviate the work-load to several services within a hospital (pharmacy service, documentation service,...) that have to read these reports. Event detection was thoroughly tackled in the Natural Language Processing for Clinical Data 2010 Challenge. Since then, cause-effect event extraction has emerged as a field of interest in the Biomedical domain (Björne et al., 2010; Mihaila et al., 2013). The motivation is, above all, practical. Electronic Health Records (EHRs) are studied by several services in the hospital, not only by the doctor in charge of the patient but also by the pharmacy and documentation services, amongst others. There are some attempts in the literature that aim to make the reading of the reports in English easier and less time-consuming by means of an automatic annotation toolkit (Rink et al., 2011; Botsis et al., 2011; Toldo et al., 2012). This work is a first approach on automatic learning of relations between drugs causing diseases in Spanish EHRs.

This work presents a system that entails two stages in cascade: 1) the first one carries out the annotation of drugs or substances (from now onwards both of them shall be referred to as DRUG) and diseases or symptoms (referred to as DISEASE); 2) the second one determines whether a given (DRUG, DISEASE) pair of concepts represents a cause-effect reaction. Note that we are interested in highlighting events involving (DRUG, DISEASE) pairs where the drug caused an adverse reaction or a disease. By contrast, often, (DRUG, DISEASE) pairs would entail a drug prescribed to combat a disease, but these correspond to a different kind of events (indeed, diametrically opposed). Besides, (DRUG, DISEASE) pairs might represent other sort of events or they might even be unrelated at all. Finally, the system should present the ADRs marked in a friendly front-end. To this end, the aim is to represent the text in the framework provided by Brat (Stenetorp et al., 2012). Figure 1 shows an example, represented in Brat, of some cause-effect events manually tagged by experts.

There are related works in this field aiming at a variety of biomedical event extraction, such as binary protein-protein interaction (Wong, 2001), biomolecular event extraction (Kim et al., 2011), and drug-drug interaction extraction (Segura-Bedmar et al., 2013). We are focusing on a variety of interaction extraction: drugs causing diseases. There are previous works in the literature that try to warn whether a document contains or not this type of events. There are more recent works that

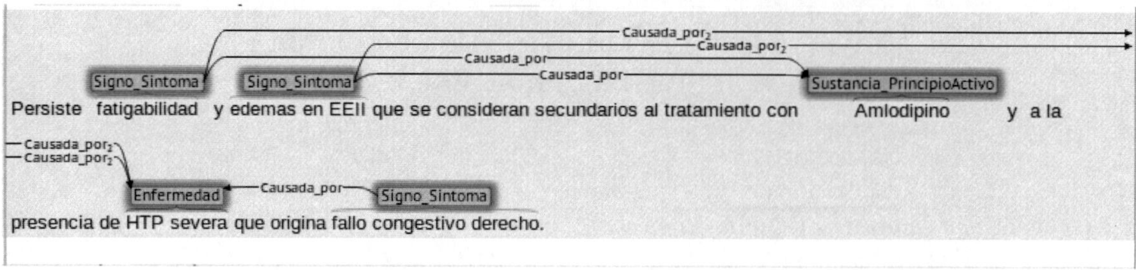

Figure 1: Some cause-effect events manually annotated in the Brat framework.

cope with event extraction within the same sentence, that is, intra-sentence events. By contrast, in this work we have realised that around 26% of the events occur between concepts that are in different sentences. Moreover, some of them are at very long distance. Hence, our method aims at providing all the (DRUG, DISEASE) concepts within the document that represent a cause-effect relation.

We cope with real discharge EHRs written by around 400 different doctors. These records are not written in a template, that is, the EHRs do not follow a pre-determined structure, and this, by itself entails a challenge. The EHRs we are dealing with are written in a free structure using natural language, non-standard abbreviations etc. Moreover, we tackle Spanish language, for which little work has been carried out. In addition, we do not only aim at single concept-words but also at concepts based on multi-word terms.

2 System overview

The system, as depicted in Figure 2 entails two stages.

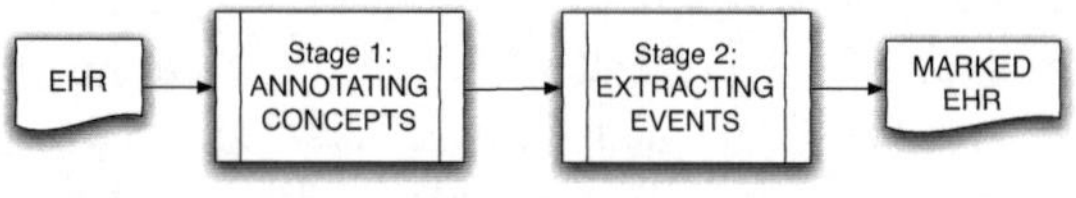

Figure 2: The ADR event extraction system.

In the first stage, relevant pairs of concepts have to be identified within an EHR. Concept annotation is accomplished by means of a shallow analyser system (described in section 2.1). Once the analyser has detected (DRUG, DISEASE) pairs in a document, all the pairs will be examined by an inferred supervised classifier (described in section 2.2).

2.1 Annotating concepts by shallow analysis

The first stage of the system has to detect and annotate two types of semantic concepts: drugs and diseases. Each concept, as requested by the pharmacy service, should gather several sub-concepts stated as follows:

1. DRUG concept:
   (a) Generic names for pharmaceutical drugs: e.g. corticoids;
   (b) Brand-names for pharmaceutical drugs: e.g. Aspirin;
   (c) Active ingredients: e.g. vancomycin;
   (d) Substances: e.g. dust, rubber;
2. DISEASE concept:
   (a) Diseases
   (b) Signs
   (c) Symptoms

These concepts were identified by means of a general purpose analyser available for Spanish, called FreeLing (Padró et al., 2010), that had been enhanced with medical ontologies and dictionaries, such as SNOMED-CT, BotPLUS, ICD-9-CM, etc. (Oronoz et al., 2013). This toolkit is able to identify multi-word context-terms, lemmas and also POS tags. An example of the morphological, semantic and syntactic analysis, provided by this parser is given in Figure 3. In the figure two pieces of information can be distinguished: for example, given the word "secundarios" (meaning secondaries) 1) the POS tag provided is AQOM corresponding to Qualificative Adjective Ordinal Masculine Singular; and 2) the provided lemma is "secundario" (secondary). Besides, in a third layer, the semantic tag is given, that is, the tag "ENFERMEDAD" (meaning disease) involves the multiword concept "HTP severa" (severe pulmonary hypertension).

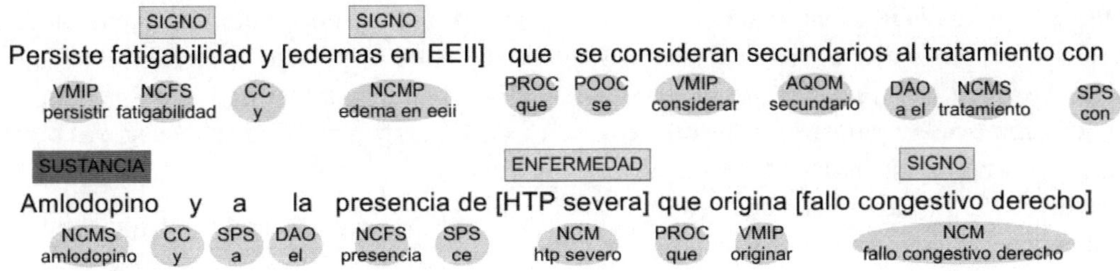

Figure 3: Lemmas, POS-tags and semantic tags are identified by the clinic domain analyser (diseases in yellow and drugs or substances in violet).

2.2 Extracting adverse drug reaction events using inferred classifiers

The goal of the second stage is to determine if a given (DRUG, DISEASE) pair represents an ADR event or not. On account of this, we resorted to supervised classification models. These models can be automatically inferred from a set of documents in which the target concepts had been previously annotated. Hence, first of all, a set of annotated data representative for the task is required. To this end, our starting point is a manually annotated corpus (presented in section 2.2.1). Besides, in order to automatically learn the classifier, the (DRUG, DISEASE) pairs have to be described in an operative way, that is, in terms of a finite-set of features (see section 2.2.2). The supervised classification model selected was a type of ensemble classifier: Random Forests (for further details turn to section 2.2.3).

2.2.1 Producing an annotated set

A supervised classifier was inferred from annotated real EHRs. The annotation was carried out by doctors from the same hospital that produced the EHRs. Given the text with the concepts marked on the first stage (turn to section 2.1) and represented within the framework provided by Brat[1], around 4 doctors from the same hospital annotated the events. This annotated set would work as a source of data to get instances that would serve to train supervised classification models, as the one referred in section 2.2.

2.2.2 Operational description of events

As it is well-known, the success of the techniques based on Machine Learning relies upon the features used to describe the instances. Hence, we selected the following features that eventually have proven useful to capture the semantic relations between ADRs. The features can be organised in the following sets:

- Concept-words and context-words: to be precise, we make use of entire terms including both single-words and multi-words.
  - DRUG concept-word together with left and right context words (a context up to 3, yielding, thus, 7 features).
  - DISEASE concept-word together with left and right context words (7 features).
- Concept-lemmas and context-lemmas for both drug and disease (14 features overall)
- Concept-POS and context-POS for both drug and disease (14 features)
- Negation and speculation: these are binary valued features to determine whether the concept words or their context was either negated or speculated (2 features).
- Presence/absence of other drugs in the context of the target drug and disease (12 features)
- Distance: the number of characters from the DRUG concept to the DISEASE concept (1 feature).

2.2.3 Inferring a supervised classifier

Given the operational description of a set of (DRUG, DISEASE) pairs, this stage has to deter-

[1]Brat is the framework a priori selected as the output front-end shown in Figure 1

mine if there exists an ADR event (that is, a cause-effect relation) or not. To do so, we resorted to Random Forests (RFs), a variety of ensemble models. RFs combine a number of decision trees being each tree built on the basis of the C4.5 algorithm (Quinlan, 1993) but with a distinctive characteristic: some randomness is introduced in the order in which the nodes are generated. Particularly, each time a node is generated in the tree, instead of chosing the attribute that maximizes the Information Gain, the attribute is randomly selected amongst the k best options. We made use of the implementation of this algorithm available in Weka-6.9 (Hall et al., 2009). Ensemble models were proved useful on drug-drug interaction extraction tasks (Thomas et al., 2011).

3 Experimental results

We count on data consisting of discharge summaries from Galdakao-Usansolo Hospital. The records are semi-structured in the sense that there are two main fields: the first one for personal data of the patient (age, dates relating to admittance) that were not provided by the hospital for privacy issues; and the second one, our target, a single field that contains the antecedents, treatment, clinical analysis, etc. This second field is an unstructured section (some hospitals rely upon templates that divide this field into several subfields, providing it with further structure). The discharge notes describe a chronological development of the patient's condition, the undergone treatments, and also the clinical tests that were carried out.

Given the entire set of manually annotated documents, 34% were randomly selected without replacement to produce the evaluation set. The resulting partition is presented in Table 1 (where the train and evaluation sets are referred to as Train and Eval respectivelly).

	Documents	**Concepts**	**Relations**
Train	144	6,105	4,675
Eval	50	2,206	1,598

Table 1: Quantitative description of the data.

All together, there are 194 EHRs manually tagged with more than 8,000 concepts (entailing diseases, symptoms, drugs, substances and procedures). From these EHRs all the (DRUG,DISEASE) pairs are taken into account as event candidates, and these are referred to as relations in Table 1.

The system was assessed using per-class averaged precision, recall and f1-measure as presented in Table 2.

Precision	**Recall**	**F1-measure**
0.932	0.849	0.883

Table 2: Experimental results.

Semantic knowledge and contextual features have proven very relevant to detect cause-effect relations. Particularly, those used to detect the concepts and also negation or speculation of the context in which the concept appear.

A manual inspection was carried out on both the false positives and false negative predictions and the following conclusions were drawn:

- The majority of false positives were caused by i) pairs of concepts at a very long distance; ii) pairs where one of the elements is related to past-events undergone while the other element is in the current treatment prescribed (e.g. the disease is in the antecedents and the drug in the current diagnostics).
- The vast majority of false negatives were due to concepts in the same sentence where the context-words are irrelevant (e.g. filler words, determiners, etc.).

4 Concluding Remarks and Future Work

This work presents a system that first identifies relevant pairs of concepts in EHRs by means of a shallow analysis and next examines all the pairs by an inferred supervised classifier to determine if a given pair represents a cause-effect event. A relevant contribution of this work is that we extract events occurring between concepts that are in different sentences. In addition, this is one of the first works on medical event extraction for Spanish.

Our aim for future work is to determine whether the (DRUG, DISEASE) pair represents either a relation where 1) the drug is to overcome the disease; 2) the drug causes the disease; 3) there is no relationship between the drug and the disease.

The aim of context features is to capture characteristics of the text surrounding the relevant concepts that trigger a relation. More features could also be explored such as trigger words, regular patterns, n-grams, etc.

Acknowledgments

The authors would like to thank the Pharmacy and Pharmacovigilance services of Galdakao-Usansolo Hospital.

This work was partially supported by the European Commission (325099 and SEP-210087649), the Spanish Ministry of Science and Innovation (TIN2012-38584-C06-02) and the Industry of the Basque Government (IT344-10).

References

Jari Björne, Filip Ginter, Sampo Pyysalo, Jun'ichi Tsujii, and Tapio Salakoski. 2010. Complex event extraction at pubmed scale. Bioinformatics [ISMB], 26(12):382–390.

Taxiarchis Botsis, Michael D. Nguyen, Emily Jane Woo, Marianthi Markatou, and Robert Ball. 2011. Text mining for the vaccine adverse event reporting system: medical text classification using informative feature selection. JAMIA, 18(5):631–638.

Mark Hall, Eibe Frank, Geoffrey Holmes, Bernhard Pfahringer, Peter Reutemann, and Ian H. Witten. 2009. The WEKA data mining software: An update. SIGKDD Explorations, 11(1):10–18.

Jin-Dong Kim, Sampo Pyysalo, Tomoko Ohta, Robert Bossy, Ngan Nguyen, and Jun'ichi Tsujii. 2011. Overview of bionlp shared task 2011. In Proceedings of the BioNLP Shared Task 2011 Workshop, pages 1–6. Association for Computational Linguistics.

Claudiu Mihaila, Tomoko Ohta, Sampo Pyysalo, and Sophia Ananiadou. 2013. Biocause: Annotating and analysing causality in the biomedical domain. BMC Bioinformatics, 14:2.

Maite Oronoz, Arantza Casillas, Koldo Gojenola, and Alicia Perez. 2013. Automatic annotation of medical records in Spanish with disease, drug and substance names. In Lecture Notes in Computer Science, volume 8259, pages 536–547. Springer-Verlag.

Lluis Padró, S. Reese, Eneko Agirre, and Aitor Soroa. 2010. Semantic Services in Freeling 2.1: WordNet and UKB. In Global Wordnet Conference, Mumbai, India.

Ross Quinlan. 1993. C4.5: Programs for Machine Learning. Morgan Kaufmann Publishers, San Mateo, CA.

Bryan Rink, Sanda Harabagiu, and Kirk Roberts. 2011. Automatic extraction of relations between medical concepts in clinical texts. JAMIA, 18:594–600.

Isabel Segura-Bedmar, P Martínez, and Marıa Herrero-Zazo. 2013. Semeval-2013 task 9: Extraction of drug-drug interactions from biomedical texts (ddiextraction 2013). Proceedings of Semeval, pages 341–350.

Pontus Stenetorp, Sampo Pyysalo, Goran Topić, Tomoko Ohta, Sophia Ananiadou, and Jun'ichi Tsujii. 2012. Brat: A web-based tool for nlp-assisted text annotation. In In Proceedings of the Demonstrations Session at EACL 2012.

Philippe Thomas, Mariana Neves, Illés Solt, Domonkos Tikk, and Ulf Leser. 2011. Relation extraction for drug-drug interactions using ensemble learning. 1st Challenge task on Drug-Drug Interaction Extraction (DDIExtraction 2011), pages 11–18.

Luca Toldo, Sanmitra Bhattacharya, and Harsha Gurulingappa. 2012. Automated identification of adverse events from case reports using machine learning. In Workshop on Computational Methods in Pharmacovigilance.

Limsoon Wong. 2001. A protein interaction extraction system. In Pacific Symposium on Biocomputing, volume 6, pages 520–531. Citeseer.

Reducing VSM data sparseness by generalizing contexts: application to health text mining

Amandine Périnet
INSERM, U1142, LIMICS, Paris, France
Sorbonne Universités, UPMC Univ Paris 06, Paris, France
Université Paris 13, Sorbonne Paris Cité, Villetaneuse, France
amandine.perinet@edu.univ-paris13.fr

Thierry Hamon
LIMSI-CNRS, Orsay, France
Université Paris 13, Sorbonne Paris Cité
Villetaneuse, France
hamon@limsi.fr

Abstract

Vector Space Models are limited with low frequency words due to few available contexts and data sparseness. To tackle this problem, we generalize contexts by integrating semantic relations acquired with linguistic approaches. We use three methods that acquire hypernymy relations on a EHR corpus. Context Generalization obtains the best results when performed with hypernyms, the quality of the relations being more important than the quantity.

1 Introduction

Distributional Analysis (DA) (Harris, 1954; Firth, 1957) computes a similarity between target words from the contexts shared by those two words. This hypothesis is applied with geometric methods, such as the Vector Space Model (VSM) (Turney and Pantel, 2010). The advantage of the VSM is that the similarity of word meaning can be easily quantified by measuring their distance in the vector space, or the cosine of the angle between them (Mitchell and Lapata, 2010). On the other hand, a major inconvenience is data sparseness within the matrix that represents the vector space (Turney and Pantel, 2010). The data sparseness problem is the consequence of the word distribution in a corpus (Baroni et al., 2009): in any corpus, most of the words have a very low frequency and appear only a few times. Thus, those words have a limited set of contexts and similarity is difficult to catch. Thus, methods based on DA perform better when more information is available (Weeds and Weir, 2005; van der Plas, 2008) and are efficient with large corpora of general language. But with specialized texts, as EHR texts that are usually of smaller size, reducing data sparseness is a major issue and methods need to be adapted.

Semantic grouping of contexts should decrease their diversity, and thus increase the frequency of the remaining generalized contexts. We assume that generalizing contexts may influence the distributional context frequencies. Information for generalization can be issued from existing resources or can be computed by linguistic approaches. In this paper, we propose to use semantic relations acquired by relation acquisition methods to group words in contexts. We define a method that switches words in DA contexts for their hierarchical parent or morphosyntactic variant that have been computed on the corpus with linguistic approaches before applying the VSM method.

In the following, we first present the related work, then our method and we finally describe the different experiments we led. The results obtained on the EHR corpus are then evaluated in terms of precision and MAP, and analyzed.

2 Related work

Our approach relates with works that influence distributional contexts to improve the performance of VSMs. Some of them intend to change the way to consider contexts; Broda et al. (2009) do not use the raw context frequency in DA, but they first rank contexts according to their frequency, and take the rank into account. Other models use statistical language models to determine the most likely substitutes to represent the contexts (Baskaya et al., 2013). They assign probabilities to arbitrary sequences of words that are then used to create word pairs to feed a co-occurrence model, before performing a clustered algorithm (Yuret, 2012). The limit of such methods is that their performance is proportional to vocabulary size and requires the availability of training data.

Influence on contexts may also be performed by embedding additional semantic information. The semantic relations may be issued from an existing resource or automatically computed. With a method based on bootstrapping, Zhitomirsky-Geffet and Dagan (2009) modify the weights of the elements in contexts relying on the semantic neighbors found with a distributional similarity measure. Based on this work, Ferret (2013) uses a set of examples selected from an original distributional thesaurus to train a supervised classifier. This classifier is then applied for reranking the neighbors of the thesaurus selection. Within Vector Space Model, Tsatsaronis and Panagiotopoulou (2009) use a word thesaurus to interpret the orthogonality of terms and measure semantic relatedness.

With the same purpose of solving the problem of data sparseness, other methods are based on dimensionality reduction, such as Latent Semantic Analysis (LSA) in (Padó and Lapata, 2007) or Non-negative Matrix Factorization (NMF) (Zheng et al., 2011). Matrix decomposition techniques are usually applied to reduce the dimensionality of the original matrix, thereby rendering it more informative (Mitchell and Lapata, 2010).

Our approach differs from the aforementioned ones in that we add semantic information in contexts to reduce the number of contexts and to increase their frequency. Contrary to these latter approaches, we do not reduce the contexts by removing information but by generalyzing information and integrating extra semantic knowledge.

3 VSM and context generalization

The contexts in which occurs a target word have associated frequencies which may be used to form probability estimates. The goal of our method is to influence the distributional context frequencies by generalizing contexts.

Step 1: target and context definition During this step, we define targets and contexts, with different constraints for their extraction. To adapt our method to specialized texts, we identify terms (specific terminological entities that denote an event) with a term extractor (YaTeA (Aubin and Hamon, 2006)). Target words are both nouns and terms (T). Their distributional contexts correspond to a graphical window of n number of words around the targets (Wilks et al., 1990; Schütze, 1998; Lund and Burgess, 1996). We consider two different window sizes defined in section 4.

Linguistic approaches During the generalization process, we use three existing linguistic approaches: two that acquire hypernymy relations and one to get morphosyntactic variants. Lexico-syntactic Patterns (LSP) acquire hypernymy relations. We use the patterns defined by (Hearst, 1992). Lexical Inclusion (LI) acquires hypernymy relations and uses the syntactic analysis of the terms. Based on the hypothesis that if a term is lexically included in another, generally there is a hypernymy relation between the two terms (*kidney transplant - cadaveric kidney transplant*) (Bodenreider et al., 2001). Terminological Variation (TV) acquires both hypernyms and synonyms. TV uses rules that define a morpho-syntactic transformation, mainly the insertion (*blood transfusion - blood cell transfusion* (Jacquemin, 1996).

Step 2: context generalization Once targets and contexts are defined, we generalize contexts with the relations acquired by the three linguistic approaches we mentioned. To integrate the relations in contexts, we replace words in context by their hypernym or morphosyntactic variant. We define two rules: (1) if the context matches with one hypernym, context is replaced by this hypernym. (2) if the context matches with several hypernyms or variants, we take the hypernym or variant frequency into account, and choose the most frequent hypernym/variant. The generalization step is individually or sequentially performed when several relation sets are available.

Step 3: computation of semantic similarity After the generalization step, similarity between target words is computed. As we previously decrease diversity in contexts, we choose a measure that favors words appearing in similar contexts. We use the Jaccard Index (Grefenstette, 1994) which normalizes the number of contexts shared by two words by the total number of contexts of those two words.

Parameter: thresholds The huge number of relations we obtain after computing similarity between targets leads us to remove the supposed wrong relations with three thresholds: (i) number of shared lemmatized contexts (2 for a large window, 1 for a small window) ; (ii) number of the lemmatized contexts (2 for a large window, 1 for a small window) ; (iii) number of the lemmatized targets (3 for both window sizes). For each parameter, the threshold is automatically computed, according to the corpus, as the mean of the values of parameters on the corpus. And we experiment two thresholds on similarity score we empirically defined : $sim > 0.001$ and $sim > 0.0005$.

4 Experiments

In this section, we present the material we use for the experiments and evaluation, and the distributional parameter values of the VSM automatically determined from the data. We then describe the generalization sets we experiment and the evaluation measures we used for evaluation.

4.1 Corpus

We use the collection of anonymous clinical English texts provided by the 2012 i2b2/VA challenge (Sun et al., 2013).

The corpus is pre-processed within the Ogmios platform (Hamon et al., 2007). We perform morphosyntactic tagging and lemmatization with Tree Tagger (Schmid, 1994), and term extraction with YATEA (Aubin and Hamon, 2006).

4.2 Distributional parameters

We consider two window sizes: a large window of 21 words ($\pm$ 10 words, centered on the target, henceforth W21) and a narrow one of 5 words ($\pm$ 2 words, centered on the target, W5).

The window size influences on the type, the volume and the quality of the acquired relations. Generally, the smaller windows allow to acquire more relevant contexts for a target, but increase the data sparseness problem (Rapp, 2003). They give better results for classical types of relations (eg. synonymy), whereas larger windows are more appropriate for domain relations (eg. collocations)(Sahlgren, 2006; Peirsman et al., 2008).

4.3 Generalizing distributional contexts

We define several sets of context generalization. We experiment in step 2 different ways of generalizing contexts. We use as a baseline the VSM without any generalization in the contexts (VSMonly), and compare the generalization sets to it.

Regarding context generalization, we first exploit the relations acquired from only one linguistic approach. We apply the method described at the section 3 (step 2) by separately using the three different sets of relations automatically acquired. Distributional contexts are replaced by their hypernym acquired with lexico-syntactic patterns (VSM/LSP) and lexical inclusion (VSM/LI), and by their morphosyntactic variants acquired with terminological variation (VSM/TV). Then, we replace contexts with relations acquired by two approaches (TV then LI, LSP then TV, etc.). This generalization is done sequentially: we generalize all the contexts with the relations acquired by one method (e.g. LI), and then with the relations acquired by another method (e.g. TV). And finally, similarly to what we perform with two methods, we experiment the generalization of contexts by relations acquired with the three different linguistic approaches (e.g. LSP then LI then TV). We experiment all the possible combinations. With both the single and multiple generalization, we aim at evaluating the contribution of each method but also the impact of the order of the methods.

4.4 Evaluation

In order to evaluate the quality of the acquired relations, we compare our relations to the 53,203 UMLS relations between terms occurring in our EHR corpus. We perform the evaluation with the Mean Average Precision (MAP) (Buckley and Voorhees, 2005) and the macro-precision computed for each target word: semantic neighbors found in the resource by the total semantic neighbors acquired by our method. We consider three sets of neighbors: precision after examining 1 (P@1), 5 (P@5) and 10 (P@10) neighbors.

5 Results and discussion

Best results are obtained with a large window of 21 words, with a precision P@1 of 0.243 against 0.032 for a 5 word window, both for VSMonly, with a threshold of 0.001. Thus, a high threshold on the similarity score is not always relevant. We observe on this corpus that the generalization with the several linguistic approaches does not improve the results. For instance, VSM/LI obtains 0.250 of P@1 with a $>$ 0.001 threshold, and this precision is the same with VSM/LI+TV and with VSM/LI+LSP. This is an interesting behavior, different from what have been observed so far on more general French corpora that contains cooking recipes (Périnet and Hamon, 2013).

We discuss here the results we obtain for terms, for the two thresholds on the similarity score: a low and a higher thresholds, with relations with a similarity above 0.0005 and above 0.001. We observe that with a higher threshold, the precision is higher, with a P@1 of 0.243 against 0.187 for the lower threshold (when considering VSMonly). As for the number of relations acquired, with a lower threshold we obtain more relations (3,936 relations acquired for the baseline) than with a higher threshold (326 relations for the baseline).

We evaluate precison after examining three groups of neighbors. The best results are obtained with P@1, and in most cases, precision decreases when we consider more neighbors: the more neighbors we consider, the lower precision is. For a 0.001 threshold, the generalized experiment sets obtain a higher precision than VSMonly, in any case. While for a 0005 threshold, the use of LI to generalize contexts decreases the precision. We also observe that when considering generalisation with TV or LSP only, or their combination, the P@10 is slightly better than P@5.

The MAP values are higher when the thresold on the similarity measure is low, with 0.446 for VSM/LI against 0.089 with the > 0.001 threshold. It means that some correct relations are not well ranked with the similarity score, but are still present. We observe that the MAP values are always higher with the generalization sets than with the baseline with both thresholds: 0.089 for VSM/LI, 0.446 for VSM/LI+LSP, etc.

Comparison of the experimental sets When considering the relations found in the UMLS, we observe that the generalization with LSP brings the same relations that the baseline VSMonly plus 22 relations, the generalization with TV brings 16 more relations that VSMonly, and finally that the generalization with LI decreases the number of relations acquired. When the generalization of the contexts is performed with LI, only with LI or with LI combined to another method, it decreases the number of relations acquired as well as the number of relations found in the resource. On the contrary, generalizing contexts with LSP increases the number of relations acquired as well as the number of relations found in the UMLS resource. We obtain the highest number of relations when generalizing contexts with LSP, with 454 relations, and the highest precision with 0.273 for P@1.

Comparing those results with the relations acquired with the linguistic approaches on the EHR corpus shows a correlation between the quality of the relations acquired with the generalized sets and the relations used for generalization. Indeed, LI gives the highest number of relations with 14,437 relations, then TV gives 631 relations, and finally LSP acquires only three relations: *pancreatic complication - necrosis*, *pancreatic complication - abscess*, *gentle laxative - milk of magnesia*.

With these relations, if the second term (eg. *necrosis*) is found in the context, it is replaced by the first term (eg. *pancreatic complication*). These three relations used for generalization give better results in terms of precision that the many relations given by the two other approaches. We could deduce that the number of relations may not be as important as their quality when they are used for generalization. But when the LSP are used after TV or LI, they do not improve the results. From this observation, we make the hypothesis that these second terms may have already been replaced during the generalization with LI or TV. To confirm or reject this hypothesis, we look closer to the relations acquired with TV and LI. In TV, we find no relation including any of these second terms. On the contrary, with LI, we found the relation *milk - milk of magnesia* that inhibits one of the three relations acquired with the LSP.

We deduce that even if the quality of the relations used for generalization is more important than their number, the number of relations still matters. If generalization is first performed with a great number of relations, then a small number of relations used for generalization is not enough and does not improve the results.

6 Conclusion and perspectives

In this work, we face the problem of data sparseness of distributional methods. This problem especially arises from specialized corpora which have a smaller size and in which words and terms have lower frequencies.

To achieve this goal, we propose to generalize distributional contexts with hypernyms and variants acquired by three existing approaches. We focus on the acquistion of relations between terms. We experimented several generalization sets, using one, two or the three methods sequentially to replace words in context by their hypernym or variant. Evaluation of the method has been performed on an EHR English text collection. Generalization obtains the best results when realized with hypernyms. The quality of the relations matters much more than their number: few but good relations used to generalize contexts give better results than many relations of poorer quality. For future work, we plan to use for generalization relations issued from different distributional and terminological resources. Finally, we will intend to combine the methods before normalization.

References

Sophie Aubin and Thierry Hamon. 2006. Improving term extraction with terminological resources. In *Advances in Natural Language Processing*, number 4139 in LNAI, pages 380–387. Springer.

Marco Baroni, Silvia Bernardini, Adriano Ferraresi, and Eros Zanchetta. 2009. The wacky wide web: a collection of very large linguistically processed web-crawled corpora. *Language Resources and Evaluation*, 43(3):209–226.

Osman Baskaya, Enis Sert, Volkan Cirik, and Deniz Yuret. 2013. Ai-ku: Using substitute vectors and co-occurrence modeling for word sense induction and disambiguation. In *Proceedings of SemEval - 2013*, pages 300–306, Atlanta, Georgia, USA. Association for Computational Linguistics.

Olivier Bodenreider, Anita Burgun, and Thomas Rindflesch. 2001. Lexically-suggested hyponymic relations among medical terms and their representation in the umls. In *TIA 2001*, pages 11–21.

Bartosz Broda, Maciej Piasecki, and Stan Szpakowicz. 2009. Rank-based transformation in measuring semantic relatedness. In Yong Gao and Nathalie Japkowicz, editors, *Canadian Conference on AI*, volume 5549, pages 187–190. Springer.

Chris Buckley and Ellen Voorhees. 2005. Retrieval system evaluation. In Ellen Voorhees and Donna Harman, editors, *TREC: Experiment and Evaluation in Information Retrieval*, chapter 3. MIT Press.

Olivier Ferret. 2013. Sélection non supervisée de relations sémantiques pour améliorer un thésaurus distributionnel. In *TALN 2013*, pages 48–61, Les Sables d'Olonne, France.

J.R. Firth. 1957. A synopsis of linguistic theory 1930-1955. *Studies in linguistic analysis*, pages 1–32.

Gregory Grefenstette. 1994. Corpus-derived first, second and third-order word affinities. In *Sixth Euralex International Congress*, pages 279–290.

T. Hamon, A. Nazarenko, T. Poibeau, S. Aubin, and J. Derivière. 2007. A robust linguistic platform for efficient and domain specific web content analysis. In *RIAO 2007*, Pittsburgh, USA.

Zellig Harris. 1954. Distributional structure. *Word*, 10(23):146–162.

Marti A. Hearst. 1992. Automatic acquisition of hyponyms from large text corpora. In *International Conference on Computational Linguistics*, pages 539–545, Nantes, France.

Christian Jacquemin. 1996. A symbolic and surgical acquisition of terms through variation. In *CoRR*, pages 425–438.

K. Lund and C. Burgess. 1996. Producing high-dimensional semantic spaces from lexical co-occurrence. *Behavior Research Methods, Instrumentation, and Computers*, 28:203–208.

Jeff Mitchell and Mirella Lapata. 2010. Composition in distributional models of semantics. *Cognitive Science*, 34(8):1388–1429.

Sebastian Padó and Mirella Lapata. 2007. Dependency-based construction of semantic space models. *Comput. Linguist.*, 33(2):161–199.

Yves Peirsman, Heylen Kris, and Geeraerts Dirk. 2008. Size matters. tight and loose context definitions in english word space models. In *ESSLLI Workshop on Distributional Lexical Semantics*, Hamburg, Germany.

Amandine Périnet and Thierry Hamon. 2013. Hybrid acquisition of semantic relations based on context normalization in distributional analysis. In *Proceedings of TIA 2013*, pages 113–120, Paris, France.

Reinhard Rapp. 2003. Word sense discovery based on sense descriptor dissimilarity. In *MT Summit'2003*, pages 315–322.

Magnus Sahlgren. 2006. *The Word-Space Model: Using Distributional Analysis to Represent Syntagmatic and Paradigmatic Relations between Words in High-Dimensional Vector Spaces*. Ph.D. thesis, Stockholm University, Stockholm, Sweden.

H. Schmid. 1994. Probabilistic part-of-speech tagging using decision trees. In *New Methods in Language Processing*, pages 44–49, Manchester, UK.

Hinrich Schütze. 1998. Automatic word sense discrimination. *Comput. Linguist.*, 24(1):97–123.

Weiyi Sun, Anna Rumshisky, and Özlem Uzuner. 2013. Evaluating temporal relations in clinical text: 2012 i2b2 challenge. *JAMIA*, 20(5):806–813.

George Tsatsaronis and Vicky Panagiotopoulou. 2009. A generalized vector space model for text retrieval based on semantic relatedness. In *EACL 2009*, pages 70–78, Stroudsburg, PA, USA.

Peter D. Turney and Patrick Pantel. 2010. From frequency to meaning: Vector space models of semantics. *JAIR*, 37:141–188.

Lonneke van der Plas. 2008. *Automatic lexico-semantic acquisition for question answering*. Thèse de doctorat, University of Groningen, Groningen.

Julie Weeds and David Weir. 2005. Co-occurrence retrieval: A flexible framework for lexical distributional similarity. *Comput. Linguist.*, 31(4):439–475.

Yorick A. Wilks, Dan, James E. Mcdonald, Tony Plate, and Brian M. Slator. 1990. Providing machine tractable dictionary tools. *Journal of Machine Translation*, 2.

Deniz Yuret. 2012. Fastsubs: An efficient and exact procedure for finding the most likely lexical substitutes based on an n-gram language model. *IEEE Signal Process. Lett.*, 19(11):725–728.

Wenbin Zheng, Yuntao Qian, and Hong Tang. 2011. Dimensionality reduction with category information fusion and non-negative matrix factorization for text categorization. In Hepu Deng, Duoqian Miao, Jingsheng Lei, and Fu Lee Wang, editors, *AICI*, volume 7004 of *LNCS*, pages 505–512.

Maayan Zhitomirsky-Geffet and Ido Dagan. 2009. Bootstrapping distributional feature vector quality. *Comput. Linguist.*, 35(3):435–461.

Disambiguation of Period Characters in Clinical Narratives

Markus Kreuzthaler and **Stefan Schulz**
Institute for Medical Informatics, Statistics and Documentation
Medical University of Graz
`<markus.kreuzthaler,stefan.schulz>@medunigraz.at`

Abstract

The period character's meaning is highly ambiguous due to the frequency of abbreviations that require to be followed by a period. We have developed a hybrid method for period character disambiguation and the identification of abbreviations, combining rules that explore regularities in the right context of the period with lexicon-based, statistical methods which scrutinize the preceding token. The texts under scrutiny are clinical discharge summaries. Both abbreviation detection and sentence delimitation showed an accuracy of about 93%. An error analysis demonstrated potential for further improvements.

1 Introduction

The full stop, or period character, is ambiguous. As well as its use as a sentence delimiter, it is often collocated with abbreviations ("Prof."), occurs in numeric expressions ("13.2 mg"), including dates, and appears in a series of special names such as Web addresses. Minor variations exist between languages and dialects (for example the use of the period as decimal delimiter), and rule variations exist that guide its collocation with abbreviations. The character-wise analysis of text can produce a clear distinction between (i) period characters that are enclosed between two alphanumeric characters, and (ii) period characters that are adjacent to at least one non-alphabetic character. Whereas in the former case the period character can be considered an internal part of a token, the latter allows for two interpretations:

1. Period characters that are mandatorily collocated with abbreviations; and

2. Period characters as sentence delimiters.

We focus on text produced by physicians at the point of care, either directly or via dictation. The sublanguage of clinical narratives is characterized, among other peculiarities such as misspellings, punctuation errors, and incomplete sentences, by the abundance of acronyms and abbreviations (Meystre et al., 2008). It is for this reason that we focus here on the use of the period character to distinguish between sentence limits and abbreviations.

A snippet from a medical text illustrates some typical phenomena:

```
 3. St.p. TE eines exulz.
sek.knot.SSM (C43.5) li Lab.
majus. Level IV, 2,42 mm
Tumordurchm.
```

In "`3.`" the period marks an ordinal number; "`St.p.`" is the abbreviation of "Status post" (state after); "`TE`" is an acronym derived from "Totale Exzision". "`Exulz.`" and "`Tumordurchm.`" are ad-hoc abbreviations for "exulzerierendes" and "Tumordurchmesser" (tumour diameter), respectively. "`sek.knot.SSM`" is an ill-formed agglutination of two abbreviations and one acronym. In correctly formatted text, they would be separated by spaces ("`sek. knot. SSM`"). The abbreviation "`sek.`" (secondary) is written in a common lexicalized form, whereas "`knot.`" is, once again, an ad-hoc creation. "`SSM`" is an acronym for "Superfiziell Spreitendes Melanom". "`C43.5`" is a code from the International Classification of Diseases[1]. "`Lab.`" means "Labium", a common anatomical abbreviation. "`IV`" is not an acronym, but a Roman number. "`2,42`" is a decimal number, demonstrating that the comma rather than the period is used as a decimal separator in German texts. Finally, the abbreviation "`Tumordurchm.`" exemplifies that

[1] http://www.who.int/classifications/icd/en/

the period can play a double role, *viz.* to mark an abbreviation and to conclude a sentence.

In this paper we will describe and evaluate a methodology that is able to identify and distinguish the following: (i) periods that act as sentence delimiters after ordinary words (such as the period after "majus") marked as **NSD** (normal sentence delimiter); (ii) periods as abbreviation markers in the middle of a sentence, marked as **MAM** (mid-sentence abbreviation marker), and (iii) periods that are both abbreviation markers and sentence delimiters, marked as **EAM** (end-sentence abbreviation marker). From this ternary distinction, two binary tasks can be derived, *viz.* the detection of abbreviations (MAM and EAM), and the detection of sentence endings (NSD and EAM).

2 Materials and Methods

2.1 Data

We used 1,696 discharge summaries extracted and anonymized from a clinical information system. They had an average word count of 302, with a mean of 55 period characters per document. The texts were divided into a learning set (1.526 documents) and an evaluation set (170 documents). Two word lists were created in advance: (i) a medical domain dictionary (MDDict) with a high coverage of domain-specific terms, excluding abbreviations, and (ii) a closed-class dictionary (CCDict) containing common, domain-independent word forms.

For **MDDict**, words were harvested from three sources: a free dictionary of contemporary German[2], a word list created out of raw text extracted from a medical dictionary on CD-ROM (Pschyrembel, 1997), and medical texts and forum postings from a patient-centered website[3]. The final list comprised approximately 1.45 million types, which were subsequently indexed with Lucene[4]. This dictionary was modified during a second step by two Web resources containing German abbreviations[5,6]. We accumulated about 5,800 acronym and abbreviation tokens, which were then removed from the Lucene-indexed dictionary, in order to transform MDDict into a resource mostly devoid of abbreviations.

[2]http://sourceforge.net/projects/germandict/
[3]http://www.netdoktor.at/
[4]https://lucene.apache.org/core/
[5]http://de.wikipedia.org/wiki/Medizinische_Abkürzungen
[6]http://de.wiktionary.org/wiki/Kategorie:Abkürzung

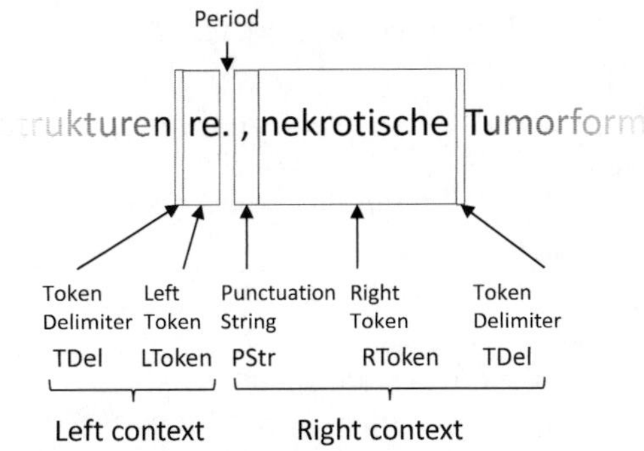

Figure 1: Period pattern and zoning of left and right context.

For **CCDict** we harvested closed-class words from a German web resource[7], i.e. prepositions, determiners, conjunctions, and pronouns, together with auxiliary and modal verbs. The purpose of this was to arrive at a comprehensive list of word forms that can only be capitalized at the beginning of a sentence.

Figure 1 shows the pattern used to identify periods of interest for this study. The right and the left context were zoned as followed: The string to the left of the period until the preceding token delimiter is the "Left Token" (**LToken**). The sequence of spaces, line breaks, or punctuation marks to the right of the period ("Punctuation String") is identified as **PStr**. The following token, spanning from the first alphanumeric character to the character left to the next delimiter, is named **RToken**.

2.2 Context evaluation

The right context is evaluated first (Algorithm 1). It is based on the following assumptions: (i) Whenever a period terminates a sentence, the first character in the following token is capitalized. For a subset of words this can be ascertained by looking up the closed word class dictionary CCDict (the restriction to "closed classes" is due to the fact that German nouns are mandatorily capitalized, including nominalized adjectives and verbs); (ii) A sentence can never be split by a line break, therefore a period that precedes the break necessarily marks the end of the previous sentence; (iii) Most punctuation signs that follow a period strongly indicate that the period character here plays the role of an abbreviation marker and does not coincide with an end-of-sentence marker. Only in the case where a decision could not be achieved using the

[7]http://www.deutschegrammatik20.de/

if *RToken begins with lower case character* **then**
  → MAM;
else
  if *decapitalized RToken matches closed class token* **then**
    → EAM or NSD;
  else
    if *If PStr contains punctuation character* **then**
      → MAM;
    else
      if *If PStr contains a line break* **then**
        → NSD or EAM;
      else
        → NSD or MAM or EAM;
      end
    end
  end
end

Algorithm 1: Rule-based decision algorithm for the right context of a period.

algorithm is the left context investigated.

The evaluation of the left context extends the approach from Kiss and Strunk (2002), who used the *log likelihood ratio* (Dunning, 1993) for abbreviation detection:

$$log\lambda = -2log(L(H_0)/L(H_A))$$

H_0 is the hypothesis that the occurrence of a period is independent of the preceding word, H_A the hypothesis that it is not independent.

We use four scaling functions S_1 – S_4. The period character is symbolized by $\bullet$; $C(word, \bullet)$ and $C(word, \neg\bullet)$ describe the co-occurrence frequency counts. The primary $log\lambda$ is modified by sequential composition. Following Kiss and Strunk (2002), S_1 enhances the initial $log\lambda$ if $C(word, \bullet)$ is greater than $C(word, \neg\bullet)$. S_2 varies from -1 to 1 depending on $C(word, \bullet)$ and $C(word, \neg\bullet)$. S_3 leads to a reduction of $log\lambda$ depending on the length of the preceding word. We introduced a fourth scaling function S_4, which reflects the fact that most abbreviations are proper substrings of the shortened original word (e.g. "exulz." = "exulzerierend"), with N being the sum of all found substring matches in the form $subword_i*$ for every $subword_i$ in $subword_1 \bullet subword_2 \bullet \ldots subword_n \bullet$ in a Lucene search result.

$$S_4(log\lambda) : log\lambda + N(word, \bullet)$$

This also includes those abbreviations which have an internal period, such as "St.p". The reason why the last scaling function contains an addition, is to accommodate for cases where $C(word, \bullet) < C(word, \neg\bullet)$ even when $word$ is an abbreviation. These cases, for which the weighted $log\lambda$ is negative, could then nevertheless be pushed to the positive side in the result of a strong S_4.

For the final decision in favor of an abbreviation, we required that the following two conditions hold: (i) $(S_1 \circ S_2 \circ S_3 \circ S_4)(log\lambda) > 0$; (ii) the length of the abbreviation candidate was within the 95% confidence interval, given the statistical distribution of all abbreviation candidates that exhibited a significant collocation ($p < 0.01$), $C(word, \bullet) > C(word, \neg\bullet)$, and MDDict not containing $word$.

3 Results

For the evaluation methodology, a gold standard was created by a random selection of 500 text frames, centered around a period with its left and right context (each 60 characters) from the evaluation set. The two authors rated each period in the center of the snippet as being an NSD, a MAM or an EAM. A subset of 100 was rated by both authors in order to compute the inter-rater agreement. We obtained a Cohen's kappa (Di Eugenio and Glass, 2004, Hripcsak and Heitjan, 2002) of 0.98, when rating both abbreviation vs. non-abbreviation, and sentence delimiter vs. non sentence delimiter, respectively. Accuracy, true and false negative rates (Manning et al., 2008), are computed for the two processing steps in isolation. This required making some default assumptions for the cases in which the result was ambiguous. The assumptions are based on frequency distributions of the three values in the learning set. The left context processing detects abbreviations, but is unable to distinguish between EAM and MAM. As the frequency of MAM is much higher, this value is set wherever NSD is discarded. In the processing of the right context, the algorithm may fail to disambiguate between NSD vs. EAM, or even terminate with any decision (NSD vs. EAM vs. MAM), cf. Algorithm 1. In the latter case MAM is set, as this was determined to be the most frequent phenomenon in the learning data (0.53). In the former case, NSD is given preference over EAM, which has a low frequency in the learning set (0.03). Table 1 shows accuracy and false positive / negative rates obtained by left, right and combined context evaluations.

	Accuracy	Fpos	Fneg
Abbreviation detection			
Left	0.914	0.035	0.136
Right	0.880	0.162	0.051
L & R	0.928	0.060	0.082
Sentence delimitation			
Left	0.902	0.107	0.077
Right	0.884	0.014	0.211
L & R	0.934	0.062	0.065

Table 1: Abbreviation detection and sentence delimitation results.

It is remarkable that the combination of both algorithms only produces a moderate gain in accuracy. For the minimization of certain false negatives and false positives, it can be advantageous to consider the right or left context separately. For instance, the right context algorithm alone is better at minimizing false positive sentence recognitions, whereas the left context algorithm is better suited at minimizing cases of false positive abbreviation detections. Apart from known issues such as the above mentioned parsing problems, for which the reader needs to be familiar with the domain and the style of the documents, the analysis of misclassifications revealed several weaknesses: sensitivity to spelling and punctuation errors (especially missing spaces after periods) and abbreviations that can also be read as a normal word (e.g. "Mal." for "Malignität" or "Mal" (time)), and abbreviations that are still present in MDDict.

4 Related Work

The detection of short forms (abbreviations, acronyms) is important due to their frequency in medical texts (Meystre et al., 2008). Several authors studied their detection, normalization, and context-dependent mapping to long forms (Xu et al., 2012). CLEF 2013 (Suominen et al., 2013) started a task for acronym/abbreviation normalization, using the UMLS[8] as target terminology. An F-Measure of 0.89 was reported by Patrick et al. (2013). Four different methods for abbreviation detection were tested by Xu et al. (2007). The fourth method (a decision tree classifier), which additionally used features from knowledge resources, performed best with a precision of 91.4% and a recall of 80.3%. Therefore Wu et al. (2011) compared machine learning methods for abbreviation detection. Word formation, vowel combinations, related content from knowledge bases, word frequency in the overall corpus, and local context were used as features. The random forest classifier performed best with an F-Measure of 94.8%. A combination of classifiers lead to the highest F-Measure of 95.7%. Wu et al. (2012) compared different clinical natural language processing systems on handling abbreviations in discharge summaries, resulting in MedLEE performing best with an F-Score of 0.60. A prototypical system, meeting real-time constraints, is described in Wu et al. (2013).

[8]http://www.nlm.nih.gov/research/umls/

5 Conclusion and Outlook

We have presented and evaluated a method for disambiguating the period character in German-language medical narratives. It is a combination of a simple rule set and a statistical approach supported by lexicons. Whereas the crafting of the rule base considers peculiarities of the document language, primarily by exploiting language-specific capitalization rules, the processing of the external language resources and the statistical methodology are unsupervised. Given these parameters, the accuracy values of about 93% for both abbreviation detection and sentence delineation are satisfactory, especially when one considers that the texts are error laden and highly compact, which also resulted in large numbers of ad-hoc abbreviations. We expect that with a limited training effort this rate can still be raised further. We are aware that the described period disambiguation procedure should be embedded into an NLP processing pipeline, where it must be preceded by a cleansing process that identifies "hidden" periods and restores the adherence to basic punctuation rules by inserting white spaces where necessary. An improved result can facilitate the creation of a sufficiently large, manually annotated corpus, which could then be used as the basis for the application of machine learning methods. Furthermore, the impact of the different modifications regarding the left context approach must be evaluated in more detail.

References

Barbara Di Eugenio and Michael Glass. 2004. The kappa statistic: A second look. *Computational linguistics*, 30(1):95–101.

T Dunning. 1993. Accurate methods for the statistics of surprise and coincidence. *Computational Linguistics*, 19(1):61–74.

George Hripcsak and Daniel F Heitjan. 2002. Measuring agreement in medical informatics reliability studies. *Journal of biomedical informatics*, 35(2):99–110.

T Kiss and J Strunk. 2002. Scaled log likelihood ratios for the detection of abbreviations in text corpora. In *Proceedings of the 19th International Conference on Computational Linguistics – Volume 2*, pages 1–5. Association for Computational Linguistics.

Christopher D Manning, Prabhakar Raghavan, and Hinrich Schütze. 2008. *Introduction to information retrieval*, volume 1. Cambridge university press Cambridge.

S M Meystre, GK Savova, KC Kipper-Schuler, and JF Hurdle. 2008. Extracting information from textual documents in the electronic health record: a review of recent research. *Yearbook of Medical Informatics*, 35:128–144.

JD Patrick, L Safari, and Y Ou. 2013. ShaARe/CLEF eHealth 2013 Normalization of Acronyms/Abbreviation Challenge. In *CLEF 2013 Evaluation Labs and Workshop Abstracts - Working Notes*.

Pschyrembel. 1997. Klinisches Wörterbuch. CD-ROM Version 1/97.

Hanna Suominen, Sanna Salanterä, Sumithra Velupillai, Wendy W Chapman, Guergana Savova, Noemie Elhadad, Sameer Pradhan, Brett R South, Danielle L Mowery, Gareth JF Jones, et al. 2013. Overview of the share/clef ehealth evaluation lab 2013. In *Information Access Evaluation. Multilinguality, Multimodality, and Visualization*, pages 212–231. Springer.

Y Wu, ST Rosenbloom, JC Denny, A Miller, S Mani, Giuse DA, and H Xu. 2011. Detecting abbreviations in discharge summaries using machine learning methods. In *AMIA Annual Symposium Proceedings*, volume 2011, pages 1541–1549.

Y Wu, JC Denny, ST Rosenbloom, RA Miller, DA Giuse, and H Xu. 2012. A comparative study of current clinical natural language processing systems on handling abbreviations in discharge summaries. In *AMIA Annual Symposium Proceedings*, volume 2012, pages 997–1003.

Y Wu, JC Denny, ST Rosenbloom, Randolph A Miller, Dario A Giuse, Min Song, and Hua Xu. 2013. A prototype application for real-time recognition and disambiguation of clinical abbreviations. In *Proc. of the 7th International Workshop on Data and Text Mining in Biomedical Informatics*, pages 7–8.

H Xu, PD Stetson, and C Friedman. 2007. A study of abbreviations in clinical notes. In *AMIA Annual Symposium Proceedings*, volume 2007, pages 821–825.

H Xu, PD Stetson, and C Friedman. 2012. Combining corpus-derived sense profiles with estimated frequency information to disambiguate clinical abbreviations. In *AMIA Annual Symposium Proceedings*, volume 2012, pages 1004–1013.

*** Formatting Issue - Best Available Paper/Graphic ***

Tuning HeidelTime for identifying time expressions in clinical texts in English and French

Thierry Hamon
LIMSI-CNRS, BP133, Orsay
Université Paris 13
Sorbonne Paris Cité, France
hamon@limsi.fr

Natalia Grabar
CNRS UMR 8163 STL
Université Lille 3
59653 Villeneuve d'Ascq, France
natalia.grabar@univ-lille3.fr

Abstract

We present work on tuning the Heideltime system for identifying time expressions in clinical texts in English and French languages. The main amount of the method is related to the enrichment and adaptation of linguistic resources to identify Timex3 clinical expressions and to normalize them. The test of the adapted versions have been done on the i2b2/VA 2012 corpus for English and a collection of clinical texts for French, which have been annotated for the purpose of this study. We achieve a 0.8500 F-measure on the recognition and normalization of temporal expressions in English, and up to 0.9431 in French. Future work will allow to improve and consolidate the results.

1 Introduction

Working with unstructured narrative texts is very demanding on automatic methods to access, formalize and organize the information contained in these documents. The first step is the indexing of the documents in order to detect basic facts which will allow more sophisticated treatments (*e.g.*, information extraction, question/answering, visualization, or textual entailment). We are mostly interested in indexing of documents from the medical field. We distinguish two kinds of indexing: conceptual and contextual.

Conceptual indexing consists in finding out the mentions of notions, terms or concepts contained in documents. It is traditionally done thanks to the exploitation of terminological resources, such as MeSH (NLM, 2001), SNOMED International (Côté et al., 1993), SNOMED CT (Wang et al., 2002), etc. The process is dedicated to the recognition of these terms and of their variants in documents (Nadkarni et al., 2001; Mercer and Di Marco, 2004; Bashyam and Taira, 2006; Schulz and Hahn, 2000; Davis et al., 2006).

The purpose of contextual indexing is to go further and to provide a more fine-grained annotation of documents. For this, additional information may be searched in documents, such as polarity, certainty, aspect or temporality related to the concepts. If conceptual indexing extracts and provides factual information, contextual indexing is aimed to describe these facts with more details. For instance, when processing clinical records, the medical facts related to a given patient can be augmented with the associated contextual information, such as in these examples:

(1) *Patient has the stomach aches.*

(2) *Patient denies the stomach aches.*

(3) *After taking this medication, patient started to have the stomach aches.*

(4) *Two weeks ago, patient experienced the stomach aches.*

(5) *In January 2014, patient experienced the stomach aches.*

In example (1), the information is purely factual, while it is negated in example (2). Example (3) conveys also aspectual information (the medical problem has started). In examples (4) and (5), medical events are positioned in the time: relative (*two weeks ago*) and absolute (*in January 2014*). We can see that the medical history of patient can become more precise and detailed thanks to such contextual information. In this way, factual information related to the stomach aches of patient may receive these additional descriptions which make each occurrence different and non-redundant. Notice that the previous I2B2 contests[1] addressed the information extraction tasks related to different kinds of contextual information.

[1] *https://www.i2b2.org/NLP*

Temporality has become an important research field in the NLP topics and several challenges addressed this taks: ACE (ACE challenge, 2004), SemEval (Verhagen et al., 2007; Verhagen et al., 2010; UzZaman et al., 2013), I2B2 2012 (Sun et al., 2013). We propose to continue working on the extraction of temporal information related to medical events. This kind of study relies on several important tasks when processing the narrative documents : identification and normalization of linguistic expressions that are indicative of the temporality (Verhagen et al., 2007; Chang and Manning, 2012; Strötgen and Gertz, 2012; Kessler et al., 2012), and their modelization and chaining (Batal et al., 2009; Moskovitch and Shahar, 2009; Pustejovsky et al., 2010; Sun et al., 2013; Grouin et al., 2013). The identification of temporal expressions provides basic knowledge for other tasks processing the temporality information. The existing available automatic systems such as HeidelTime (Strötgen and Gertz, 2012) or SUTIME (Chang and Manning, 2012) exploit rule-based approaches, which makes them adaptable to new data and areas. During a preliminary study, we tested several such systems for identification of temporal relations and found that HeidelTime has the best combination of performance and adaptability. We propose to exploit this automatic systems, to adapt and to test it on the medical clinical documents in two languages (English and French).

In the following of this study, we introduce the corpora (Section 2) and methods (Section 3). We then describe and discuss the obtained results (Section 4.2) and conclude (Section 5).

2 Material

Corpora composed of training and test sets are the main material we work with. The corpora are in two languages, English and French, and has comparable sizes. All the processed corpora are deidentified. Corpora in English are built within the I2B2 2012 challenge (Sun et al., 2013). The training corpus consists of 190 clinical records and the test corpus of 120 records. The reference data contain annotations of temporal expressions according to the Timex3s guidelines: date, duration, frequency and time (Pustejovsky et al., 2010). Corpora in French are built on purpose of this study. The clinical documents are issued from a French hospital. The training corpus consists of 182 clinical records and the test corpus of 120 records. 25 documents from the test set are annotated to provide the reference data for evaluation.

3 Method

HeidelTime is a cross-domain temporal tagger that extracts temporal expressions from documents and normalizes them according to the Timex3 annotation standard, which is part of the markup language TimeML (Pustejovsky et al., 2010). This is a rule-based system. Because the source code and the resources (patterns, normalization information, and rules) are strictly separated, it is possible to develop and implement resources for additional languages and areas using HeidelTime's rule syntax. HeidelTime is provided with modules for processing documents in several languages, *e.g.* French (Moriceau and Tannier, 2014). In English, several versions of the system exist, such as general-language English and scientific English.

HeidelTime uses different normalization strategies depending on the domain of the documents that are to be processed: news, narratives (*e.g.* Wikipedia articles), colloquial (*e.g.* SMS, tweets), and scientific (*e.g.* biomedical studies). The *news* strategy allows to fix the document creation date. This date is important for computing and normalizing the relative dates, such as *two weeks ago* or *5 days later*, for which the reference point in time is necessary: if the document creation date is *2012/03/24*, *two weeks ago* becomes *2012/03/10*.

Our method consists of three steps: tuning HeidelTime to clinical data in English and French (Section 3.1), evaluation of the results (Section 3.2), and exploitation of the computed data for the visualization of the medical events (Section 3.3).

3.1 Tuning HeidelTime

While HeidelTime proposes a good coverage of the temporal expressions used in general language documents, it needs to be adapted to specialized areas. We propose to tune this tool to the medical domain documents. The tuning is done in two languages (English and French). Tuning involves three aspects:

1. The most important adaptation needed is related to the enrichment and encoding of linguistic expressions specific to medical and especially clinical temporal expressions, such as *post-operative day #*, *b.i.d.* meaning *twice a day*, *day of life*, etc.

2. The admission date is considered as the reference or starting point for computing relative dates, such as *2 days later*. For the identification of the admission date, specific preprocessing step is applied in order to detect it within the documents;

3. Additional normalizations of the temporal expressions are done for normalizing the durations in approximate numerical values rather than in the undefined 'X'-value; and for external computation for some durations and frequencies due to limitations in HeidelTime's internal arithmetic processor.

3.2 Evaluating the results

HeidelTime is tuned on the training set. It is evaluated on the test set. The results generated are evaluated against the reference data with:

- precision $\mathcal{P}$: percentage of the relevant temporal expressions extracted divided by the total number of the temporal expressions extracted;
- recall $\mathcal{R}$: percentage of the relevant temporal expressions extracted divided by the number of the expected temporal expressions;
- APR: the arithmetic average of the precision and recall values $\frac{\mathcal{P}+\mathcal{R}}{2}$;
- F-measure $\mathcal{F}$: the harmonic mean of the precision and recall values $\frac{\mathcal{P}*\mathcal{R}}{\mathcal{P}+\mathcal{R}}$.

3.3 Exploiting the results

In order to judge about the usefulness of the temporal information extracted, we exploit it to build the timeline. For this, the medical events are associated with normalized and absolute temporal information. This temporal information is then used to order and visualize the medical events.

4 Experiments and Results

4.1 Experiments

The experiments performed are the following. Data in English and French are processed. Data in two languages are processed by available versions of HeidelTime: two existing versions (general language and scientific language) and the medical version created thanks to the work performed in this study. Results obtained are evaluated against the reference data.

4.2 Results

We added several new rules to HeidelTime (164 in English and 47 in French) to adapt the recognition of temporal expressions in medical documents. Some cases are difficult to annotate. For instance, it is complicated to decide whether some expressions are concerned with dates or durations. The utterance like *2 years ago* (*il y a 2 ans*) is considered to indicate the date. The utterance like *since 2010* (*depuis 2010*) is considered to indicate the duration, although it can be remarked that the beginning of the duration interval marks the beginning of the process and its date. Another complex situation appears with the relative dates:

- as already mentioned, date like *2 years ago* (*il y a 2 ans*) are to be normalized according to the reference time point;
- a more complex situation appears with expressions like *the day of the surgery* (*le jour de l'opération*) or *at the end of the treatment by antiobiotics* (*à la fin de l'antibiothrapie*), for which it is necessary first to make the reference in time of the other medical event before being able to define the date in question.

In Table 1, we present the evaluation results for English. On the training corpus, with the general language version and the scientific version of HeidelTime, we obtain F-measure around 0.66: precision (0.77 to 0.79) is higher than recall (0.56). The values of F-measure and APR are identical. The version we adapted to the medical language provides better results for all the evaluation measures used: F-measure becomes then 0.84, with precision up to 0.85 and recall 0.84. This is a good improvement of the automatic tool which indicates that specialized areas, such as medical area, use indeed specific lexicon and constructions. Interestingly, on the test corpus, the results decrease for the general language and scientific versions of HeidelTime, but increase for the medical version of HeidelTime, with F-measure 0.85. During the I2B2 competition, the maximal F-measure obtained was 0.91. With F measure 0.84, our system was ranked 10/14 on the English data. Currently, we improve these previous results.

In Table 2, we present the results obtained on the French test corpus (26 documents). Two versions of HeidelTime are applied: general language, that is already available, and medical, that has been developed in the presented work. We can

***** Formatting Issue - Best Available Paper/Graphic *****

Versions of HeidelTime	Training				Test			
	$\mathcal{P}$	$\mathcal{R}$	*APR*	$\mathcal{F}$	$\mathcal{P}$	$\mathcal{R}$	*APR*	$\mathcal{F}$
general language	0.7745	0.5676	0.6551	0.6551	0.8000	0.5473	0.6499	0.6499
scientific	0.7877	0.5676	0.6598	0.6598	0.8018	0.5445	0.6486	0.6486
medical	0.8478	0.8381	0.8429	0.8429	0.8533	0.8467	0.8500	0.8500

Table 1: Results obtained on training and test sets in English.

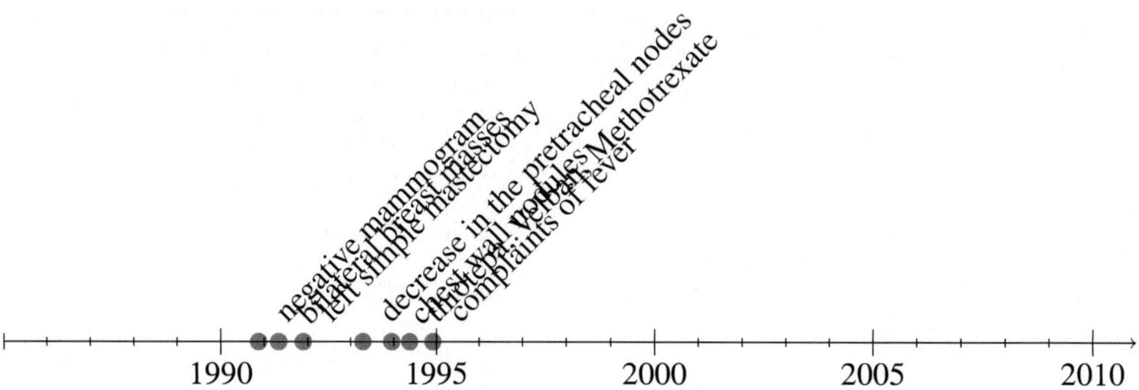

Figure 1: Visualization of temporal data.

Versions of HeidelTime	Test		
	$\mathcal{P}$	$\mathcal{R}$	$\mathcal{F}$
general language	0.9030	0.9341	0.9183
medical	0.9504	0.9341	0.9422

Table 2: Results obtained on test set in French.

observe that the adapted version suits better the content of clinical documents and improves the F-measure values by 3 points, reaching up to 0.94.

The main limitation of the system is due to the incomplete coverage of the linguistic expressions (*e.g. au cours de, mensuel* (*during, monthly*)). Among the current false positives, we can find ratios (*2/10* is considered as date, while it means lab results), polysemous expressions (*Juillet* in *rue du 14 Juillet* (*14 Juillet street*)), and segmentation errors (*few days* detected instead of *the next few days*). These limitations will be fixed in the future work.

In Figure 1, we propose a visualization of the temporal data, which makes use of the temporal information extracted. In this way, the medical events can be ordered thanks to their temporal anchors, which becomes a very useful information presentation in clinical practice (Hsu et al., 2012). The visualization of unspecified expressions (*e.g. later, sooner*) is being studied. Although it seems that such expressions often occur with more specific expressions (*e.g. later that day*).

5 Conclusion

HeidelTime, an existing tool for extracting and normalizing temporal information, has been adapted to the medical area documents in two languages (English and French). It is evaluated against the reference data, which indicates that its tuning to medical documents is efficient: we reach F-measure 0.85 in English and up to 0.94 in French. More complete data in French are being annotated, which will allow to perform a more complete evaluation of the tuned version. We plan to make the tuned version of HeidelTime freely available. Automatically extracted temporal information can be exploited for the visualization of the clinical data related to patients. Besides, these data can be combined with other kinds of contextual information (polarity, uncertainty) to provide a more exhaustive picture of medical history of patients.

Acknowledgments

This work is partially performed under the grant ANR/DGA Tecsan (ANR-11-TECS-012). The authors are thankful to the CHU de Bordeaux for making available the clinical documents.

*** Formatting Issue - Best Available Paper/Graphic ***

References

ACE challenge. 2004. The ACE 2004 evaluation plan. evaluation of the recognition of ace entities, ace relations and ace events. Technical report, ACE challenge. http://www.itl.nist.gov/iad/mig/tests/ace/2004.

V Bashyam and Ricky K Taira. 2006. Indexing anatomical phrases in neuro-radiology reports to the UMLS 2005aa. In *AMIA*, pages 26–30.

Iyad Batal, Lucia Sacchi, Riccardo Bellazzi, and Milos Hauskrecht. 2009. A temporal abstraction framework for classifying clinical temporal data. In *AMIA Annu Symp Proc. 2009*, pages 29–33.

Angel X. Chang and Christopher D. Manning. 2012. SUTIME: A library for recognizing and normalizing time expressions. In *LREC*, pages 3735–3740.

Roger A. Côté, D. J. Rothwell, J. L. Palotay, R. S. Beckett, and Louise Brochu. 1993. *The Systematised Nomenclature of Human and Veterinary Medicine: SNOMED International*. College of American Pathologists, Northfield.

Neil Davis, Henk Harlema, Rob Gaizauskas, Yikun Guo, Moustafa Ghanem, Tom Barnwell, Yike Guo, and Jon Ratcliffe. 2006. Three approaches to GO-tagging biomedical abstracts. In Udo Hahn and Michael Poprat, editors, *SMBM*, pages 21 – 28, Jena, Germany.

Cyril Grouin, Natalia Grabar, Thierry Hamon, Sophie Rosset, Xavier Tannier, and Pierre Zweigenbaum. 2013. Hybrid approaches to represent the clinical patient's timeline. *J Am Med Inform Assoc*, 20(5):820–7.

William Hsu, Ricky K Taira, Suzie El-Saden, Hooshang Kangarloo, and Alex AT Bui. 2012. Context-based electronic health recond: toward patient specific healthcare. *IEEE Transactions on information technology in biomedicine*, 16(2):228–234.

Remy Kessler, Xavier Tannier, Caroline Hagge, Vronique Moriceau, and Andr Bittar. 2012. Finding salient dates for building thematic timelines. In *50th Annual Meeting of the Association for Computational Linguistics*, pages 730–739.

Robert E Mercer and Chrysanne Di Marco. 2004. A design methodology for a biomedical literature indexing tool using the rhetoric of science. In *HLT NAACL 2004, Workshop Biolink*, pages 77–84.

Vronique Moriceau and Xavier Tannier. 2014. French resources for extraction and normalization of temporal expressions with heideltime. In *LREC*.

Robert Moskovitch and Yuval Shahar. 2009. Medical temporal-knowledge discovery via temporal abstraction. In *AMIA Annu Symp Proc*, pages 452–456.

P Nadkarni, R Chen, and C Brandt. 2001. Umls concept indexing for production databases: a feasibility study. *J Am Med Inform Assoc*, 8(1):80–91.

National Library of Medicine, Bethesda, Maryland, 2001. *Medical Subject Headings. www.nlm.nih.gov/mesh/meshhome.html.*

James Pustejovsky, Kiyong Lee, Harry Bunt, and Laurent Romary. 2010. ISO-TimeML: An international standard for semantic annotation. In Nicoletta Calzolari (Conference Chair), Khalid Choukri, Bente Maegaard, Joseph Mariani, Jan Odijk, Stelios Piperidis, Mike Rosner, and Daniel Tapias, editors, *Proceedings of the Seventh International Conference on Language Resources and Evaluation (LREC'10)*, Valletta, Malta, may. European Language Resources Association (ELRA).

Stefan Schulz and Udo Hahn. 2000. Morpheme-based, cross-lingual indexing for medical document retrieval. *Int J Med Inform*, 58-59:87–99.

Jannik Strötgen and Michael Gertz. 2012. Temporal tagging on different domains: Challenges, strategies, and gold standards. In *Proceedings of the Eigth International Conference on Language Resources and Evaluation (LREC'12)*, pages 3746–3753. ELRA.

Weiyi Sun, Anna Rumshisky, and Özlem Uzuner. 2013. Evaluating temporal relations in clinical text: 2012 i2b2 challenge. *JAMIA*, 20(5):806–813.

Naushad UzZaman, Hector Llorens, Leon Derczynski, James Allen, Marc Verhagen, and James Pustejovsky. 2013. Semeval-2013 task 1: Tempeval-3: Evaluating time expressions, events, and temporal relations. In *Second Joint Conference on Lexical and Computational Semantics (*SEM), Volume 2: Proceedings of the Seventh International Workshop on Semantic Evaluation (SemEval 2013)*, pages 1–9, Atlanta, Georgia, USA, June. Association for Computational Linguistics.

Marc Verhagen, Robert Gaizauskas, Frank Schilder, Mark Hepple, Graham Katz, and James Pustejovsky. 2007. Semeval-2007 task 15: Tempeval temporal relation identification. In *Proceedings of the Fourth International Workshop on Semantic Evaluations (SemEval-2007)*, pages 75–80, Prague, Czech Republic, June. Association for Computational Linguistics.

Marc Verhagen, Roser Sauri, Tommaso Caselli, and James Pustejovsky. 2010. Semeval-2010 task 13: Tempeval-2. In *Proceedings of the 5th International Workshop on Semantic Evaluation*, pages 57–62, Uppsala, Sweden, July. Association for Computational Linguistics.

AY Wang, JH Sable, and KA Spackman. 2002. The snomed clinical terms development process: refinement and analysis of content. In *AMIA*, pages 845–9.

Detecting drugs and adverse events from Spanish health social media streams

Isabel Segura-Bedmar, Ricardo Revert, Paloma Martínez
Computer Science Department,
Carlos III University of Madrid, Spain
{isegura,rrevert,pmf}@inf.uc3m.es

Abstract

To the best of our knowledge, this is the first work that does drug and adverse event detection from Spanish posts collected from a health social media. First, we created a gold-standard corpus annotated with drugs and adverse events from social media. Then, Textalytics, a multilingual text analysis engine, was applied to identify drugs and possible adverse events. Overall recall and precision were 0.80 and 0.87 for drugs, and 0.56 and 0.85 for adverse events.

1 Introduction

It is well-known that adverse drug reactions (ADRs) are an important health problem. Indeed, ADRs are the 4th cause of death in hospitalized patients (Wester et al., 2008). Thus, the field of pharmacovigilance has received a great deal of attention due to the high and growing incidence of drug safety incidents (Bond and Raehl, 2006) as well as to their high associated costs (van Der Hooft et al., 2006).

Since many ADRs are not captured during clinical trials, the major medicine regulatory agencies such as the US Food and Drug Administration (FDA) or the European Medicines Agency (EMA) require healthcare professionals to report all suspected adverse drug reactions. However, some studies have shown that ADRs are under-estimated due to the fact that they are reported by voluntary reporting systems (Bates et al., 2003; van Der Hooft et al., 2006; McClellan, 2007). In fact, it is estimated that only between 2 and 10 per cent of ADRs are reported (Rawlins, 1995). Healthcare professionals must perform many tasks during their workdays and thus finding the time to use these surveillance reporting systems is very difficult. Also, healthcare professionals tend to report only those ADRs on which they have absolute certainty of their existence. Several medicines agencies have implemented spontaneous patient reporting systems in order for patients to report ADRs themselves. Some of these systems are the MedWatch from the FDA, the Yellow Cards from the UK Medicines agency (MHRA) or the website[1] developed by the Spanish Agency of Medicines and Medical devices (AEMPS). Unlike reports from healthcare professionals, patient reports often provide more detailed and explicit information about ADRs (Herxheimer et al., 2010). Another important contribution of spontaneous patient reporting systems is to achieve patients having a more central role in their treatments. However, despite the fact that these systems are well-established, the rate of spontaneous patient reporting is very low probably because many

[1] https://www.notificaram.es/

patients are still unaware of their existence and even may feel embarrassed when describing their symptoms.

In this study, our hypothesis is that health-related social media can be used as a complementary data source to spontaneous reporting systems in order to detect unknown ADRs and thereby to increase drug safety. In recent days, social media on health information, just like has happened in other areas, have seen a tremendous growth (Hill et al., 2013). Examples of social media sites include blogs, online forums, social networking, and wikis, among many others. In this work, we focus on health forums where patients often exchange information about their personal medical experiences with other patients who suffer the same illness or receive similar treatment. Some patients may feel more comfortable sharing their medical experiences with each other rather than with their healthcare professionals. These forums contain a large number of comments describing patient experiences that would be a fertile source of data to detect unknown ADRs.

Although there have been several research efforts devoted to developing systems for extracting ADRs from social media, all studies have focused on social media in English, and none of them have addressed the extraction from Spanish social media. Moreover, the problem is that these studies have not been compared with each other, and hence it is very difficult to determine the current "state-of-art" of the techniques for ADRs extraction from social media. This comparison has not been performed due to the lack of a gold-standard corpus for ADRs. Thus, the goal of our work is twofold: i) to create a gold-standard corpus annotated with drugs and adverse events and ii) to develop a system to automatically extract mentions of drugs and adverse events from Spanish health-related social media sites. The corpus is composed by patients' comments from Forumclinic[2], a health online networking website in Spanish. This is the first corpus of patient comments annotated with drugs and adverse events in Spanish. Also, we believe that this corpus will facilitate comparison for future ADRs detection from Spanish social media.

This is a preliminary work, in which we have only focused on the automatic detection of mentions of drugs and adverse events. Our final goal will be to develop a system to automatically extract drugs and their side effects. We hope our system will be beneficial to *AEMPS* as well as to the pharmaceutical industry in the improvement of their pharmacovigilance systems.

2 Related Work

In recent years, the application of Natural Language Processing (NLP) techniques to mine adverse reactions from texts has been explored with promising results, mainly in the context of drug labels (Gurulingappa et al., 2013; Li et al., 2013; Kuhn et al., 2010), biomedical literature (Xu and Wang, 2013), medical case reports (Gurulingappa et al., 2012) and health records (Friedman, 2009; Sohn et al., 2011). However, as it will be described below, the extraction of adverse reactions from social media has received much less attention.

In general, medical literature, such as scientific publications and drug labels, contains few grammatical and spelling mistakes. Another important advantage is that this type of texts can be easily linked to biomedical ontologies. Similarly, clinical records present specific medical terminology and can also be mapped to biomedical ontologies and resources. Meanwhile social media texts are markedly different from clinical records and scientific articles, and thereby the processing of social media texts poses additional challenges such as the management of meta-information included in the text (for example as tags in tweets) (Bouillot et al., 2013), the detection of typos and unconventional spelling, word shortenings (Neunedert et al, 2013; Moreira et al., 2013) and slang and emoticons (Balahur, 2013), among others. Moreover, these texts are often very short

[2] http://www.forumclinic.org

and with an informal nature, making the processing task extremely challenging.

Regarding the identification of drug names in text, during the last four years there has been significant research efforts directed to encourage the development of systems for detecting these entities. Concretely, shared tasks such as DDIExtraction 2013 (Segura-Bedmar et al., 2013), CHEMDNER 2013 (Krallinger et al., 2013) or the i2b2 Medication Extraction challenge (Uzuner et al., 2010) have been held for the advancement of the state of the art in this problem. However, most of the work on recognizing drugs concerns either biomedical literature (for example, MedLine articles) or clinical records, thus leaving unexplored this task in social media streams.

Leaman et al., (2010) developed a system to automatically recognize adverse effects in user comments. A corpus of 3,600 comments from the DailyStrength health-related social network was collected and manually annotated with a total of 1,866 drug conditions, including beneficial effects, adverse effects, indications and others. To identify the adverse effects in the user comments, a lexicon was compiled from the following resources: (1) the COSTART vocabulary (National Library of Medicine, 2008), (2) the SIDER database (Kuhn et al., 2010), (3) MedEffect[3] and (4) a list of colloquial phrases which were manually collected from the DailyStrength comments. The final lexicon consisted of 4,201 concepts (terms with the same CUI were grouped in the same concept). Finally, the terms in the lexicon were mapped against user comments to identify the adverse effects. In order to distinguish adverse effects from the other drug conditions (beneficial effects, indications and others), the systems used a list of verbs denoting indications (for example, help, work, prescribe). Drug name recognition was not necessary because the evaluation focused only on a set of four drugs: carbamazepine, olanzapine, trazodone and ziprasidone. The system achieved a good performance, with a precision of 78.3% and a recall of 69.9%.

An extension of this system was accomplished by Nikfarjam and Gonzalez (2011). The authors applied association rule mining to extract frequent patterns describing opinions about drugs. The rules were generated using the Apriori tool[4], an implementation of the Apriori algorithm (Agrawal and Srikant, 1994) for association rule mining. The system was evaluated using the same corpus created for their previous work (Leaman et al., 2010), and which has been described above. The system achieved a precision of 70.01% and a recall of 66.32%. The main advantage of this system is that it can be easily adapted for other domains and languages. Another important advantage of this approach over a dictionary based approach is that the system is able to detect terms not included in the dictionary.

Benton et al., (2011) created a corpus of posts from several online forums about breast cancer, which later was used to extract potential adverse reactions from the most commonly used drugs to treat this disease: tamoxifen, anastrozole, letrozole and axemestane. The authors collected a lexicon of lay medical terms from websites and databases about drugs and adverse events. The lexicon was extended with the Consumer Health Vocabulary (CHV)[5], a vocabulary closer to the lay terms, which patients usually use to describe their medical experiences. Then, pairs of terms co-occurring within a window of 20 tokens were considered. The Fisher's exact test (Fisher, 1922) was used to calculate the probability that the two terms co-occurred independently by chance. To evaluate the system, the authors focused on the four drugs mentioned above, and then collected their adverse effects from their drug labels. Then, precision and recall were calculated by comparing the adverse effects from drug labels and the adverse effects obtained by the system.

---

[3] http://www.hc-sc.gc.ca/dhp-mps/medeff/index-eng.php

[4] http://www.borgelt.net/apriori.html

[5] http://consumerhealthvocab.org

The system obtained an average precision of 77% and an average recall of 35.1% for all four drugs.

UDWarning (Wu et al., 2012) is an ongoing prototype whose main goal is to extract adverse drug reactions from Google discussions. A knowledge base of drugs and their adverse effects was created by integrating information from different resources such as SIDER, DailyMed[6], Drugs.com[7] and MedLinePlus. The authors hypothesized that unknown adverse drug effects would have a high volume of discussions over the time. Thus, the systems should monitor the number of relevant discussions for each adverse drug effect. However, to the best of our knowledge, the UDWarning's component devoted to the detection of unrecognized adverse drug effects has not been developed yet.

Bian et al., (2012) developed a system to detect tweets describing adverse drug reactions. The systems used a SVM classifier trained on a corpus of tweets, which were manually labeled by two experts. MetaMap (Aronson and Lang, 2010) was used to analyze the tweets and to find the UMLS concepts present in the tweets. The system produced poor results, mainly because tweets are riddled with spelling and grammar mistakes. Moreover, MetaMap is not a suitable tool to analyze this type of texts since patients do not usually use medical terminology to describe their medical experiences.

As it was already mentioned, the recognition of drugs in social media texts has hardly been tackled and little research has been conducted to extract relationships between drugs and their side effects, since most systems were focused on a given and fixed set of drugs. Most systems for extracting ADRs follow a dictionary-based approach. The main drawback of these systems is that they fail to recognize terms which are not included in the dictionary. In addition, the dictionary-based approach is not able to handle the large number of spelling and grammar errors in social media texts. Moreover, the detection of ADRs has not been attempted for languages other than English. Indeed, automatic information extraction from Spanish-language social media in the field of health remains largely unexplored. Additionally, to the best of our knowledge, there is no corpus annotated with ADRs in social media texts available today.

3 Method

3.1 Corpus creation

In order to create the first corpus in Spanish annotated with drugs and adverse events, we reviewed the main health-related social networks in Spanish language to select the most appropriate source of user comments. This corpus will be used to evaluate our system.

Twitter was initially our preferred option due to the tremendous amount of tweets published each day (nearly 400 millions). However, we decided to discard it because Twitter does not seem to be the preferred source for users to describe their ADRs. Gonzalez et al. (2013) gathered a total of 42,327 in a one-month period, from which only 216 described ADRs. Although Facebook is the most popular social media and many Facebook groups dedicated to specific diseases have emerged in the last years, we discarded it because most of these groups usually have restricted access to their members. Online health-related forums are an attractive source of data for our corpus due to their high dynamism, their great number of users as well as their easy access. After reviewing the main health forums in Spanish, we chose ForumClinic, an interactive program for patients, whose main goal is to provide rigorous information about specific diseases (such as breast cancer, HIV, bipolar disorder, depression, schizophrenia, ischemic heart disease, among others) and their treatments. Also, this platform aims to increase the participation of patients maintaining a discussion forum where patients can exchange information about their experiences. Figure 1 shows the distribution of user comments across the main twelve categories defined in the forum. We

[6] http://dailymed.nlm.nih.gov/dailymed/
[7] http://www.drugs.com/

implemented a web crawler to gather all user comments published in ForumClinic to date.

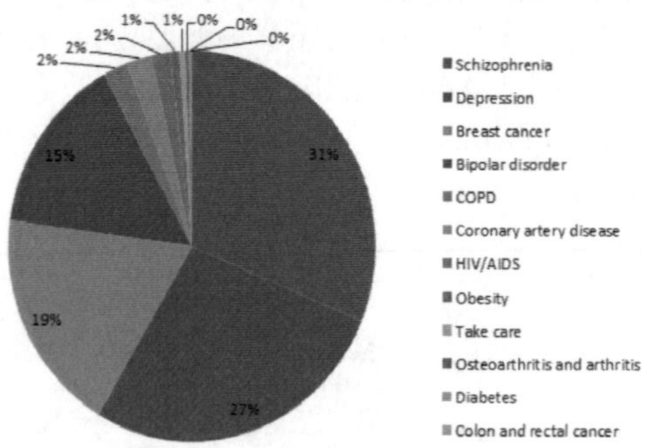

Figure 1 Distribution of user comments.

Then, we randomly selected a sample of 400 comments that were manually labeled with drugs and adverse events by two annotators with expertise in Pharmacovigilance. It should be noted that adverse events and ADRs do not refer to the same: while an adverse event may or may not be caused by a drug, an ADR is an adverse event that is suspected to be caused by a drug. A drug is a substance used in the treatment, cure, prevention or diagnosis of diseases. The corpus includes generic and brand drugs as well as drug families. Disagreements between the annotators were discussed and reconciled during the harmonization process, where a third annotator helped to make the final decision (some examples are shown in Table 1). All the mentions of drugs and adverse events were annotated, even those containing spelling or grammatical errors (for example, *hemorrajia*). Nominal anaphoric expressions, which refer to previous adverse events or drugs in the comment, were also included in the annotation. The annotators found 187 drugs (from which 40 were nominal anaphors and 14 spelling errors) and 636 adverse events (from which 48 were nominal anaphors and 17 spelling errors). The corpus is available for academic purposes[8].

To measure the inter-annotator agreement we used the F-measure metric. This metric approximates the kappa coefficient (Cohen, 1960) when the number of true negatives (TN) is very large (Hripcsak and Rothschild, 2005). In our case, we can state that the number of TN is very high since TN are all the terms that are not true positives, false positives nor false negatives. The F-measure was calculated by comparing the two corpora created by the two first annotators. The corpus labelled by the first annotator was considered the gold-standard. As it was expected, drugs exhibit a high IAA (0.89), while adverse events point to moderate agreement (0.59). As drugs have specific names and there are a limited number of them, it is possible to create a limited and controlled vocabulary to gather many of the existing drugs. On the other hand, patients can express their adverse events in many different ways due to the variability and richness of natural language.

Sentence	Final Decision
*De entre los distintos antiretrovirales, **transcriptasa inversa, proteasa, integrasa** y **fusión**, qué grupo sería el más potente y cual el menos.*	Names in bold type refer to four families of inhibitors (that is, drug families), and thereby, they should be annotated.
*Como **complemento proteico** recomendamos el de los laboratorio Vegenat. Si compras los complementos del Decathlon, asegúrate que contenga proteínas.*	The mention "complementos del Decathlon" should not be annotated as a drug since it is not a brand-marked drug.

Table **1**: Some examples of disagreements between annotators

3.2 *Constructing a dictionary for drugs and adverse events*

Since our goal is to identify drugs and adverse events from user comments, the first challenge is to create a dictionary that contains all of the drugs and known adverse events.

CIMA[9] is an online information center about medicines that provides all the daily updated official information about drugs. CIMA is

[8] http://labda.inf.uc3m.es/SpanishADRCorpus

[9] http://www.aemps.gob.es/cima/

maintained by the Spanish Agency for Medicines and Health Products (AEMPS). It includes information on all drugs authorized in Spain and their current authorization status. CIMA contains a total of 16,418 brand drugs and 2,228 generic drugs. Many brand drug names include additional information such as dosages, mode and route of administration, laboratory, among others (for example, "ESPIDIFEN 400 mg GRANULADO PARA SOLUCION ORAL SABOR ALBARICOQUE" or "ESPIDIFEN 600 mg GRANULADO PARA SOLUCION ORAL SABOR LIMON EFG, 20 sobres"). Since it is unlikely that these long names are used by patients, we implemented a method to shorten them by removing their additional information (for example, "ESPIDIFEN"). After applying this method, the resulting list of brand drug names consisted of 3,662 terms. The main limitation of CIMA is that it only provides information about drugs authorized in Spain. That is, CIMA does not contain information about drugs approved only in Latin America. CIMA is free and offers a downloadable version in XML format. Thus, it provides the information in a well-structured format that makes it possible to directly extract generic and brand drug names as well as other related information such as their ATC codes, their pharmaceutical company, among others. Unfortunately, CIMA does not provide information about drug groups. For this reason, we decided to consider the WHO ATC system[10], a classification system of drugs, as an additional resource to obtain a list of drug groups.

MedDRA [11] is a medical terminology dictionary about events associated with drugs. It is a multilingual terminology, which includes the following languages: Chinese, Czech, Dutch, French, German, Hungarian, Italian, Japanese, Portuguese and Spanish. Its main goal is to provide a classification system for efficient communication of ADRs data between countries. The main advantage of MedDRA is that its structured format allows easily obtaining a list of possible adverse events. MedDRA is composed of a five levels hierarchy. We collected the terms from the most specific level, "Lowest Level Terms" (LLTs)". This level contains a total of 72,072 terms, which express how information is communicated in practice.

By analyzing the information from these resources, we found that none of them contained all of the drugs and adverse events. Patients usually use lay terms to describe their symptoms and their treatments. Unfortunately, many of these lay terms are not included in the above mentioned resources. Therefore, we decided to integrate additional information from other resources devoted to patients to build a more complete and comprehensive dictionary. There are several online websites that provide information to patients on drugs and their side effects in Spanish language. For example, MedLinePlus and Vademecum contain information about drugs and their side effects. These websites allow users to browse by generic or drug name, providing an information leaflet for each drug in a HTML page. Since these leaflets are unstructured, the extraction of drugs and their adverse effects is a challenging task. While drug names are often located in specific fields (such as title), their adverse events are usually descriptions of harmful reactions in natural language. We only developed a web crawler to browse and download pages related to drugs from Vademecum since this website provided an easier access to its drug pages than MedLinePlus. We plan to augment the list of drugs and adverse events by crawling MedLinePlus in future work.

After extracting drugs and adverse events from these different resources, we created a dictionary of drugs and adverse events. Table 2 shows the statistics of our final dictionary.

Resource	Total
Generic drugs from CIMA	2,228
Brand drugs from CIMA	3,662

[10] http://www.whocc.no/atc_ddd_index/
[11] http://www.meddra.org/

Drug group names from the ATC system	466
Drug names (which are not in CIMA) from Vademecum	1,237
Total Drugs:	7,593

Table **2**: Number of drugs in the dictionary.

Resource	Total
Adverse events from MedDRA	72,072
Adverse events from Vademecum (which are not in MedDRA)	2,793
Total adverse events:	74,865

Table **3**: Number of adverse events in the dictionary.

3.3 Using Textalytics and gazetteers to identify drugs and adverse events

Textalytics [12] is a multilingual text analysis engine to extract information from any type of texts such as tweets, posts, comments, news, contracts, etc. This tool offers a wide variety of functionalities such as text classification, entity recognition, concept extraction, relation extraction and sentiment analysis, among others. We used a plugin that integrates Textalytics with GATE. In this paper, we applied entity recognition provided by Textalytics, which follows a dictionary-based approach to identify entities in texts. We created a dictionary for drugs and adverse events from CIMA and MedDRA. This dictionary was integrated into Textalytics. Additionally, the lists of drugs and adverse events collected from the others resources (ATC system and Vademecum) were used to create GATE gazetteers.

4 Results and error analysis

We evaluated the system on the corpus annotated with drugs and adverse events. The results of this study show a precision of 87% for drugs and 85% for adverse events, and a recall of 80% for drugs and 56% for adverse events.

We performed an analysis to determine the main sources of error in the system. A sample of 50 user comments were randomly selected and analyzed. Regarding the detection of adverse events, the major cause of false negatives was the use of colloquial expressions to describe an adverse event. Phrases like "*me deja ko* (it makes me KO)" or "*me cuesta más levantarme* (it's harder for me to wake up)" were used by patients for expressing their adverse events. These phrases are not included in our dictionary. A possible solution may be to create a lexicon containing this kind of idiomatic expressions. The second highest cause of false negatives for adverse events was due to the different lexical variations of the same adverse event. For example, '*depresión* (depression)' is included in our dictionary, but their lexical variations such as "*depremido* (depress)", "*me deprimo* (I get depressed)", "*depresivo* (depressive)" or "*deprimente* (depressing)" were not detected by our system since they are not in our dictionary. Nominalization may be used to identify all the possible lexical variations of a same adverse event. Another important error source of false negatives was spelling mistakes (eg. *hemorrajia* instead of *hemorragia).* Many users have great difficulty in spelling unusual and complex technical terms. This error source may be handled by a more advanced matching method capable of dealing with the spelling error problem. The use of abbreviations ("*depre*" is an abbreviation for "*depression*") also produces false negatives. Techniques such as lemmatization and stemming may help to resolve this kind of abbreviations.

False positives for adverse events were mainly due to the inclusion of MedDRA terms referring to procedures (such as therapeutic, preventive or laboratory procedures) and tests in our dictionary. MedDRA includes terms for diseases, signs, abnormalities, procedures and tests. We should have not included those terms referring to procedures and tests since they do not represent adverse events.

[12] https://textalytics.com/

The main source of false negatives for drugs seems to be that users often misspelled drug names. Some generic and brand drugs have complex names for patients. Some examples of misspelled drugs are *avilify* (*Abilify*) or *rivotril (ribotril).* Another important cause of false negatives was due to the fact that our dictionary does not include drugs approved in other countries than Spain (for example, *Clorimipramina*, *Ureadin* or *Paxil*). However, ForumClinic has a large number of users in Latin America. It is possible that these users have posted comments about some drugs that have only been approved in their countries. The third largest source of errors was the abbreviations for drug families. For instance, *benzodiacepinas (benzodiazepine)* is commonly used as *benzos*, which is not included in our dictionary. An interesting source of errors to point out is the use of acronyms referring to a combination of two or more drugs. For instance, *FEC* is a combination of *Fluorouracil, Epirubicin* and *Cyclophosphamide*, three chemotherapy drugs used to treat breast cancer. This combination of drugs is not registered in the resources (CIMA and Vademecum) used to create our dictionary.

Most false positives for drugs were due to a lack of ambiguity resolution. Some drug names are common Spanish words such as "*Alli*" (a slimming drug) or "*Puntual*" (a laxative). These terms are ambiguous and resolve to multiple senses, depending on the context in which they are used. Similarly, some drug names such as "alcohol" or "oxygen" can take a meaning different than the one of pharmaceutical substance. Another important cause of false positives is due to the use of drug family names as adjectives that specify an effect. This is the case of *sedante (sedative)* or *antidepresivo (antidepressant)*, which can refer to a family of drugs, but also to the definition of an effect or disorder caused by a drug (*sedative effects*).

5 Conclusion

In this research, we created the first Spanish corpus of health user comments annotated with drugs and adverse events. The corpus is available for research. In this work, we only focused on the detection of the mentions of drugs and adverse events, but not the relationships among them. In future work, we plan to extend the system to detect the relationships between drugs and their side effects. Also, we would like to identify their indications and beneficial effects.

Acknowledgments

This work was supported by the EU project TrendMiner [FP7-ICT287863], by the project MULTIMEDICA [TIN2010-20644-C03-01], and by the Research Network MA2VICMR [S2009/TIC-1542].

References

Rakesh Agrawal and Ramakrishnan Srikant. 1994. Fast algorithms for mining association rules. In *Proc. 20th Int. Conf. Very Large Data Bases,* 1215:487-499.

Alan R Aronson and Francois-Michel Lang. 2010. An overview of MetaMap: historical perspective and recent advances. *Journal of the American Medical Informatics Association*, 17(3):229-236.

Alexandra Balahur. 2013. Sentiment Analysis in Social Media Texts. *WASSA 2013*, 120.

David W. Bates, R Scott Evans, Harvey Murff, Peter D. Stetson, Lisa Pizziferri and George Hripcsak. 2003. Detecting adverse events using information technology. *Journal of the American Medical Informatics Association*, 10(2):115-128.

Adrian Benton, Lye Ungar, Shawndra Hill, Sean Hennessy, Jun Mao, Annie Chung, Charles E. Leonarda and John H. Holmes. 2011. Identifying potential adverse effects using the web: A new approach to medical hypothesis generation. *Journal of biomedical informatics*, 44(6): 989-996.

Jiang Bian, Umit Topaloglu and Fan Yu. 2012. Towards large-scale twitter mining for drug-related adverse events. In *Proceedings of the 2012 international workshop on Smart health and wellbeing*, 25-32.

CA. Bond and Cynthia L. Raehl. 2006. Adverse drug reactions in United States hospitals. *Pharmacotherapy: The Journal of Human Pharmacology and Drug Therapy*, 26(5):601-608.

Jacob Cohen. 1960. A coefficient of agreement for nominal scales. *Educational and Psychol Meas* ;20:37e46.

Ronald A. Fisher. 1922. On the interpretation of χ 2 from contingency tables, and the calculation of P. *Journal of the Royal Statistical Society*, 85(1):87-94.

Flavien Bouillot, Phan N. Hai, Nicolas Béchet, Sandra Bringay, Dino Ienco, Stan Matwin, Pascal Poncelet, Mathiue Roche and Maguelonne Teisseire. 2013. How to Extract Relevant Knowledge from Tweets?. *Communications in Computer and Information Science*.

Carol Friedman. 2009. Discovering novel adverse drug events using natural language processing and mining of the electronic health record. In *Artificial Intelligence in Medicine.* LNAI 5651:1 -5.

Graciela H. Gonzalez, Matthew L Scotch and Garrick L Wallstrom. Mining Social Network Postings for Mentions of Potential Adverse Drug Reactions. HHS-NIH-NLM (9/10/2012 - 8/31/2016).

Harsha Gurulingappa, Abdul Mateen-Rajput and Luca Toldo. 2012. Extraction of potential adverse drug events from medical case reports. *Journal of biomedical semantics.* 3(1):15.

Harsha Gurulingappa, Luca Toldo, Abdul Mateen-Rajput, Jan A. Kors, Adel Taweel and Yorki Tayrouz. 2013. Automatic detection of adverse events to predict drug label changes using text and data mining techniques. *Pharmacoepidemiology and drug safety*, *22*(11):1189-1194.

A Herxheimer, MR Crombag and TL Alves. 2010. Direct patient reporting of adverse drug reactions. A twelve-country survey & literature review. *Health Action International (HAI). Europe.* Paper Series Reference 01-2010/01.

Shawndra Hill, Raina Merchant and Lile Ungar. (2013). Lessons Learned About Public Health from Online Crowd Surveillance. *Big Data*, 1(3):160-167.

George Hripcsak and Adam S. Rothschild. 2005. Agreement, the F-measure, and reliability in information retrieval. *J Am Med Inform Assoc.*12:296e8.

Martin Krallinger, Florian Leitner, Obdulia Rabal, Miguel Vazquez, Julen Oyarzabal and Alfonso Valencia. 2013. Overview of the chemical compound and drug name recognition (CHEMDNER) task. In *BioCreative Challenge Evaluation Worksho. 2*:2-33.

Michael Kuhn, Monica Campillos, Ivica Letunic, Lars J. Jensen and Peer Bork. 2010. A side effect resource to capture phenotypic effects of drugs. *Molecular systems biology*, *6*(343):1-6.

Robert Leaman, Laura Wojtulewicz, Ryan Sullivan, Annie Skariah, Jian Yang and Graciela Gonzalez. 2010. Towards internet-age pharmacovigilance: extracting adverse drug reactions from user posts to health-related social networks. In *Proceedings of the 2010 workshop on biomedical natural language processing.* 117-125. Association for Computational Linguistics.

Anne J. Leendertse, Antoine C. Egberts, Lennar J. Stoker, & Patricia M.L.A. van den Bemt. 2008. Frequency of and risk factors for preventable medication-related hospital admissions in the Netherlands. *Archives of internal medicine*, *168*(17), 1890.

Qi Li, Louise Deleger, Todd Lingren, Haijun Zhai, Megan Kaiser, Laura Stoutenborough Anil G Jegga, Kevin B Cohen and Imre Solti. 2013. Mining FDA drug labels for medical conditions. *BMC medical informatics and decision making*, 13(1):53.

Mark McClellan. 2007. Drug Safety Reform at the FDA-Pendulum Swing or Systematic Improvement?. *New England Journal of Medicine*, 356(17):1700-1702.

Silvio Moreira, Joao Filgueiras, Bruno Martins, Francisco Couto and Mario J. Silva. 2013. REACTION: A naive machine learning approach for sentiment classification. In *2nd Joint Conference* on. *Lexical and Computational Semantics. 2:490-494.*

Melanie Neunerdt, Michael Reyer and Rudolf Mathar. 2013. A POS Tagger for Social Media Texts trained on Web Comments. *Polibits*, *48*:59-66.

Azadeh Nikfarjam and Graciela H. Gonzalez. 2011. Pattern mining for extraction of mentions of adverse drug reactions from user comments. In *AMIA Annual Symposium Proceedings,* 2011:1019-1026. American Medical Informatics Association.

Isabel Segura-Bedmar, Paloma Martınez and María Herrero-Zazo. 2013. SemEval-2013 Task 9: Extraction of Drug-Drug Interactions from

Biomedical Texts (DDIExtraction 2013). 3206(65): 341-351.

Cornelis S. van Der Hooft, Miriam CJM Sturkenboom, Kees van Grootheest, Herre J. Kingma and Bruno HCh Stricker. 2006. Adverse drug reaction-related hospitalisations. *Drug Safety*, 29(2):161-168.

Hamish Cunningham. 2002. GATE, a general architecture for text engineering. *Computers and the Humanities*, *36*(2):223-254.

M Rawlins. 1995. Pharmacovigilance: paradise lost, regained or postponed? The William Withering Lecture 1994. *Journal of the Royal College of Physicians of London*, *29*(1): 41-49.

Sunghwan Sohn, Jean-Pierre A. Kocher, Christopher G. Chute and Guergana K. Savova. 2011. Drug side effect extraction from clinical narratives of psychiatry and psychology patients. *Journal of the American Medical Informatics Association*, 18(Suppl 1):i144-i149.

Özlem Uzuner, Imre Solti and Eithon Cadag. 2010. Extracting medication information from clinical text. *Journal of the American Medical Informatics Association*. 17(5):514-518.

Rong Xu and QuanQiu Wang. 2013. Large-scale extraction of accurate drug-disease treatment pairs from biomedical literature for drug repurposing. *BMC Bioinformatics*, *14*(1):181.

Karin Wester, Anna K. Jönsson, Olav Spigset, Henrik Druid and Staffan Hägg. 2008. Incidence of fatal adverse drug reactions: a population based study. *British journal of clinical pharmacology*, *65*(4):573-579.

Care Episode Retrieval

Hans Moen[1], Erwin Marsi[1], Filip Ginter[2],
Laura-Maria Murtola[3,4], Tapio Salakoski[2], Sanna Salanterä[3,4],
[1]Dept. of Computer and Information Science,
Norwegian University of Science and Technology, Norway
[2]Dept. of Information Technology, University of Turku, Finland
[3]Dept. of Nursing Science, University of Turku, Finland
[4]Turku University Hospital, Finland
{hans.moen,emarsi}@idi.ntnu.no, ginter@cs.utu.fi,
{lmemur,tapio.salakoski,sansala}@utu.fi

Abstract

The documentation of a care episode consists of clinical notes concerning patient care, concluded with a discharge summary. Care episodes are stored electronically and used throughout the health care sector by patients, administrators and professionals from different areas, primarily for clinical purposes, but also for secondary purposes such as decision support and research. A common use case is, given a – possibly unfinished – care episode, to retrieve the most similar care episodes among the records. This paper presents several methods for information retrieval, focusing on care episode retrieval, based on textual similarity, where similarity is measured through domain-specific modelling of the distributional semantics of words. Models include variants of *random indexing* and a semantic neural network model called *word2vec*. A novel method is introduced that utilizes the ICD-10 codes attached to care episodes to better induce domain-specificity in the semantic model. We report on an experimental evaluation of care episode retrieval that circumvents the lack of human judgements regarding episode relevance by exploiting (1) ICD-10 codes of care episodes and (2) semantic similarity between their discharge summaries. Results suggest that several of the methods proposed outperform a state-of-the art search engine (Lucene) on the retrieval task.

1 Introduction

Information retrieval (IR) aims at retrieving and ranking documents relative to a textual query expressing the information need of a user (Manning et al., 2008). IR has become a crucial technology for many organisations that deal with vast amounts of partly structured and unstructured (free text) data stored in electronic format, including hospitals and other health care providers. IR is an essential part of the clinical practice; e.g., on-line IR systems are associated with substantial improvements in clinicians decision-making concerning clinical problems (Westbrook et al., 2005).

The different stages of the clinical care of a patient are documented in *clinical care notes*, consisting mainly of free text. A *care episode* consists of a sequence of individual clinical care notes, concluded by a discharge summary, as illustrated in Figure 1. Care episodes are stored in electronic format in *electronic health record* (EHR) systems. These systems are used throughout the health care sector by patients, administrators and professionals from different areas, primarily for clinical purposes, but also for secondary purposes such as decision support and research (Häyrinen et al., 2008). IR from EHR in general is therefore a common and important task.

This paper focuses on the particular task of retrieving those care episodes that are most similar to the sequence of clinical notes for a given patient, which we will call *care episode retrieval.* In conventional IR, the query typically consists of several keywords or a short phrase, while the retrievable units are typically documents. In contrast, in care episode retrieval, the query consist of the clinical notes contained in a care episode. The discharge summary is used separately for evalu-

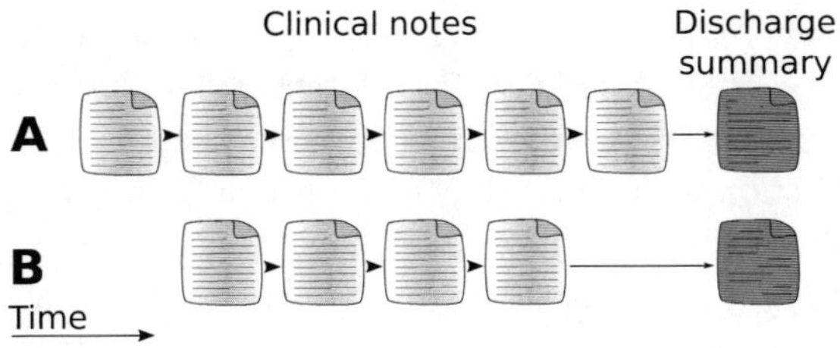

Figure 1: Illustration of care episode retrieval. The two care episodes (A and B) are composed of a number of individual clinical notes and a single discharge summary. Given an ongoing care episode (minus the discharge summary), the task is to retrieve other, similar care episodes.

ation purposes, and is assumed to be unavailable for constructing a query at retrieval time. Retrievable units are thus complete care episodes without summaries.

We envision a number of different use cases for a care episode retrieval system. Firstly, it could facilitate clinicians in decision-making. For example, given a patient that is being treated in a hospital, an involved clinician may want to find previous patients that are similar in terms of their health history, symptoms or received treatments. Supplementary input from the clinician would enable the system to give heightened weight to keywords of particular interest within the care episodes, which would further be emphasized in the semantic similarity calculation during IR. It may help considerably to see what similar patients have received in terms of medication and further treatment, what related issues such as bi-conditions or risks occurred, how other clinicians have described certain aspects, what clinical practice guidelines have been utilized, and so on. This relates to the underlying principle in textual case-based reasoning (Lenz et al., 1998). Secondly, it could help management to get almost real time information concerning the overall situation on the unit for a specific follow-up period. Such a system could for example support managerial decision-making with statistical information concerning care trends on the unit, adverse events or infections. Thirdly, it could facilitate knowledge discovery and research. For instance, it could enable researchers to map or cluster similar care episodes to find common symptoms or conditions. In sum, care episode retrieval is likely to improve care quality and consistency in hospitals.

From the perspective of NLP, care episode retrieval – and IR from EHRs in general – is a challenging task. It differs from general-purpose web search in that the vocabulary, the information needs and the queries of clinicians are highly specialised (Yang et al., 2011). Clinical notes contain highly domain-specific terminology (Rector, 1999; Friedman et al., 2002; Allvin et al., 2010) and generic text processing resources are therefore often suboptimal or inadequate (Shatkay, 2005). At the same time, development of dedicated clinical NLP tools and resources is often difficult and costly. For example, popular data-driven approaches to NLP are based on supervised learning, which requires substantial amounts of tailored training data, typically built through manual annotation by annotators who need both linguistic and clinical knowledge. Additionally, variations in the language and terminology used in sub-domains within and across health care organisations greatly limit the scope of applicability of such training data (Rector, 1999).

Recent work has shown that distributional models of semantics, induced in an unsupervised manner from large corpora of clinical and/or medical text, are well suited as a resource-light approach to capturing and representing domain-specific terminology (Pedersen et al., 2007; Koopman et al., 2012; Henriksson et al., 2014). This raises the question to what extent distributional models of semantics can alleviate the aforementioned problems of NLP in the clinical domain. The work reported here investigates to what extent distributional models of semantics, built from a corpus of clinical text in an fully unsupervised manner, can be used for care episode retrieval. Models include several variants of *random indexing* and a semantic neural network model called *word2vec*, which will be described in more detail in Section 4.

It has been argued that clinical NLP should exploit existing knowledge resources such as knowledge bases about medications, treatments, diseases, symptoms and care plans, despite these not having been explicitly built for doing clinical NLP (Friedman et al., 2013). Along these lines, a novel method is proposed here that utilizes the ICD-10 codes – diagnostic labels attached to care episodes by clinicians – to better induce domain-specificity in the semantic model. Experimental results suggest that this method outperforms a state-of-the art search engine (Lucene) on the task of care episode retrieval.

Apart from issues related to clinical terminology, another problem in care episode retrieval is the lack of benchmark data, such as the relevance scores produced by human judges commonly used for evaluation of IR systems. Although collections of care episodes may be available, producing gold standard similarity scores required for evaluation is costly. Another contribution of this paper is the proposal of evaluation procedures that circumvent the lack of human judgements regarding episode similarity. This is accomplished by exploiting either (1) ICD-10 codes of care episodes or (2) semantic similarity between their discharge summaries. Despite our focus on the specific task of care episode retrieval, we hypothesize that the methods and models proposed here have the potential to increase performance of IR on clinical text in general.

2 Data

The data set used in this study consists of the electronic health records from patients with any type of heart related problem that were admitted to one particular university hospital in Finland between the years 2005-2009. Of these, only the clinical notes written by physician are used. A supporting statement for the research was obtained from the Ethics Committee of the Hospital District (17.2.2009 §67) and permission to conduct the research was obtained from the Medical Director of the Hospital District (2/2009). The total set consist of 66884 care episodes, which amounts to 398040 notes and 64 million words in total. This full set was used for training of the semantic models. To make the experimentation more convenient, we chose to use a subset for evaluation. This comprises 26530 care episodes, amounting to 155562 notes and 25.7 million words in total.

Notes are mostly unstructured, consisting of free text in Finnish. Some meta-data – such as names of the authors, dates, wards, and so on – is present, but is not used for retrieval.

Care episodes have been manually labeled according to the 10th revision of the International Classification of Diseases (ICD-10) (World Health Organization and others, 2013), a standardised tool of diagnostic codes for classifying diseases. Codes are normally applied at the end of the patient's stay, or even after the patient has been discharged from the hospital. Care episodes have one primary ICD-10 code attached and optionally a number of additionally relevant codes. In this study, only the primary one is used, because extraction of the secondary codes is non-trivial.

ICD-10 codes have an internal structure that reflects the classification system ranging from broad categories down to fine-grained subjects. For example, the first character (J) of the code J21.1 signals that it belongs to the broad category *Diseases of the respiratory system*. The next two digits (21) classify the subject as belonging to the subcategory *Acute bronchiolitis*. Finally, the last digit after the dot (1) means that it belongs to the sub-subclass *Acute bronchiolitis due to human metapneumovirus*. There are 356 unique "primary" ICD-10 codes in the evaluation data set.

3 Task

The task addressed in this study is retrieval of care episodes that are similar to each other. In contrast to the normal IR setting, where the search query is derived from a text stating the user's information need, here the query is based on another care episode, which we refer to as the *query episode*. As the query episode may document ongoing treatment, and thus lack a discharge summary and ICD-10 code, neither of these information sources can be relied upon for constructing the query. The task is therefore to retrieve the most similar care episodes using only the information contained in the free text of the clinical notes in the query episode.

Evaluation of retrieval results generally requires an assessment of their relevancy to the query. Since similarity judgements by humans are currently lacking, and obtaining these is time-consuming and costly, we explored alternative ways of evaluating performance on the task. The first alternative is to assume that care episodes are similar if they have the same ICD-10 code. That is, a retrieved care episode is considered correct if its ICD-10 code is identical to the code of the query episode. It should be noted that ICD-10 codes are not used in the query in any of the experiments.

Closer inspection shows that the free text content in care episodes with the same ICD-10 code is indeed quite similar in many cases, but not always. Considering all of them equally similar amounts to an arguably coarse approximation of relevance. The second alternative tries to remedy this issue by measuring the similarity between discharge summaries. That is, if the discharge summary of a retrieved episode is semantically similar to the discharge summary of the query episode, the retrieved episode is assumed to be correct. In practice, textual similarity between discharge summaries, and therefore the relevance score, is continuous rather than binary. It is measured using the same models of distributional semantics used for retrieval, which will be described in Section 4. It should be stressed that the discharge summaries are not taken into consideration during retrieval in any of the experiments and are only used for evaluation.

4 Method

4.1 Semantic models

A crucial part in retrieving similar care episodes is having a good similarity measure. Here similarity between care episodes is measured as the similarity between the words they contain (see Section 4.2). Semantic similarity between words is in turn measured through the use of word space models (WSM), without performing an explicit query expansion step. Several variants of these models were tested, utilizing different techniques and parameters for building them. The models trained and tested in this paper are: (1) classic random indexing with a sliding window using term index vectors and term context vectors (RI-Word); (2) random indexing with index vectors for documents (RI-Doc); (3) random indexing with index vectors for ICD-10 codes (RI-ICD); (4) a version of random indexing where only the term index vectors are used (RI-Index); and (5) a semantic neural network model, using *word2vec* to build word context vectors (Word2vec).

RI-Word

Random Indexing (RI) (Kanerva et al., 2000) is a method for building a (pre) compressed WSM with a fixed dimensionality, done in an incremental fashion. RI consist of the following two steps: First, instead of allocating one dimension in the multidimensional vector space to a single word, each word is assigned an "index vector" as its unique signature in the vector space. Index vectors are generated vectors consisting of mostly zeros together with a randomly distributed set of several 1's and -1's, uniquely distributed for each unique word; The second step is to induce "context vectors" for each word. A context vector represents the *contextual meaning* of a word in the WSM. This is done using a sliding window of a fixed size to traverse a training corpus, inducing context vectors for the center/target word of the sliding window by summing the index vectors of the neighbouring words in the window.

As the dimensionality of the index vectors is fixed, the dimensionality of the vector space will not grow beyond the size $W \times Dim$, where W is the number of unique words in the vocabulary, and Dim being the pre-selected dimensionality to use for the index vectors. As a result, RI models are significantly smaller than plain word space models, making them a lot less computationally expensive. Additionally, the method is fully incremental (additional training data can be added at any given time without having to retrain the existing model), easy to parallelize, and scalable, meaning that it is fast and can be trained on large amounts of text in an on-line fashion.

RI-Doc

Contrary to sliding window approach used in RI-Word, a RI model built with *document index vectors* first assigns unique index vectors to every document in the training corpus. In the training phase, each word in a document get the respective document vector added to its context vector. The resulting WSM is thus a compressed version of a term-by-document matrix.

RI-ICD

Based on the principle of RI with document index vectors, we here explore a novel way of constructing a WSM by exploiting the ICD-10 code classification done by clinicians. Instead of using document index vectors, we here use *ICD-code index vectors*. First, a unique index vector is assigned to each chapter and sub-chapter in the ICD-10 taxonomy. This means assigning a unique index vector to each "node" in the ICD-10 taxonomy, as illustrated in Figure 2. For each clinical note in the training corpus, the index vector of the their primary ICD-10 code is added to all words within it. In addition, all the index vectors for the ICD codes higher in the taxonomy are added, each weighted according to their position in the hierarchy. A weight of 1 is given to the full code, while the weight is halved for each step upwards in the hierarchy. The motivation for the latter is to capture a certain degree of similarity between codes that share an initial path in the taxonomy. As a result,

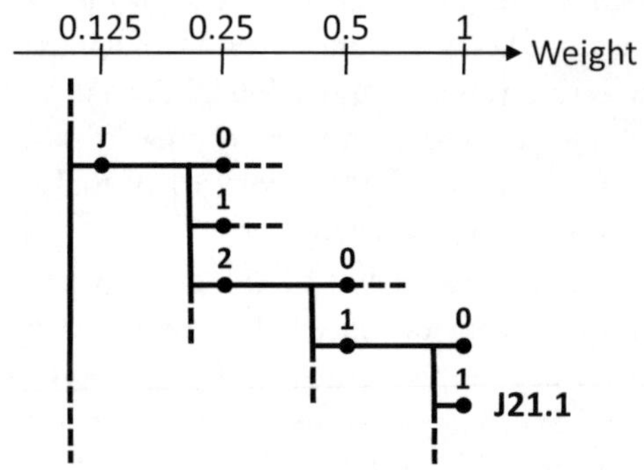

Figure 2: Weighting applied to ICD-code index vectors when training WSMs based on ICD-10 codes (RI-ICD).

this similarity is encoded in the resulting WSM. As a example: for a clinical note labelled with the code $J21.1$, we add the following index vectors to the context vectors of all its constituting words: $iv(J) \times 0.125$, $iv(J2) \times 0.25$, $iv(J21) \times 0.5$ and $iv(J21.1) \times 1.0$. The underlying hypothesis for building a WSM in this way is that it may capture relations between words in a way that better reflects the clinical domain, compared to the other domain-independent methods for constructing a WSM.

RI-Index

As an alternative to using word's (semantic) context vectors, we simply only use their index vectors as their "contextual meaning". When constructing document vectors directly from word index vectors (see Section 4.2), the resulting document vectors represent a compressed version of a document-by-term matrix.

Word2vec

Recently, a novel method for inducing WSMs was introduced by Mikolov et al. (2013a), stemming from the research in deep learning and neural network language models. While the overall objective of learning a continuous vector space representation for each word based on its textual context remains, the underlying algorithms are substantially different from traditional methods such as Latent Semantic Analysis and RI. Considering, in turn, every word in the training data as a target word, the method induces the representations by training a simplified neural network to predict the nearby context words of each target word (skip-gram architecture), or alternatively the target word based on all words in its immediate context (BoW architecture). The vector space representation is subsequently extracted from the learned weights within the neural network. One of the main practical advantages of the word2vec method lies in its scalability, allowing quick training on large amounts of text, setting it apart from the majority of other methods of distributional semantics. Additionally, the word2vec method has been shown to produce representations that surpass in quality traditional methods such as Latent Semantic Analysis, especially on tasks measuring the preservation of important linguistic regularities (Mikolov et al., 2013b).

4.2 Computing care episode similarity

After having computed a WSM, the next step is to build episode vectors to use for the actual retrieval task. This is done by first normalizing the word vectors and multiplying them with a word's TF*IDF weight. An episode vector is then obtained by summing the word vectors of all its words and dividing the result by the total number of words in the episode. Similarity between episodes is determined by computing the cosine similarity between their vectors.

4.3 Baselines

Two baselines were used in this study. The first one is random retrieval of care episodes, which can be expected to give very low scores and serves merely as a sanity check. The second one is Apache Lucene (Cutting, 1999), a state-of-the-art search engine based on look-up of similar documents through a reverse index and relevance ranking based on a TF*IDF-weighted vector space model. Care episodes were indexed using Lucene. Similar to the other models/methods, all of the free text in the query episode, excluding the discharge summary, served as the query string provided to Lucene. Being a state-of-the-art IR system, the scores achieved by Lucene in these experiments should indicate the difficulty of the task.

5 Experiments

In these experiments we strove to have a setup that was as comparable as possible for all models and systems, both in terms of text pre-processing and in terms of the target model dimensionality when inducing the vector space models. The clinical notes are split into sentences, tokenized, and lemmatized using a Constraint-Grammar based morphological analyzer and tagger extended with clinical vocabulary (Karlsson, 1995). After stop words were removed[1], the total training corpus contained 39 million words (minus the query episodes), while the evaluation subset contained 18.5 million words. The vocabulary consisted of 0.6 million unique terms. Twenty care episodes were randomly selected to serve as the query episodes during testing, with the requirement that each had different ICD-10 codes and consisted of a minimum of six clinical notes. The average number of words per query episode is 830.

RI-based and word2vec models have a predefined dimensionality of 800. For RI-based models, 4 non-zeros were used in the index vectors. For the RI-Word model, a narrow context window was employed (5 left + 5 right), weighting index vectors according to their distance to the target word ($weight_i = 2^{1-dist_{it}}$). In addition, the index vectors were shifted once left or right depending on what side of the target word they were located, similar to *direction vectors* as described in (Sahlgren et al., 2008) These parameters for RI were chosen based on previous work on semantic textual similarity (Moen et al., 2013). Also a much larger window of 20+20 was tested, but without noteworthy improvements. The word2vec model is trained with the BoW architecture and otherwise default parameters. In addition to Apache Lucene (version 4.2.0)[2], the word2vec tool[3] was used to train the word2vec model, and the RI-based methods utilized the JavaSDM package[4]. Scores were calculated using the *trec_eval* tool[5].

5.1 Experiment 1: ICD-10 code overlap

In this experiment retrieved episodes with a primary ICD-10 code identical to that of the query episode were considered to be correct. The number of correct episodes varies between 49 and 1654. The total is 7721, and the average is 386. The high total is mainly due to three query episodes with ICD-10 codes that occur very frequently in the episode collection (896, 1590, and 1654 times). When conducting the experiment all care episodes were retrieved for each of the 20 query episodes.

IR model	MAP	P@10
Lucene	0.1379	0.3000
RI-Word	0.0911	0.2650
RI-Doc	0.1015	0.3300
RI-ICD	**0.3261**	**0.5150**
RI-Index	0.1187	0.3200
Word2vec	0.1768	0.3350
Random	0.0154	0.0200

Table 1: Mean average precision and precision at 10 for retrieval of care episodes with the same primary ICD-10 code as the query episode

Performance was measured in terms of mean average precision (MAP) and precision among the top-10 results (P@10), averaged over all 20 queries, as shown in in Table 1. The best MAP score is achieved by RI-ICD, almost twice that of word2vec, which achieved the second best MAP score, whereas RI-Word performed worst of all. All models score well above the random baseline, whereas RI-ICD outperforms Lucene by a large margin. P@10 scores follow the same ranking. The latter scores are more representative for most use cases where users will only inspect the top-n retrieval results.

5.2 Experiment 2: Discharge summary overlap

In this experiment retrieved episodes with a discharge summary similar to that of the query episode were considered to be correct. Using the discharge summaries of the query episodes, the top 100 care episodes with the most similar discharge summary were selected as the most similar care episodes (disregarding the query episode). This was repeated for each of the methods – i.e. the five different semantic models and Lucene – resulting in six different tests. The top 100 was used rather than a threshold on the similarity score, because otherwise six different thresholds would have to be chosen. This procedure thus resulted in six different test collections, each consisting of 20 query episodes with their corresponding 100 most similar collection episodes.

Subsequently a 6-by-6 experimental design was followed where each retrieval method was tested against each test set construction method. At retrieval time, for each query episode, the system retrieves and ranks 1000 care episodes. It can be expected that when identical methods are used for re-

[1] http://www.nettiapina.fi/finnish-stopword-list/

[2] http://archive.apache.org/dist/lucene/java/

[3] https://code.google.com/p/word2vec/

[4] http://www.nada.kth.se/~xmartin/java/

[5] http://trec.nist.gov/trec_eval/

trieval and test set construction, the resulting bias gives rise to relatively high scores. In contrast, averaging over the scores for all six construction methods is assumed to be a less biased indicator of performance.

Table 2 shows the number of correctly retrieved episodes by the different models, with the maximum being 2000 (20 queries times 100 most similar episodes). This gives an indication of the recall among a 1000 retrieved episodes per query, but without caring about precision or ranking. In general, the numbers are relatively good when the same model is used for both retrieval and construction of the test set (cf. values on the diagonal), although in a couple of cases (e.g. with word2vec) results are better with different models. The RI-ICD model performs best when used for both retrieval and test construction. Looking at the averages, which presumably are less biased indicators, RI-ICD and word2vec seem to have comparable performance, with both of them outperforming Lucene. Other models are less successful, although still much better than the random baseline.

The MAP scores in Table 3 show similar results, although here RI-ICD yields the best average score. Both models RI-ICD and word2vec outperform Lucene. Again the RI-ICD model performs exceptionally well when used for both retrieval and test construction.

Finally Table 4 presents precision for top-10 retrieved care episodes. Here RI-Doc yields the best average scores, while RI-ICD and word2vec both perform slightly worse.

6 Discussion

The goal of the experiments was primarily to determine which distributional semantic models work best for care episode retrieval. The experimental results show that several models outperform Lucene at the care episode retrieval task. This suggests that models of higher order semantics contribute positively to calculating document similarities in the clinical domain, compared with straight forward boolean word matching (cf. RI-Index and Lucene).

The relatively good performance of the RI-ICD model, particularly in Experiment 1, suggests that exploiting structured or encoded information in building semantic models for clinical NLP is a promising direction that calls for further investigation. This approach concurs with the arguments in favor of reuse of existing information sources in Friedman et al. (2013). On the one hand, it may not be surprising that the RI-ICD model is performing well on Experiment 1, given how it induces semantic relations between words occurring in episodes with the same ICD-10 code. On the other hand, being able to accurately retrieve care episodes with similar ICD-10 codes evidently has practical value from a clinical perspective.

The different ranking of models in experiments 1 versus 2 confirms that there is a difference between the two indicators of episode similarity, i.e. similarity in terms of their ICD-10 codes versus similarity with regard to their discharge summaries. In our data a single care episode can potentially span across several hospital wards. A better correlation between the similarity measures is to be expected when narrowing the definition of a care episode to only a single ward. Also, taking into consideration all ICD-10 codes for care episodes – not only the primary one – could potentially improve discrimination among care episodes. This could be useful in two ways: (1) to create more precise test sets of the type used in Experiment 1; (2) to extend RI-ICD models with index vectors also for the secondary ICD-10 codes.

Input to the models for training was limited to the free text in the clinical notes, with the exception of the use of ICD-10 codes in the RI-ICD model. Other sources of information could, and probably should, be utilized in a practical care episode retrieval system applied in a hospital, such as the structured and coded information commonly found in EHR systems. Another potential information source is the internal structure of the care episodes, as episodes containing similar notes in the same sequential order are intuitively more likely to be similar. We tried computing exhaustive pairwise similarities between the individual notes from two episodes and then taking the average of these as a similarity measure for the episodes. However, this did not improve performance on any measure. An alternative approach may be to apply sequence alignment algorithms, as commonly used in bioinformatics (Gusfield, 1997), in order to detect if both episodes contain similar notes in the same temporal order. We leave this to future work.

IR model \ Test set	Lucene	RI-Word	RI-Doc	RI-ICD	RI-Index	Word2vec	Average	Rank
Lucene	889	700	670	687	484	920	725	2
RI-Word	643	800	586	600	384	849	644	5
RI-Doc	665	630	859	697	436	795	680	4
RI-ICD	635	459	659	**1191**	490	813	707	3
RI-Index	690	491	607	654	576	758	629	6
Word2vec	789	703	702	870	516	**1113**	**782**	1
Random	74	83	86	67	84	85	79	7

Table 2: Number of correctly retrieved episodes (max 2000) for different IR models (rows) when using different models for measuring discharge summary similarity (columns)

IR model \ Test set	Lucene	RI-Word	RI-Doc	RI-ICD	RI-Index	Word2vec	Average	Rank
Lucene	0.0856	0.0357	0.0405	0.0578	0.0269	0.0833	0.0550	3
RI-Word	0.0392	0.0492	0.0312	0.0412	0.0151	0.0735	0.0416	6
RI-Doc	0.0493	0.0302	0.0677	0.0610	0.0220	0.0698	0.0500	4
RI-ICD	0.0497	0.0202	0.0416	**0.1704**	0.0261	0.0712	**0.0632**	1
RI-Index	0.0655	0.0230	0.0401	0.0504	0.0399	0.0652	0.0473	5
Word2vec	0.0667	0.0357	0.0404	0.0818	0.0293	0.1193	**0.0622**	2
Random	0.0003	0.0003	0.0005	0.0002	0.0003	0.0004	0.0003	7

Table 3: Mean average precision for different IR models (rows) when using different models for measuring discharge summary similarity (columns)

IR model \ Test set	Lucene	RI-Word	RI-Doc	RI-ICD	RI-Index	Word2vec	Average	Rank
Lucene	0.2450	0.1350	0.1200	0.1650	0.0950	0.1900	0.1583	5
RI-Word	0.1350	0.1500	0.1000	0.1350	0.0600	0.2100	0.1316	6
RI-Doc	0.2000	0.1250	0.2050	0.2200	0.0900	0.2400	**0.1800**	1
RI-ICD	0.1700	0.0650	0.1350	**0.3400**	0.0950	0.2050	0.1683	2
RI-Index	0.2000	0.1250	0.1550	0.1250	0.1700	0.2050	0.1633	3
Word2vec	0.1800	0.1200	0.1150	0.2100	0.0850	0.2650	0.1625	4
Random	0.0000	0.0000	0.0050	0.0000	0.0000	0.0000	0.0008	7

Table 4: Precision at top-10 retrieved episodes for different IR models (rows) when using different models for measuring discharge summary similarity (columns)

7 Conclusion and future work

In this paper we proposed the task of *care episode retrieval* as a way of evaluating several distributional semantic models in their performance at IR. As manually constructing a proper test set of classified care episodes is costly, we experimented with building test sets by exploiting either ICD-10 code overlap or semantic similarity of discharge summaries. A novel method for generating semantic models utilizing the ICD-10 codes of care episodes in the training corpus was presented (RI-ICD). The models, as well as the Lucene search engine, were applied to the care episode retrieval task and their performance was evaluated against the test sets using different evaluation measures. The results suggest that the RI-ICD model is better suited to IR tasks in the clinical domain compared with models trained on local distributions of words, or those relying on direct word matching. The word2vec model performed relatively well and outperformed Lucene in both experiments.

In the results reported here, the internal sequence of clinical notes is ignored. Future work should focus on exploring the temporal (sub-) sequence similarities between care episode pairs for doing care episode retrieval. Further work should also focus on expanding on the RI-ICD method by exploiting other types of structured and/or encoded information related to clinical notes for training semantic models tailored for NLP in the clinical domain.

Acknowledgments

This study was partly supported by the Research Council of Norway through the EviCare project (NFR project no. 193022), the Turku University Hospital (EVO 2014), and the Academy of Finland (project no. 140323). The study is a part of the research projects of the Ikitik consortium (`http://www.ikitik.fi`). We would like to thank Juho Heimonen for assisting us in preprocessing the data and the reviewers for their helpful comments.

References

Helen Allvin, Elin Carlsson, Hercules Dalianis, Riitta Danielsson-Ojala, Vidas Daudaravičius, Martin Hassel, Dimitrios Kokkinakis, Heljä Lundgren-Laine, Gunnar Nilsson, Øystein Nytrø, et al. 2010. Characteristics and analysis of finnish and swedish clinical intensive care nursing narratives. In *Proceedings of the NAACL HLT 2010 Second Louhi Workshop on Text and Data Mining of Health Documents*, pages 53–60. Association for Computational Linguistics.

Doug Cutting. 1999. Apache Lucene open source package.

Carol Friedman, Pauline Kra, and Andrey Rzhetsky. 2002. Two biomedical sublanguages: a description based on the theories of zellig harris. *Journal of biomedical informatics*, 35(4):222–235.

Carol Friedman, Thomas C Rindflesch, and Milton Corn. 2013. Natural language processing: State of the art and prospects for significant progress, a workshop sponsored by the national library of medicine. *Journal of biomedical informatics*, 46(5):765–773.

Dan Gusfield. 1997. *Algorithms on strings, trees and sequences: computer science and computational biology*. Cambridge University Press.

Kristiina Häyrinen, Kaija Saranto, and Pirkko Nykänen. 2008. Definition, structure, content, use and impacts of electronic health records: a review of the research literature. *International journal of medical informatics*, 77(5):291–304.

Aron Henriksson, Hans Moen, Maria Skeppstedt, Vidas Daudaravi, Martin Duneld, et al. 2014. Synonym extraction and abbreviation expansion with ensembles of semantic spaces. *Journal of biomedical semantics*, 5(1):6.

Pentti Kanerva, Jan Kristofersson, and Anders Holst. 2000. Random indexing of text samples for latent semantic analysis. In *Proceedings of 22nd Annual Conference of the Cognitive Science Society*, page 1036.

Fred Karlsson. 1995. *Constraint grammar: a language-independent system for parsing unrestricted text*. Mouton de Gruyter, Berlin and New York.

Bevan Koopman, Guido Zuccon, Peter Bruza, Laurianne Sitbon, and Michael Lawley. 2012. An evaluation of corpus-driven measures of medical concept similarity for information retrieval. In *Proceedings of the 21st ACM international conference on Information and knowledge management*, pages 2439–2442. ACM.

Mario Lenz, André Hübner, and Mirjam Kunze. 1998. Textual cbr. In *Case-based reasoning technology*, pages 115–137. Springer.

Christopher D Manning, Prabhakar Raghavan, and Hinrich Schütze. 2008. *Introduction to information retrieval*, volume 1. Cambridge University Press Cambridge.

Tomas Mikolov, Ilya Sutskever, Kai Chen, Greg S. Corrado, and Jeff Dean. 2013a. Distributed representations of words and phrases and their compositionality. In *Advances in Neural Information Processing Systems 26*, pages 3111–3119.

Tomas Mikolov, Wen-tau Yih, and Geoffrey Zweig. 2013b. Linguistic regularities in continuous space word representations. In *Proceedings of the 2013 Conference of the North American Chapter of the Association for Computational Linguistics: Human Language Technologies*, pages 746–751. Association for Computational Linguistics, June.

Hans Moen, Erwin Marsi, and Björn Gambäck. 2013. Towards dynamic word sense discrimination with random indexing. *ACL 2013*, page 83.

Ted Pedersen, Serguei VS Pakhomov, Siddharth Patwardhan, and Christopher G Chute. 2007. Measures of semantic similarity and relatedness in the biomedical domain. *Journal of biomedical informatics*, 40(3):288–299.

Alan L Rector. 1999. Clinical terminology: why is it so hard? *Methods of information in medicine*, 38(4/5):239–252.

Magnus Sahlgren, Anders Holst, and Pentti Kanerva. 2008. Permutations as a means to encode order in word space. In *Proceedings of the Annual Meeting of the Cognitive Science Society*.

Hagit Shatkay. 2005. Hairpins in bookstacks: information retrieval from biomedical text. *Briefings in Bioinformatics*, 6(3):222–238.

Johanna I Westbrook, Enrico W Coiera, and A Sophie Gosling. 2005. Do online information retrieval systems help experienced clinicians answer clinical questions? *Journal of the American Medical Informatics Association*, 12(3):315–321.

World Health Organization and others. 2013. International classification of diseases (icd).

Lei Yang, Qiaozhu Mei, Kai Zheng, and David A Hanauer. 2011. Query log analysis of an electronic health record search engine. In *AMIA Annual Symposium Proceedings*, volume 2011, page 915. American Medical Informatics Association.

Author Index

Alnazzawi, Noha, 69
Ananiadou, Sophia, 1, 69

Bjødstrup Jensen, Peter, 64
Brunak, Søren, 64

Casillas, Arantza, 85
Collier, Nigel, 11
Cormack, James, 75

Eklund, Ann-Marie, 2
Engel Thomas, Cecilia, 64

Ginter, Filip, 116
Gojenola, Koldo, 85
Grabar, Natalia, 101

Hamon, Thierry, 90, 101

Kokkinakis, Dimitrios, 2
Kreuzthaler, Markus, 96

Marsi, Erwin, 116
Martínez, Paloma, 106
Milward, David, 75
Moen, Hans, 116
Moradi, Farnaz, 2
Murtola, Laura-Maria, 116

Ng, Hwee Tou, 21

Olovsson, Tomas, 2
Oronoz, Maite, 38, 85

Paster, Ferdinand, 11
Perez, Alicia, 85
Perez-de-Viñaspre, Olatz, 38
Périnet, Amandine, 90

Quan, Changqin, 54

Ren, Fuji, 54
Revert, Ricardo, 106
Riccardi, Giuseppe, 30
Roller, Roland, 80

Salakoski, Tapio, 116
Salanterä, Sanna, 116
Santiso, Sara, 85
Schulz, Stefan, 96
Segura-Bedmar, Isabel, 106
Shivade, Chaitanya, 75
Stepanov, Evgeny, 30
Stevenson, Mark, 80

Tan, He, 46
Thompson, Paul, 69
Tran, Mai-vu, 11
Tsigas, Philippas, 2

Werge, Thomas, 64

Zhao, Shanheng, 21

Association for Computational Linguistics
209 N. Eighth Street
Stroudsburg, Pennsylvania 18360

CURRAN ASSOCIATES INC
proceedings.com